CHRISTMAS AND THE IRISH

CW01466811

COME, LET US ADORE

CHRISTMAS AND THE IRISH

A MISCELLANY

Edited by
Salvador Ryan

WORDWELL BOOKS

First published 2023 by Wordwell Books
Dublin, Ireland

www.wordwellbooks.com

First edition

Wordwell Books is an imprint of the Wordwell Group

Wordwell Books
The Wordwell Group
Unit 9, 78 Furze Road
Sandyford
Dublin, Ireland

© The authors, 2023

ISBN: 978-1-913934-93-4 (Paperback)
ISBN: 978-1-913934-98-9 (Ebook)

The right of Salvador Ryan to be identified as the Editor
of this work has been asserted in accordance with the
Copyright, Designs and Patents Act 1988.

All rights reserved. No part of this book may be reprinted
or reproduced or utilised in any form or by any electronic,
mechanical or other means, now known or hereafter invented,
including photocopying and recording, or in any information
storage or retrieval system, without the permission in writing
from the Publishers.

British Library Cataloguing in Publication Data.
A catalogue record for this book is available from the National Library of
Ireland and the British Library.

Typesetting and design by the Wordwell Group
Copyediting by Emer Condit
Printed in Ireland by Sprint Print

CONTENTS

CONTENTS

INTRODUCTION AND ACKNOWLEDGEMENTS

Christmas can be a magical time. It often evokes the most powerful memories of childhood, family, gift-giving and togetherness. Accounts from the 'Schools Collection', gathered in 1937–8 by schoolchildren across the country for the fledgling National Folklore Commission, portray the lead-up to Christmas as a busy time, consumed by both material and spiritual preparation. For a child in Killahan, Co. Kerry, 'the first sign of Christmas is the houses are whitewashed and the places cleaned'. An account from Golden, Co. Tipperary, recalls how 'there is always great joy at Christmas. Every woman is busy. My mother is very busy at Christmas always, cleaning and dusting. She has to white-wash and then everything is tossed about, dressers tables and pictures. Then all these things have to be washed and painted.' In Bracknagh, Co. Offaly, one entry recounts how 'on Christmas Eve the people make chains of berries and hang them at the doors, in the centre of them there is a cross made of berries. They put up holly and ivy in the house also.'

Meanwhile, an entry from Cregganbane, Co. Mayo, prescribes the following actions (complete with words spelt as they were pronounced): 'It is right to white wash the house in honner of our loard. It is right to clain the chimney with ivy. It is right to have holly and ivy up on every spot and cornar of the house … It is right to leave every dowar opened on Christmas night and if the dowar is opened the holy gosht will stay a copla minnits in every house.'

Candles were also a popular feature at Christmastime. A child from Shanakill, Co. Tipperary, recalls how 'people of this district light a candle on Christmas Eve Night. It is in memory of the time when the Holy Family were wandering around Bethlehem looking for somewhere to stay the night and the lights in the windows of the houses are supposed to show that they are welcome in each house.' Another account, from Ballycastle, Co. Mayo, recalls how on Christmas night 'the photographs of the absent ones were placed on the supper table and it was an unwritten law that all families kept to their own homes on that night. Visitors were looked upon as intruders, but all doors were open to the homeless.'

There was also a custom around Tulrahan, Co. Mayo, of lighting a three-branched tallow candle on Christmas Eve to commemorate the Trinity. The account notes that, when the candle was extinguished at midnight, 'the triple candle remains were, however, carefully preserved until the following year as a protection against the visits of all evil spirits except whiskey'! Meanwhile, a story from Ballybunion convent school, Co. Kerry, tells how a woman who had quenched candles and put them in a drawer after midnight got up the next morning to find the candles still lighting at both ends, and 'she took it as a lesson that the Christmas candles would not burn anything' [*editorial advisory note: please don't try this one at home*].

Other traditions, such as the following practice, survive in some parts of the country to this day. An account from Ballindine, Co. Mayo, relates how on Christmas morning, when people went to Mass, they took a few wisps of straw from the crib, brought them home and put one under the rafters of each cabin and under the beds.

Some stories from 1937 relate how certain Christmas traditions presented initial difficulties for those unfamiliar with them. A tale from Fethard, Co. Tipperary, recounts how a gentleman gave a present to his workman of a plum pudding at Christmas, and the man brought the gift home to his wife. The account continues:

Apparently neither had ever seen a plum-pudding. It was put down in the pot to boil in the morning. They spent most of the day tasting the water, without results, so the woman procured a rather strong fork and started prodding it. About five o'clock in the evening, when she got tired and vexed, she took the famous pudding back to the donor, thanking him, but saying she boiled it all day long and could not get a taste of soup from it.

Something of the wonder surrounding the Christmas feast is captured in an account from Arklow, Co. Wicklow: 'On Christmas Eve in Ireland we could compare the country with the sky lit up with stars … no wonder Our Blessed Lady likes visiting the windows when she sees how she is welcomed!'

As charming as some of these accounts from the Schools Collection are, the reality for many people who celebrate the feast can often be very different. This collection comprises 75 articles examining what Irish people thought of Christmas and how they experienced it, both at home and abroad, over a period of some 1,500 years—and not all of it was either pretty or magical. The contributions certainly cover theological and spiritual readings of the Christmas feast; accounts of medieval feasting at Christmastime, and the history of Christmas foods in Ireland over the centuries; the often-fascinating origins of Christmas songs and carols; and the social niceties surrounding gift-giving and card-sending. But they also discuss less festive experiences of this time of year: Christmas in time of plague; Christmas while engaged in war; drunkenness, domestic violence and public order offences at Christmastime; spending Christmas in the poorhouse, in prison or sick in hospital; and the experience of Christmas when one is far away from home and family. And sometimes, too, it is the powerful associations that Christmas has— and how the 'perfect Christmas' is often commercially portrayed—that can make it most painful when life is not as one would like it to be.

It is my hope that readers will find the essays in this volume to be, in turn, informative, engaging, thought-provoking, poignant and often humorous. They may also prompt us to reflect anew on our own cherished Christmas traditions: what they are; why we perform them; and what they mean to us.

***

I would like to acknowledge a number of institutions and individuals for their support in the preparation of this volume. First, I wish to thank those who have assisted in the sourcing of images, and those who have granted permission for their use: R.D. Ballard for the image of the mummer's mask; Ita Callagy for supplying the images of Christmas Eve Mass in Galway cathedral, and for her image of the Sligo Christmas Swim; Patrick Comerford for his photographs; Bill Corr for allowing me to use his image 'Hope at Christmas'; Liam Doherty and Clodagh Doyle, Irish Folklife Division, Castlebar, for their help in sourcing the image of the open prison cell from Mountjoy, 1941; Fiona Dunne of the Design Department of DWM cards, Co. Roscommon, for the wonderful frontispiece image of the nativity with the backdrop of an Irish round tower; Seán Gannon for supplying images to accompany his article on Irish policing in Palestine; Max McCoubrey for permission to use the image from her tour of the Lebanon in 1986; Karin Morrow for allowing me to use her image of the Menorah; Yvonne McDermott for her sketches; the National Library of Ireland; the National Museum of Ireland; the RTÉ Stills Department for permission to use the image of the *Late Late Toy Show*; Paddy Waldron for allowing me to use some Christmas card images from his family collection, and Dr Paul O'Brien for having sourced them; JP Ryan for his image of 'The Caroler', specially drawn for this volume and Dr Críostóir Mac Cárthaigh, Director of the National Folklore Collection, for granting permission to quote from the Schools' Manuscript Collection.

This book would simply not exist without the interest shown by its contributors, and their willingness to research and write up the articles which make up this collection. To them I owe a particular debt of gratitude. My deep thanks, too, to the Maynooth Scholastic Trust for its generous publication grant.

I am also grateful to my colleagues at St Patrick's Pontifical University, Maynooth, for their continued support of my work; the beautiful Maynooth campus really is the most congenial of settings in which to research, write and edit. In addition, I wish to thank the team at Wordwell, especially Fiona Murphy, Emer Condit and Ronan Colgan, for their customary efficiency and professionalism in bringing this volume to press. Finally, my deepest gratitude goes to my wonderful family, and to Trish for her constant support and encouragement.

Salvador Ryan
Thursday 15 June 2023

THE LIGHT OF CHRISTMAS IN EARLY IRISH TEXTS

Conor McDonough OP

My earliest memory of Christmas lights doesn't involve multicoloured lights on a tree or fancy street lights but a single candle, sending out its warm glow against a dark window in our house.

It's an archetypal image but it's deeply biblical too, resonating with Jesus's own description of himself as 'the light of the world' (John 8:12). Shortly before his death, he spoke of his own birth in the same terms: 'I have come into the world as a light' (John 12:46). It's in John's Prologue, of course, that the light-imagery of the Incarnation is at its most pronounced: 'The light shines in the darkness, and the darkness has not overcome it ... The true light that enlightens every man was coming into the world' (John 1:5, 9).

These New Testament texts are themselves drawing on similar imagery in the Old Testament, from the pillar of fire of Exodus to the people of whom the prophet Isaiah spoke, 'who walked in darkness [and] have seen a great light' (Isaiah 9:2).

As Christians came to reflect creatively on the Christmas story, not only receiving it in faith but also producing new texts, they naturally made use of this imagery of light shining in darkness. Early Christian wordsmiths like Prudentius, Ambrose and Sedulius honoured the

Incarnation by weaving together these and other biblical texts in works that dazzled and delighted those who read and sang them.

In the first few centuries of Irish Christianity, we see the very same creativity at work, and in texts on the birth of Jesus the imagery of light shining in darkness is central.

The earliest Irish Christian text, the *Confessio* of St Patrick, takes up this theme in a brief moment of polemic against worship of the sun. It is Christ, says Patrick, who is 'the true Sun', whose light will outlast that of the visible sun. Patrick looks forward, too, to the resurrection of the body, which will take place 'on the appointed day in the brightness of the sun, that is, in the glory of Christ Jesus our redeemer'.

Patrick isn't speaking about the Nativity here, though. The first Irish text to bring out the theme of luminosity in a Christmas context is the Bangor Antiphonary, one of the oldest of our surviving books. Its home now is the Bibliotheca Ambrosiana in Milan, but it was written in the great monastery of Bangor near the end of the seventh century. It contains hymns and antiphons to be sung in the celebration of the Eucharist and the Divine Office. The oldest Latin copy of the *Gloria* and the *Te Deum*, for example, are found in this manuscript. There's only one short antiphon explicitly linked to the feast of Christmas, but it's extremely beautiful for all its brevity:

> From this day on, the night decreases and the day grows, the shadows are shaken and the light spreads, and debts to darkness give way to dividends of light.

The antiphon works on two levels. It's true, of course, that after the winter solstice the day—the period of visible light—is lengthening (is this the first reference in Irish history to the famous 'grand stretch in the evenings'?), but the liturgical context makes it clear that the real 'day' being referred to is the birth of Christ. From that day on, while natural rhythms of day and night endure, the light of salvation spreads inexorably.

This antiphon is written in—and was sung in—the Latin language, but there does exist liturgical material in the Irish language from this early period. In the early decades of the ninth century, probably in the reforming monastery of Tallaght, St Oengus composed a long poem known as the *Félire Óengusso*, giving brief notices for all the liturgical celebrations of the year. When it comes to 25 December (identified as 'great Christmas', as opposed to the 'little Christmas' of 6 January), this is how Oengus sums up the feast:

In notlaic mór mírbuil
Críst ó Mairi bánglain
génair la díth ndorchae,
rí sorchae síl Ádaim.

At great marvellous Christmas, Christ from white-pure Mary was born, bringing the ruin of darkness, Christ, the bright king of Adam's race.

Here again the consequential nature of Christ's birth is underlined: the light that began to shine in Bethlehem is no fragile, flickering flame but entails the definitive destruction of darkness.

Around the time that the *Félire Óengusso* was being composed, a missal was written, probably also in Tallaght. The Stowe Missal is a rare and precious witness to early Irish liturgical practices, especially in the short vernacular treatise it contains on the significance of various gestures and practices. Various moments in the celebration of the Sunday Eucharist are linked, for example, to moments in Christ's life. Interestingly, the moment associated with the Nativity is the elevation of the uncovered chalice. What's the connection? It's not entirely clear, but it's worth noting that the author connects this moment not only with Christ's birth but also with 'his glory through signs and miracles', and it seems likely that it is precisely the luminosity of this moment in the Mass—the elevated chalice glowing in candlelight—which made this generation of Irish Christians think of the birth of Christ.

A generation or so later, many great Irish centres—including Tallaght and Bangor—had been greatly weakened by Viking attacks. Many monastic scholars sought refuge on the Continent, among them a certain Sedulius Scotus, who could turn his hand to biblical commentary, scribal work (even in Greek), political advice and poetry. One of his poems describes a Christmas celebration led by a bishop, surrounded by the Church at prayer. It opens with striking natural imagery:

> It is the time of snow, gleaming with perfect light,
> now is the season in which Lord Jesus was born.
> O brothers, shine like the purest snow,
> and glisten with unblemished souls.

The poem goes on to make a tongue-in-cheek comparison between the Magi, coming from the East with their gifts, and newly arrived Irish scholars, coming from western lands, 'bringing their precious gifts of learning'. After that bit of self-congratulation, the poem returns to the theme of light-in-darkness:

> When the joyous day arrives, let all rejoice as one,
> and let gladness and love rule every man's heart.
> Divine radiance attests to Christ's birth,
> and heaven's splendour adores our True Light.
> Let us walk happily in the light of Christ,
> and go directly to his sacred land. Amen.

Wandering scholars like Sedulius often settled down in Continental schools, and one of them, Moengall of St Gallen, had a particularly distinguished teaching career. Several of his students excelled in various arts, including one—Notker the Stammerer—in music. Notker was a pioneer in the art of composing sequences, a kind of extended musical poem for use in the liturgy, then in its infancy as a genre. In his own writings, he describes taking his early compositions to his Irish teacher, who received them 'with joy' and gave them to his students to sing. One of Notker's sequences, *Natus ante saecula*, became greatly loved in succeeding generations and featured in Christmas celebrations for centuries. In its imagery it's entirely consistent with the Irish tradition which shaped his teacher:

> This present little day proclaims,
> all bright, its length increased,
> that the true Sun by the ray
> of his light has driven off
> the old shadows of the world.

Notker's use of the phrase 'true Sun' brings us back, full circle, to Patrick, with whom we began. Neither of these men was Irish, but they bookend our period neatly, a period in which, for Irish Christians, the birth of Christ was above all conceived of as a victory for light, a defeat for darkness, a definitive dawn.

SOURCES AND FURTHER READING

The Antiphonary of Bangor, ed. F.E. Warren (2 vols, London, 1895).
The Martyrology of Oengus the Culdee, ed. and trans. W. Stokes (London, 1905).
St Patrick, *Confessio*, online edition and translation at confessio.ie.

THE CHRISTMAS STORY IN
THE POEMS OF BLATHMAC

David Stifter and Siobhán Barrett

The first formulation of the Christmas narrative as a literary text in the Irish language comes as part of the so-called 'Poems of Blathmac', two long poems in eighth-century Old Irish. The poems survive in a single seventeenth-century copy, nine centuries after their composition. Manuscript G50, today kept in the National Library of Ireland in Dublin, was perhaps written by Cú Choigríche Ó Cléirigh, one of the Four Masters. Although no scribal signature proves Cú Choigcríche's penmanship, the handwriting is very similar to that of other manuscripts suspected to be in his hand. In any case, the manuscript was owned in the early nineteenth century by a descendant of Cú Choigcríche, from whom it was acquired, together with other manuscripts, by the Irish scholar Edward O'Reilly.

A heading at the beginning of the poems ascribes the verses to a poet called Blathmac, son of Cú Brettan son of Congus from the Fir Rois, a people who inhabited parts of the modern counties Louth and Monaghan. Other sources associate Cú Brettan rather with the Uí Ségáin, a people among the Airgíalla. Even though the poet Blathmac is not known to us from any other source, we have some information about his father and his brother Donn Bó, who both were kings of their people. According to annalistic evidence, Cú Brettan died in 740 and Donn Bó was killed in a battle in 759. If we can trust this information, this allows us to locate Blathmac approximately in the middle of the eighth century in eastern Ulster. From the devotional contents of his poems, from his ample use of religious writing and liturgical formulae and from the literary genre of the poems, an invocation of Mary, we may deduce that Blathmac was a cleric.

Poem 1 extends over 149 stanzas and poem 2 over at least 154 stanzas (numbers 150–303), of which the last 30 or so are only fragmentary. The second poem must have originally been longer still, but unfortunately the rest is lost because of the lamentable state of the manuscript.

In the opening stanzas of the first poem, which may be the earliest surviving Irish keen, Blathmac greets Mary and invites her to join him in keening the death of her first-born son, Jesus Christ. This is followed by a long section praising Jesus's beauty, generosity and wisdom, and part of this, namely stanzas 10–23, contain the Christmas story. The rest of the poem is an account of Christ's salvific work and a detailed description of his Passion. For his Christmas story, Blathmac has blended the accounts in the Gospels of Luke (2:4–20) and Matthew (2:1–18). He is viewing the biblical story through local, Irish eyes: the word he uses for the Magi is the Old Irish *druí*, the inherited word for 'druid'. When the Magi return to their own land, Blathmac speaks of *túath*, the term for the small medieval Irish kingdoms and their people, of which there existed over 150 on the island.

Old Irish text

10 *Soër ngein ro·génair úait,*
    rot·rath, a Maire, mórbúaid.
    Críst mac Dé Athar do nim,
    é ro·n-ucais i mBeithil.

11 *Ba suäichnid dia·mbá, a bé*
    cot mac i mBeithil Iude,
    ad·fét aingel co clú gil
    a gein donaib augairib.

12   *Ad·ces rétglu co mméit móir*
       tairrngert Bálam mac Bëóir.
       Ba sí do·deraid anair
       na tri druídea co ndánaib.

13   *Tadallsat ind fir cen úaill*
       Ierosalem co Hirúaid.
       Íarmi·foächtat loc glé
       i·ngénair rí na nIudae.

14   *As·bert Heróaid: 'Aidlid lib*
       dús ind·fogbaid i mBeithil.
       Má ro·fessid phort i·mbé
       tísid conda·radar-se.'

15   *Inmailli ferais in rí*
       do chuingid in tairngerthai,
       condid·tetairsed tri mrath.
       Níbu ar onóir nó adrad.

16   *Íar sin fúaratar do mac*
       it chomair, a Mairenat.
       Na tri druïd no·rádu
       ad·opartat degdánu.

17   *Batar é na dána trá*
       aurum, tus et mirrha.
       Ba coindfe do Ísu uile,
       rí ba Día, ba fírduine.

18   *Do·fied aingel Dé de nim*
       sét n-aile donaib druídib.

Lotar as slán chéill dia túaith,
ní·adallsat co Hirúaith.

19   *Ad·fíad alaile—fó chíall—*
    isind aislingiu do Iosíab:
    'Dul lat dé Mairi for fecht
    ocus do mac i nÉgept.'

20   *Oc cuingid Chríst—ba trúag sé—*
    ortae macrad Bethele.
    Heróid cródu cech airiuch,
    las·tarda fo glaschlaidiub.

21   *Céin·mair in macraid moíth maith,*
    táthus subae i mbithflaith.
    Táthai Heroäid—tróg delb—
    bithbrón ocus bithifernn.

22   *Fersai do longas nach sel*
    i nÉgept, a nóebingen,
    oc díte Chríst cosind rath.
    Ba huisse a imdídnad.

23   *†Nond babair† níbar toirsich*
    hi comair for móethloingsich,
    Coimdiu gréine gile glé,
    oirdnidiu in fócarthae.

Translation

10   A noble being was born from you,
    a great gift has been bestowed on you, Mary.

Christ, son of God, the Father in Heaven,
it is he whom you have borne in Bethlehem.

11   It was manifest, woman, when you were
with your son in Bethlehem of Juda,
an angel with bright fame announces
his birth to the shepherds.

12   A star of great size was seen,
which Balaam, son of Beöir, had prophesied.
It was it that had guided from the east
the three magi with gifts.

13   The men visited without haughtiness
Herod at Jerusalem.
They enquired about the bright spot
in which the king of the Jews was born.

14   Herod said: 'Go ye to see
if ye find him in Bethlehem.
If ye find out the place in which he is,
come so that I may adore him.'

15   The king expressed longing
to find the prophesied one,
so that he might seize him through treachery.
It was not for honour or worship.

16   After that they found your son
in your company, dear Mary.
The three magi that I mention
offered fine gifts.

17   These, then, were the gifts,
aurum, tus et myrrha (gold, frankincense and myrrh).
All this was fitting for Jesus,
a king who was God, who was true man.

18   An angel of God from Heaven showed
another way to the magi.
They left safely for their own country,
they did not visit Herod.

19   Another (angel)—good sense—
told Joseph in a vision:
'Go away from here with Mary
and your son on a journey to Egypt.'

20   In the search for Christ—this was pitiful—
the boys of Bethlehem were slain.
It was Herod, bloodier than any prince,
by whom they were put to the grey sword.

21   Blessed the good, tender boys,
they have happiness in an eternal kingdom.
Herod—a miserable figure—
has eternal sorrow and eternal hell.

22   You spent your exile for a while
in Egypt, holy maiden,
protecting Christ with grace.
It was right to protect him.

23   †...† ye were not sorrowful
in the company of your tender exile,

the Lord of the clear bright sun,
a most eminent outlaw.

NOTES

17b: This line is in Latin.
23a: This line is corrupt; the meaning of the first two words is unclear.

SOURCES AND FURTHER READING

Siobhán Barrett, 'A study of the lexicon of the poems of Blathmac son of Cú Brettan' (Ph.D thesis, Maynooth University, 2017) (https://mural.maynoothuniversity.ie/10042/).

Siobhán Barrett and David Stifter, 'Blathmac's stanzas 260–303 on Judgement Day', *Celtica* **31** (2019), 19–89.

James Carney (ed.), *The Poems of Blathmac Son of Cú Brettan together with The Irish Gospel of Thomas and A Poem on the Virgin Mary* (Irish Texts Society, Dublin, 1964).

Pádraig Ó Riain (ed.), *The Poems of Blathmac Son of Cú Brettan: reassessments* (Irish Texts Society, London, 2015).

David Stifter, 'The language of the Poems of Blathmac', in Pádraig Ó Riain (ed.), *The Poems of Blathmac Son of Cú Brettan*, 47–103.

Image of manuscript NLI G50 p. 123. The page contains stanzas 13–25, i.e. most of the Christmas narrative in the *Poems of Blathmac*. Courtesy of the National Library of Ireland. Source: Irish Script On Screen (School of Celtic Studies, Dublin Institute for Advanced Studies).

(NOT) DREAMING OF A WHITE CHRISTMAS IN 'PRE-NORMAN' IRELAND

Niamh Wycherley

One of the first surviving written mentions of Christmas in Ireland describes the awe-inspiring opportunities presented by some remarkably cold weather. In the year 818 the Annals of Ulster recorded:

> Unusual ice and much snow lasted from Little Christmas (*notlaic stelle*) until Shrovetide. People crossed the Boyne and other rivers dry-footed; similarly, the loughs. Herds and armed companies went across Loch nEchach; deer were hunted. After that the materials for an oratory were brought by a company across Loch nEirne from the lands of Connacht into the land of the Uí Chremthainn; and other novel things occurred this year because of the frost and the hail.

Annals are short yearly accounts of major events, such as the death of important people (bishops, kings), battles, attacks on churches, extreme weather, bad and good harvests, disease and famine. Significant snow fell rarely enough in medieval Ireland to warrant inclusion. In 855, for example, the annals claimed that the snow was 'as deep as men's belts on the 23rd of April'. Unlike the 818 reference above, most of the mentions of the white stuff lament the destruction wrought on the countryside, which usually experienced a more temperate climate. In the years 635, 670, 748, 799, 895, 917, 1047, 1095, 1107, 1111 and 1115, severe snowfall killed many people and animals and led to crop failure and famine.

This scarcity of sunlight dominated the Christmas discourse in the medieval Irish texts. In one early Irish chant for the first hour of Christmas Day there is no mention of the birth of Christ. The antiphon, from the Antiphonary of Bangor, possibly dating from as early as *c.* 690, instead focuses on the joy of the monks at the prospect of shrinking hours of darkness following the winter solstice and the promise of longer days to come.

While we brighten the winter gloom with a seemingly ever-increasing abundance of twinkling Christmas fairy lights, our medieval ancestors relied on candlelight. In the (arguably) ninth-century Irish text 'The Voyage of St Brendan the Abbot', Brendan and his monks celebrate Christmas on the island of St Ailbe, 'during which they observe the altar lamps being magically set alight by a flying arrow, the candles burning without being consumed because the light is of a spiritual kind'. This tale has been termed a medieval best-seller on account of its popularity across medieval Europe and was the inspiration for Tim Severin's famous Atlantic voyage in 1976.

Christmas in medieval Ireland was, by definition, the celebration of the Nativity (the birth of Christ). This meaning was clearly preserved in the Irish language. The Old Irish word *notlaic* (modern *Nollaig*) derived from the Latin *natalicia*, 'birth'. While *Notlaic Mór* denoted 25 December, the big day itself, the feast of the Epiphany on 6 January was often referred to as *Notlaic Becc*, 'Little Christmas', or *Notlaic Stéille*, 'Christmas of the star'. The early ninth-century text *Félire Óengusso* ('The Martyrology of Oengus') poetically commemorates the birth of Jesus under 25 December: 'At great marvellous Christmas, Christ was born from white-pure Mary' (*In notlaic mór mírbuil, Críst ó Mairi bánghlain génair*).

In 'pre-Norman' Ireland, Christmas was not the big festival that it is today, and it receives much less attention in texts like 'The Voyage of

St Brendan the Abbot' than Easter, which marked the pinnacle of the liturgical calendar. We can also see this in Irish iconography. There is potentially only one depiction of the Nativity on Irish high crosses, while representations of the Crucifixion and the Passion are almost ubiquitous. There are enough references in the written texts, however, to indicate that it was a special time, marked by feasting and rest. According to early Irish law, for example, commoners were allowed bread (most likely wheaten) on Easter, Christmas and Sundays. Similarly, Dublittir (d. 796), abbot of Finglas, a church which observed a strict abstinent lifestyle, permitted a relaxation of the rules during the feasts of Christmas, Easter and Whitsun, while another set of monks' rules laments the drunkenness of some clerics during these same holy festivals.

Brennu-Njáls Saga, a later medieval Icelandic literary tale, provides an evocative depiction of a lavish Christmas feast/political summit attended by Sitric Silkenbeard, 'Hiberno-Norse' king of Dublin, in 1013. While this account is dramatic fiction, it does convey how Christmas was a time for significant political events and displays of hospitality. There are a number of references in the sources to kings spending Christmas in important monasteries such as Clonmacnoise, and that taxes and dues were also to be paid at that time. After a victory over Dublin in 989, Máel Sechnaill, the king of Tara, demanded an ounce of gold per each *garðr* ('enclosure', 'yard') from the Dubliners every Christmas. Christmas was sometimes seen as a convenient time for attack. The churches of Clonmore (836) and Iona (986) were both attacked by 'heathen foreigners' on Christmas Eve.

According to *Brennu-Njáls Saga*, Sitric Silkenbeard was at the court of fellow so-called 'Viking' leader Earl Sigurd of Orkney to drum up support against Brian Boru, recently acknowledged as 'Emperor of the Irish', for what became the Battle of Clontarf. Dublin was resisting the overlordship of the man from Munster (nothing new here, then!). According to another literary account of the events surrounding the Battle of Clontarf, the 'War of the Irish against the foreigners' (*Cogadh Gaedhel re Gallaibh*), Brian Boru tired of his siege of Dublin in the winter of 1013 and returned home to Munster for Christmas, to rest and regroup. He returned east in January, according to the story, rested after the break, and intensified his efforts to bring the Dubs to heel, ultimately culminating in the Battle of Clontarf at Easter 1014.

SOURCES AND FURTHER READING

Annals of Ulster, digital edition: https://celt.ucc.ie/published/ T100001A/.

W.R.J. Barron and Glyn S. Burgess (eds), *The Voyage of Saint Brendan: representative versions of the legend in English translation* (Exeter, 2002).

SALVATION HISTORY AND MIRACLES IN ROME AT THE TIME OF CHRIST'S BIRTH: EXPLORING TWO FRANCISCAN SOURCES FROM LATER MEDIEVAL IRELAND

Diarmuid Scully

Two Franciscan sources from later medieval Ireland—the anonymous *Liber Exemplorum* and Friar John Clyn's Annals of Ireland—describe miracles in Rome at the time of Christ's birth. A temple collapsed, oil streamed from the ground and a sign was seen in the heavens. The sources' accounts of these miracles provide an insight into their understanding of salvation history. The first of these sources, the *Liber Exemplorum* or 'Book of Examples' (*c.* 1275), was a collection of short narratives designed as preaching aids. It was compiled by an English Franciscan resident in Ireland. The Annals of Ireland, best remembered today for their terrifying account of the Black Death, were compiled by Friar John Clyn of Kilkenny between 1333 and 1349.

Clyn's aim was to locate Ireland within the flow of universal history under divine providence. His annals begin with the birth of Christ and use the *Anno Domini* ('Year of the Lord') incarnational dating system to emphasise the central importance of Christ's first coming for the salvation of humanity. The annals' opening sentence connects Christ with Rome and indicates Clyn's historiographical perspective and model. It cites Orosius's early fifth-century *Seven books of history against the pagans*, a hugely influential work in the Middle Ages: 'According to Orosius, [there were] 4,484 years from the foundation of the world to the foundation of the city of Rome. And from the foundation of the city to the birth of Christ 715 years.' Orosius believed that God ordained the rise of the Roman Empire and synchronised its achievement of global rule under Augustus (r. 27 BC–AD 14) with the birth of Christ. God wished to secure worldwide conversion to Christianity through the *pax Romana* (Roman peace) and indicated his power and purpose through miracles in Rome that foretold or announced the Saviour's birth.

Clyn's first entry in the annals matches Orosius in recounting Christ's birth under Augustus, who 'reduced the whole world into one kingdom ... ordered that no one should call him Lord, that all captives should be freed ... There was total peace everywhere.' Patristic and medieval tradition saw a prefiguring of the universal Church and heavenly peace and joy under the one true God in the Augustan experience of universal peace, imperial humility and justice on earth. Concerning Rome at that time Clyn says: 'At the birth of Christ three miracles were visible. A temple at Rome collapsed; a fountain of oil burst forth across the Tiber from Taberna [or 'tavern']; on that day a circle appeared like an arch in the heavens around the sun'. The second and third of these miracles derive from Orosius. The *Liber Exemplorum* also contains versions of the three miracles or, more accurately, the first two miracles and an account of a sign in the heavens that may be a variant of the third.

The *Liber Exemplorum* identifies Peter Comestor's biblical history, the *Historia Scholastica* (c. 1170), as the source of the first of the three miracles in Rome: the collapsing temple. The Romans, enjoying a long period of peace, asked the god Apollo how long it would last. They were told that it would last until a virgin gave birth and remained a virgin after the birth. 'Believing that this was not possible, they build an enormous and wonderful temple to peace as if it would last forever. But when he was born who came to send not peace but a sword [Matthew 10:34], it fell to the ground.' Patristic commentators on Scripture believed that Christ's statement in Matthew's Gospel foretold spiritual warfare between good and evil. Satan was behind the pagan gods and their misleading promises and the trumperies of their idols and temples. Christ's birth silenced the oracles and overthrew the false gods of Antiquity, as foretold in Isaiah 19:1—'the idols of Egypt will tremble at his presence' (a biblical precedent for the collapse of the temple in Rome). Master Gregory's early thirteenth-century *The marvels of Rome*, reporting a variant of the collapsing temple story, concludes: 'We can also believe that the evil enemy [Satan] lost its ability to deceive mankind when God took human form'. The first miracle in Rome at Christ's birth therefore marks a decisive moment in salvation history.

The *Liber Exemplorum* also identifies Peter Comestor as its source for the second miracle in Rome, but the story ultimately comes from Orosius. Clyn knew the Orosian version. In Orosius, this miracle occurred before the birth of Christ and indicated that he would be born when Augustus achieved global rule. Orosius's interpretation of the miracle rests on belief in Jesus as 'the Christ', meaning the Messiah, the anointed one; in the Old Testament the ceremony of anointing involves sacred oil. Orosius says that on the day that Augustus (then Octavian) entered Rome and received 'permanent tribunician power' after victories over his Roman rivals:

> a spring of oil flowed all day out of a lodging house. What could be more obvious than that this sign declared the birth of Christ would occur when Caesar ruled the whole world? For Christ in the language of that race into which and from which he was born, means the anointed.

The *Liber Exemplorum* specifies that the spring of oil appeared 'across the Tiber where the Church of St Mary now stands' (Santa Maria in

Trastevere). This makes its account all the more reliable and powerful: pilgrims can visit the place where the miracle occurred; they can see it for themselves. The fact that the tavern has been replaced by a church again affirms the triumph of Christianity in once-pagan Rome.

The third miracle in Rome involves a sign in the heavens. Clyn's version comes from Orosius, who puts it before his account of the miraculous oil, intending both stories to 'show that Caesar's rule had been ordained in advance entirely to prepare for the future coming of Christ'. Orosius describes Augustus entering Rome after the murder of his uncle, Julius Caesar, which provoked civil war; 'a circle of light like a rainbow surrounded the sun in a clear, serene, sky as if to mark him as the one, mightiest man in the world and by himself the most glorious man on the earth in whose days would come he [Christ] who by himself made and rules over the sun and the whole world'. The *Liber Exemplorum* reports a different kind of sign in the heavens in Rome, and dates it to the time 'when the Heavenly King was born'. The text cites Athanasius's 'book on the constitutions of the primitive Church' as its source, but this work has not been found. In the *Liber Exemplorum*, Augustus took advice from the Tiburtine Sybil, removed his imperial regalia and prayed to the Lord in sackcloth and ashes. 'And behold, he saw Heaven open wide and the Virgin holding a little baby in her arms. And he heard the words: This is the altar of the living God.' The *Liber Exemplorum* again reports that a church now stands at the site of this miracle: 'It is called the church of St Mary of the Altar of God or of Heaven [Santa Maria in Aracoeli]'.

The *Liber Exemplorum*'s respect for the Tiburtine Sybil, a pagan oracle, may seem contradictory, given medieval Christian hostility to paganism and the book's own account of the collapsing temple. Many Christian authorities believed, however, that God had revealed spiritual truths and foreknowledge of Christ and the Virgin Mary to good and wise pagans. The *Liber Exemplorum* shares this belief. It tells how a philosopher, 'though an unbeliever', foretold Christ's virgin birth when he predicted that a virgin would be born in 'the sign of the Virgin' and would give birth to a son: 'Doubtless, he means that the Blessed Virgin was born in the autumn, when the sun is in the sign of Virgo'. The *Liber Exemplorum* comments on the implications of such prophecies:

> For Christ was born not only on account of the Jews but also so that all peoples might be blessed in him, as God promised Abraham [Genesis 22:18]; thus it was not unfitting that the nativity of Christ, who would be born of a virgin, should be revealed not only to the holy prophets of God's people but to just men and women who belonged to heathen peoples.

This generous and inclusive vision of salvation is particularly meaningful in texts from medieval Ireland and Britain—islands of the gentiles at the ends of the earth. The stories in Friar Clyn's annals and the *Liber Exemplorum* concerning the miracles in Rome at Christ's birth pinpoint the moment in history when salvation was first extended to the gentiles. The conversion of these islands, foretold in Scripture, as medieval historians, exegetes and missionaries believed, was the final act in the extension of universal salvation that God initiated at that time. Thus Bede, who was greatly respected by Friar Clyn, concluded his *Ecclesiastical history of the English people* (*c.* 731): 'let the multitude of isles be glad and give thanks at the remembrance of his holiness [Psalm 96 (97):1, 12]'.

SOURCES AND FURTHER READING

A.T. Fear (trans.), *Orosius: Seven books of history against the pagans* (Liverpool, 2010).

David Jones (trans.), *Friars' tales: thirteenth-century exempla from the British Isles* (Manchester, 2011).

Bernadette Williams (ed. and trans.), *The Annals of Ireland by Friar John Clyn* (Dublin, 2007).

'MAY I REACH THE ANNIVERSARY OF THIS GREAT EVE ONCE MORE': CHRISTMAS IN A TIME OF PLAGUE (1350–1)

Denis Casey

When at Christmas 2021 contributions were first sought for this volume, Ireland was experiencing the rapid spread of Omicron, the most easily transmissible variant of the coronavirus SARS-CoV-2 known to that point. With a second muted Christmas and concerns of increased morbidity in the air, my thoughts turned to a different Christmas, that of 1350, when the Black Death/ bubonic plague was brutalising Ireland, and to the reactions of two different men, one an Anglo-Irish and the other a Gaelic writer.

Readers may be familiar with the oft-quoted final entry to the chronicle of Franciscan Friar John Clyn of Kilkenny (1348):

Now I, Friar John Clyn of the order of Minors and convent of Kilkenny, have written in this book these noteworthy deeds that happened in my time, that [I know] by faithful eye witness or by worthy reliable report. And lest these notable records should be lost with time and recede from memory of future people, [I] seeing these many evils and the whole world as it were in a bad situation, among the dead, expecting death when it should come, I have brought together in writing, just as I have truthfully heard and examined. And lest the writing should perish with the writer and the work fail together with the worker, I am leaving parchment for the work to continue if, by chance, in the future a man should remain surviving, and anyone of the race of Adam should be able to escape this plague and [live] to continue this work [I] commenced.

Living 'among the dead, expecting death', his pessimism was justified; the next year of his chronicle, in a different hand, sees the words *Videtur quod Author hic obiit* ('Here it seems the author died').

Clyn's understandable resignation to his fate was not, however, shared by all in Ireland. Two years later, on Christmas Eve, a Gaelic scribe facing the same plague as Friar Clyn prayed with his pen, invoking his own youth in a plea for preservation from the pestilence, a plea that deserves to be known at least as well as that of Friar Clyn. He expressed his fears in the margins of a legal manuscript owned by his father and now preserved in Trinity College Dublin:

It is one thousand three hundred and fifty years to-night since Jesus Christ was born, and in the second year after the coming of the plague to Ireland was this written, and I myself am full twenty-one years old; … and let every reader in pity recite a 'pater' for my soul. It is Christmas Eve to-night, and under the protection of the King of heaven and earth am I on this Eve to-night. May the end of my life be holy, and may this great plague pass by me and my friends, and restore us once more to joy and gladness. Amen. Pater noster. Hugh, son of Connor Mac Egan, wrote this on his father's book, the year of the great plague.

Hugh placed himself under the *commairge* ('protection') of God. In the early medieval period the ability to offer 'protection' to another—physically from harm or from legal proceedings—was enjoyed by all free men, with the level and duration dependent upon rank. In the law texts of the seventh to ninth centuries it was often referred to by the words *snádud* or *turtugud*, while in later literature it was usually called *fóesam* or *commairge* (the latter being used by Hugh). Naturally, much had changed since the early medieval period, which was as far removed from Hugh as Hugh is from us, but in fourteenth-century society the honour of a superior and his ability to extend protection could still be the difference between life and death. For the plague to violate God's protection was to dishonour Him and risk His retribution. Perhaps the prayers of Hugh's readers proved effective, for on Christmas Eve 1351 he wrote:

> It is just a year to-night since I wrote the lines on the margin below; and, if it be God's will, may I reach the anniversary of this great Eve once more. Amen. Pater noster.

He lived but a few years more. Hugh, son of Connor Mac Egan, 'the choicest of the brehons of Ireland', died in 1359, the year of his 30th birthday.

These marginalia's editor and translator, the Revd Charles Plummer, wrote in 1926 (perhaps with the effects of the Spanish influenza fresh in his mind) that, 'even after the lapse of more than five and a half centuries, it seems almost sacrilege to unveil the record of feelings so intimate and so sacred'. While his hesitancy does him credit, Plummer worried excessively. The margins of medieval manuscripts were a semi-public forum where the writer could interact with the text and also with fellow readers, and Hugh wrote his words in the hope that they would be read and acted upon. What Plummer did, through a translation sensitive to the depths of Hugh's worry and piety, was to give us a rare glimpse into the emotional turmoil of a Christmas Eve where the usual celebrations of a birth that promised the salvation of humanity seemed to be mocked by a devastation that threatened the extinction of 'the race of Adam'.

There are many in Ireland, doubtless some who possess a copy of this book, who empathised with Hugh's worry during the Christmas Eves of

2020 and 2021, and in their own ways prayed 'may this great plague pass by me and my friends, and restore us once more to joy and gladness'. And there are those family members and friends who will not 'reach the anniversary of this great Eve once more', but who remain in their hearts.

Amen. Pater noster.

SOURCES AND FURTHER READING

Charles Plummer, 'On the colophons and marginalia of Irish scribes', *Proceedings of the British Academy* **12** (1926), 11–44.

Bernadette Williams (ed. and trans.), *The Annals of Ireland by Friar John Clyn* (Dublin, 2007).

Bernadette Williams, 'The Black Death in Kilkenny', in Salvador Ryan (ed.), *Death and the Irish: a miscellany* (Dublin, 2016), 39–41.

CHRISTMAS 1397—FEASTING AT THE COURT OF NIALL ÓG Ó NÉILL

Tara Shields

L ate in the year 1397, the Catalan knight and diplomat Ramon de
Perellós, distraught at the death of his beloved patron King John
I of Aragon, was determined to discover his lord's fate and speak
with him one last time. But how? There was only one thing he could do:
he must travel to Ireland, the edge of the then-known world, and enter a
pit in a remote north-western corner of the island. This pit, known as St
Patrick's Purgatory, was believed to be the earthly entrance to Purgatory,
and during the Middle Ages it was famed throughout Europe; it was here
that Ramon could search for the late King John. And so, like many other
Continental pilgrims, he made the arduous journey to Ireland, unaware
of what lay in store. Embarking upon this expedition, Ramon could
hardly have imagined that he would end up celebrating Christmas at the
household of the 'greatest king' in Ireland.

Luckily, Ramon wrote an account of his travels—the *Viatge al
Purgatori Sant Patrici*—which gives the modern reader a unique insight
into medieval Ireland from an outsider's perspective. Whilst the visionary
account of his experiences within the purgatory itself makes for fascinat-
ing reading, what is perhaps even more interesting are his descriptions of
Ireland, its people and its customs, including one of the fullest accounts

of an élite Irish Christmas celebration that we have from the Middle Ages.

Throughout his journey Ramon meets and interacts with individuals at the highest levels of society, both within the Pale and beyond it. A distinguished knight and diplomat, it is no surprise that he was well received by the likes of Roger Mortimer, earl of March and lord lieutenant of Ireland, and John Colton, archbishop of Armagh. Ramon's ultimate destination, the purgatory, lay on a small island in Lough Derg, which lies in the south of modern-day County Donegal. At the end of the fourteenth century this was deep within Gaelic territory, and well beyond the jurisdiction of the English colony. Both Mortimer and Colton did their utmost to dissuade Ramon from continuing his journey. The earl of March warned him that he would have to 'go through strange places inhabited by wild people', and Archbishop Colton emphasised the danger of being in Ó Néill lands, above and beyond the dangers of the purgatory itself. It was with this impression of Gaelic Ireland that Ramon, resolute in his conviction to make it to Lough Derg, crossed beyond the Pale.

Upon entering Gaelic territory, Ramon and his retinue soon came upon Niall Óg Ó Néill, who was the king of Tír Eoghain at the time. In contrast to the reception that his contacts in the colony had prepared Ramon to expect, Niall Óg was welcoming, even sending him a gift of food. Ramon gives a lengthy description of Irish customs, providing us with invaluable eyewitness testimony. Noting that Irish 'customs and habits seem very strange to us', Ramon resolved to report 'a few things about their manners and way of life, about what I observed of them while with the king, with whom, on my return, I celebrated the feast of Christmas'.

Having arrived in Ireland in November 1397, Ramon travelled through the cities of Dublin, Drogheda and Dundalk before he turned west and entered Gaelic territory. Briefly hosted by Ó Néill, he and his company headed westward to the purgatory; it was on his return journey from Lough Derg that Niall Óg again received him 'very well and with great pleasure' over the Christmas period. Ramon tells us that he 'celebrated Christmas Day where he [Niall Óg] held great court according to their custom, which to us here is very strange for a king to do, albeit he had so many people'. It is evident that Ó Néill's feast made an impression on him, and he wanted to record the details of these 'strange' Irish Christmas customs in writing, so that he could share his experiences with audiences on the Continent.

Ramon painted a vivid picture of the festivities, evoking all the senses of his readers. He began by providing a detailed description of the dress of those in attendance:

> The great lords wear an unlined tunic that comes down to the knees, with a very low neckline, like that worn by women. And they wear great long-tailed hoods that come down to the waist, with the pointed end as narrow as a finger. And they wear no leggings, or shoes, or breeches but wear their spurs on their bare heels. It was in this fashion that the king appeared on Christmas Day, and all his clerics and knights and bishops and abbots and other great lords.

In a not-so-subtle dig at the male royal attendants, he also noted: 'you can well imagine how badly dressed the squires were'.

Although one might expect such an account to focus solely on the upper echelons of society, Ramon also provided some detail on the 'common' people, who

> go about as best they can—they are badly dressed—but most of them wear a frieze mantle, and both men and women display all their private parts with absolutely no shame. The poor people go naked but they all wear those mantles—good or bad—including ladies.

He continued with a description of female attire:

> The queen and her daughter and her sister were dressed, and had their hair tied up, in green, but wore no shoes. The queen's maidens, who numbered

about twenty, were dressed as I have described above, and showed their private parts with as little shame as people here show their faces.

Quite the spectacle indeed! (This account of nakedness underneath the long mantle, as surprising as it may be, echoes Laurent Vital's description of bare-breasted women in Kinsale in 1518.) For all their shamelessness, however, Ramon was favourably impressed with the beauty of the Irish, commenting that 'they are indeed amongst the handsomest men and the most beautiful women that I have seen in the whole world'.

Today many consider Christmas a time for charity and gift-giving, and an opportunity to spend time sharing food with family and friends. These also appear to have been important elements of the Christmas celebration in 1397. Ramon highlights Niall Óg's benevolence on Christmas Day: 'and with the king there were about three thousand horses, and also many poor people, to whom I saw the king order generous alms of beef to be given'.

With regard to the feast itself, Ramon remarked that on Christmas Day, when the king held his great court,

his table was nothing more than a great quantity of rushes spread out on the ground, and close by him they set down the finest grass they could find for wiping the mouth, and they brought him the food on two poles, just as they carry buckets [of grapes] [during the wine harvest] …

Although there was 'neither bread to eat nor wine to drink', Ramon tells us that 'as a special gift he [the king] sent me two little bread cakes as thin as wafers, and as easily folded as raw dough. They were made of oats and had an earthen appearance, and were as black as charcoal, but truly delicious.'

Ramon's *Viatge* provides the modern reader with an illuminating glimpse into Ireland's medieval past. From his unique perspective as a Catalan pilgrim, his insightful account might also be viewed as an early example of the travelogue, a genre which remains popular with modern readers seeking to learn about far-off places that they might only dream of visiting. Indeed, Ramon's account served a similar purpose for Continental contemporaries. For all the warnings that Ramon received before he crossed beyond the Pale, one gets the sense that he was generously welcomed at the Christmas feast of Ó Néill, and that he was able to enjoy some of that Irish hospitality that lives on to this day.

SOURCES AND FURTHER READING

Stephen Boyd (ed.), *Ramon de Perellós: Journey to St Patrick's Purgatory* (Woodbridge, 2022).

Michael Haren and Yolande de Pontfarcy (eds), *The medieval pilgrimage to St Patrick's Purgatory: Lough Derg and the European tradition* (Enniskillen, 1988).

THE EARLY LIFE OF IRISH CHRISTMAS FOOD

Regina Sexton

Food plays a significant and central role in the celebration of Irish Christmases past and present. Today, in the early 21st century, festive foods and dishes such as roast/baked turkey (and, to a lesser extent, goose), bread, potato and sausage stuffings and Brussels sprouts, together with sweet confections like plum puddings, mince pies, cakes and trifles, form the typical package of Christmas fare. These table items are perceived as traditional, with repetitive and clearly defined activities associated with their procurement, preparation and consumption, to the point where a festive season without all, or even one, of these dishes might be considered a disruption of the proper and prescribed way of 'doing' Christmas. Yet this typical package of festive foods is only a recent standardisation of older food practices and customs associated with the celebration of Christmas. An exploration of the evolution of Christmas food customs and associated food behaviours illustrates the interconnections and mingling of agricultural practice, religious observance and economic and commercial developments in shaping a range of Christmas food cultures in Ireland that varied with time, location, cultural outlook and economic standing.

There is little, if any, evidence of distinctive Irish early medieval food practices to celebrate the Nativity and Christmastide. References to the season emphasise food prohibitions linked to the liturgical seasons of Advent and Christmas, with no direct descriptions of elaborate feasting or indulgence. Christmas Day and Little Christmas, the latter named for either New Year's Day or the Epiphany, are mentioned in the contexts of fasting. The Advent season, starting on the fourth Sunday before Christmas or the Sunday closest to 31 November, was a time of abstinence when the consumption of meat was prohibited either for the duration of the season or on fixed days (various combinations of Wednesdays, Fridays and Saturdays were imposed as fast days through time). As a period to reflect on and prepare for the celebration of the Nativity, the Advent fast ended on the eve of Christmas, and this fast to feast relationship had implications for food traditions. The *Monastery of Tallaght*, a *c.* ninth-century text detailing the religious habits of the Céle Dé, a community of penitent monks, refers to another fast on the eve of the Epiphany, which, according to the text, was a fast that was more relaxed in its food allowance in comparison with former custom. An evening fast meal consisting of one-eighth of a bread loaf and a measure of the capacity of twelve fills of a hen's egg of good milk (possibly fresh or full-fat) with an accompanying relish was prescribed for the monastic community. The observance of seasonal and vigil fasts may suggest that their associated feast-days, Christmas Day and New Year's Day and/or the Epiphany, were days to celebrate with special foods. Nevertheless, we can only speculate that a feast routinely followed a fast, as the documentary sources do not provide descriptions of Christmas feasting.

On the other hand, the sources are rich in references to secular feasting and associated high-value and élite foods. The saga literature and early Irish laws (*Corpus iuris Hibernici*) list meats, beef (in particular the sirloin and shank cuts) and pig meat, along with wheaten bread, butter and honey, as high-status foods required as food renders and rents from clients to noble grades. Closer to Christmas time, the coshering season (*cáe*) from New Year's Day to Shrovetide was a period when servile clients were expected to provide one night's portion of winter food (*gambiadh*) to their lords and company. Winter provision included sides of bacon, cereals and butter.

The meat element of seasonal feasting is detailed further in the eighth-century law tract *Críth Gablach*, in which a cow, a yearling heifer or bullock (*colpach*) and a heifer or bull calf (*dartaid*) are listed as required renders. If a Christmas-season feast followed a fast, the inference to draw from descriptions of food renders and winter provisioning is that meat, especially beef, held high status as a desirable item for special occasions and festive celebrations. In a traditional economy, higher rates of meat consumption for certain social groups were tied to patterns of the farming year. Winter slaughter of post-harvest fattened animals and the culling of older animals saved fodder for breeding and productive stock. These seasonal agricultural practices and ritualised slaughter at the feast of St Martin of Tours (Martinmas) on 11 November became entwined with the religious observance of the Advent fast, introducing cultural complexity to meat-eating practices at this time of the year. The conflicting pairings of fast and feast, the practical strategies associated with the consumption of fresh meat, especially in organising feasts to strengthen bonds of clientship and networks of power, and the preserving of surplus imbued meat, especially fresh meat, with symbolic value and multiple meanings. Its association with élite consumption patterns gave it high status, making it an item that differentiated the everyday from the extraordinary.

High levels of meat consumption, or at least a desire to secure meat for Christmas eating, is a notable feature of food customs that remained a characteristic of the festival through time. What also lingered was the fast and feast relationship, whereby one gave definition to the other in the observance of fish days and meat days, as influenced by the liturgical cycle of the year. We must remain cautious, however, in imagining an early medieval Irish Christmas and recognise the nuances and complexities that separated the food and dietary patterns of religious and secular communities.

Of more substance is the often-cited description of the Christmas celebrations of King Henry II in Dublin in 1171, which gives insight into courtly feasting in terms of food choice and table etiquette. The cleric and writer Gerald of Wales in his *Expugnatio Hibernica* (*c.* 1189) describes the Christmas royal court where Henry accepted the submission of the Gaelic kings of north Leinster:

> As the solemn festival of Our Lord's birth drew near, the princes of that land came to Dublin in great numbers to view the king's court. There they greatly admired the sumptuous and plentiful fare of the English table and the most elegant service by the royal domestics. Throughout the great hall, in obedience to the king's wishes they began to eat the flesh of the crane [*carne gruina*], which they had hitherto loathed.

Implicit in his description are the differences between the two cultural groups and their associated foodways, with domination politics played out in the Irish conforming to new tastes. And while we must remain cautious of Gerald's bias in setting a distorted contrast between the barbaric Irish and the sophistication of the Anglo-Normans, there is still value in his reference to the selection of great birds to bring to the table for special and celebratory occasions. Provisioning the king's stay in Ireland was a considerable undertaking and it was planned not simply to sustain his entourage and troops but also to maintain, display and perform elements of Anglo-Norman food and culinary culture. Alongside the supply of staples like meat and grain, the king's table also required hundreds of pounds of almonds, spices and electuaries, suggesting the desire to recreate for the royal stay a food culture of the colonist as distinct from Irish practice. The use of spices in cooking, the preparation of almond milk as a cooking ingredient for fast days and the belief in the health-giving and medicinal benefits of sweet-based cordials and preparations indicate the beginnings, or at the least a tentative expansion, of a different food philosophy and culinary system in Ireland.

Over time, a Norman presence in Ireland and the establishment of manors to embed the socio-economic and cultural ethos of the conquering élite encouraged the transmission of new ways with food. Meat and fish pies and pasties, home-made or ready-made and shop-bought, become a feature of urban foodscapes in areas of Norman influence, while medieval manorial records highlight the popularity of the Christmas hen, which was a customary part of the food renders from servile tenants to lords at the festival. Capons and geese and fatted hogs are also listed as Christmastide renders. In medieval England, these food renders often made up the Christmas meal provided by the lord to estate tenants, which marked the festive meal as one of commensality characterised by the inclusion of a farmyard fowl and a post-harvest fattened animal in the celebrations. The popularity of the Christmas hen, capon and goose offered by tenants to lords carries through to seventeenth- and eighteenth-century indentures of land rental agreements and lease conditions. Food returns are joined by fat brawns, fat mutton, flagons of beer, loaves of bread and notably, in early eighteenth-century agreements, Christmas gifts of sugar loaves, often of prescribed grade and weight, from tenants to their landlords.

Beef remained prominent in the Christmas social celebrations and assembly dinners of certain social groups and guilds, as illustrated in the 1628 Christmas gift of beef made to the Dublin mayor by the city's Guild of Tailors. This nexus of seasonal food-related customs and associated social functions mirrors the details of Christmas foods listed by the English poet and farmer Thomas Tusser in his *Five hundred points of good Husbandrie* (1580). Here, besides meats in variety, capons, goose, puddings and shred pies are presented as typical Christmas fare, along with what is believed to be the first linkage of the turkey, a New World introduction, to the Christmas table.

By the early seventeenth century the mercantile ambitions of the expanding empire, its activities in establishing the East India Company and transatlantic trading routes brought Ireland into closer contact with the circulation of luxury and expensive ingredients like sugar and spices. Ireland's colonial status and the associated food culture of the élites and wealthy merchants supported the introduction and circulation of new ingredients and fashionable cookery styles. The high status of New World exotics like the turkey, chocolate and sugar made them desirable items to integrate into occasions of celebration and feasting as symbols of wealthy, sophisticated and modern foodways. When these exotics came together with high-status staples like meat, fat and flour, specialities like mince pies, plum porridge and pudding were grafted onto festive menus and the Christmas food template was set. That they had entered the popular psyche as desired Christmas foods is evident in the body of comic and satirical literature published in England in response to ordinances issued by the Puritan parliament to curtail the excesses of Christmas feasting. Pamphlets like *The arraignment, conviction and imprisoning of Christmas, printed by Simon Minc'd Pye for Cissely Plum-porridge* (1646) and *The exaltation of the Christmas pye* (1659) demarcate customary Christmas foods and traditions that would in time embed themselves in English festivities and, by extension, in those of the Irish colony.

The early acceptance and transmission of these Christmas food practices must have been largely confined to areas of strong colonist settlement and to certain socio-cultural groups with early integration at the upper echelons of the social hierarchy. As detailed by Taverner and Flavin, turkey is an ingredient in the Dublin Castle kitchen of William Fitzwilliam, lord deputy of Ireland in the 1570s, while directions for cooking large table birds and making all sorts of puddings and pies are well represented in mid- to late seventeenth-century handwritten recipe collections produced by high-ranking élite and gentry women in Ireland. William Penn's observation of Cork at Christmas 1669 that 'December 25 was Pie Day, none could be got to work', indicates the extension of custom into the celebrations of the general populace in urban and trading centres.

SOURCES AND FURTHER READING

Daniel Binchy, *Críth Gablach* (Dublin, 1941; repr. 1979).
Eoin MacNeill, 'Ancient Irish law. The Law of Status or Franchise', *Proceedings of the Royal Irish Academy* **36**C (1921–4), 265–316.

A.B. Scott and F.X. Martin (eds), *Expugnatio Hibernica: The conquest of Ireland* (Dublin, 1978).

Madeline Shanahan, *Christmas food and feasting: a history* (New York and London, 2019).

Charlie Taverner and Susan Flavin, 'Food and power in sixteenth-century Ireland: studying household accounts from Dublin Castle', *The Historical Journal* **66** (2022), 1–26.

FESTIVE FEASTING
AND FIGHTING
IN THE MIDDLE AGES

Yvonne Seale

Generosity and hospitality are the hallmarks of many Irish Christmases. Friends, neighbours, aunties and uncles, even distant cousins, are sure to be welcomed in and plied with liberal quantities of tea, biscuits and mince pies. The small children of the house might be coaxed to perform a party piece, or music might be played. Gatherings like these strengthen our sense of community and family—even if sometimes they can create anxiety about whether the 'good china' has been used or whether there are any 'fancy biscuits' left. This is because the perceived warmth of a welcome or lavishness of a meal can be used as a proxy to judge the wealth and social standing of the hosts. A Christmas gathering, in other words, can be an opportunity to show off the size of your wallet or the sophistication of your taste. This was as true in the Middle Ages as it is now; the élites of medieval Ireland hosted events to impress others with their power and authority.

The great feast thrown on Christmas Day 1351 by William (Uilliam) Ó Ceallaigh, ruler of Uí Mháine, was renowned for doing just that. William invited 'the learned of Ireland, travellers, the poor and the indigent, and they were all served to their satisfaction, both good and bad, noble and ignoble', to celebrate the season at his recently built Galey

Castle (today a ruinous tower-house perched precariously on the shore of Lough Ree, Co. Roscommon). The revellers likely feasted on the kinds of foods much prized in medieval Ireland: beef, pork and oatcakes slathered with butter and honey. A contemporary praise-poem tells us that William's invitation attracted so many people and from such distances that temporary wattle-built structures had to be constructed around the castle to house them. The banquet was such a success that it even gave rise to the Irish-language saying *Cuireadh fáilte Uí Cheallaigh romhainn* ('We got the O'Kelly welcome') to describe outstanding hospitality.

Such great festive banquets were not confined to the Gaelic aristocracy. James Butler, earl of Ormond, was one of the foremost magnates of Ireland in the later fourteenth century, and served as justiciar or deputy lieutenant of Ireland several times. In order for him and his household to spend Christmas 1393 at New Ross in a manner befitting his rank, he ordered the seneschal of Wexford to provide all the provisions necessary. The list of requirements was lengthy: '40 crannocks of pure wheat; 60 crannocks of oats; 60 good bullocks; 4 boars; 80 large pigs; 60 small pigs; 100 geese; 100 ducks; 200 pairs of rabbits; 100 trusses of litter; 200 trusses of hay; 600 of poultry; 6 lambs; 5 meases of herrings; 100 cod and ling fish; and 100 salted salmons', together with anything else that might be needed. This is an enormous quantity of food, even assuming that its consumption would have been spread out over the whole Christmas season. It seems safe to assume that those in the earl's household were well fed indeed.

Guests at other Christmastime festivities in medieval Ireland, even those hosted by royalty, were admittedly less impressed by the hospitality offered to them. As noted in Tara Shields's essay, in 1397 the Catalan nobleman and pilgrim Ramon de Perellós spent Christmas as the guest of Niall Óg Ó Néill, the new king of Tír Eoghain. According to Ramon, the nobles of Niall Óg's court went barefoot and scantily clad, the king wiped his mouth on grass and 'there was no bread or wine in all his court'—although 'great alms of oxflesh' were distributed to the poor.

A lack of wine does not, of course, mean a general lack of alcohol on such occasions. The Annals of Clonmacnoise record rather dryly that in

1405 Risteard Mac Raghnaill, a chieftain of Muintir Eolais (today part of south Leitrim), died 'at Christmas by taking a surfeit of *aqua vitae*, to him *aqua mortis*'.

The power of the great households of medieval Ireland was also visible in other ways at Christmas. This was often a time when leases began or rents came due. The Annals of the Four Masters tell us that in 988 Máel Sechnaill mac Domnaill, king of Meath, gained control of Dublin from its Hiberno-Norse rulers following a battle and siege. The city's inhabitants agreed to pay him 'an ounce of gold for every garden, to be paid on Christmas night, for ever'. Other such agreements did not have quite the same ring of permanency, but we can imagine medieval tenants hustling to make the midwinter instalment of their rent. In the mid-fourteenth century one Thomas Bodenham held land at Crumlin, Dublin, in return for payment of 'half a pound of pepper at Christmas', while his contemporaries who held land in the diocese of Cloyne, Cork, were required to pay either a hen or a penny each Christmas.

Christmas was also a time when élites could have demands made on them in turn. For instance, in 1401 Stephen Scrope was given the governorship of Connacht and the custody of Galway City and Athenry on Christmas Day, likely as part of his attempt as deputy lieutenant of Ireland to relieve tensions between Anglo-Irish lords and their Gaelic counterparts. While Scrope appears to have been diligent in his duties, spare a thought for the unfortunate William Roughead, bishop of Emly in Tipperary. Although summoned to a meeting of parliament in Dublin in 1329, he was unable to attend because while heading to church on Christmas Eve he fell from his horse and broke three ribs—and was initially heavily fined for his absence until it was proven that he was indeed gravely ill.

The feasts described above are examples of what scholars might term 'soft power': wooing people with goods or opportunities so that they are co-opted to your side rather than coerced. Not every medieval Irish Christmas was a peaceful one, however; 'hard power'—the use of threats and military force—was also exerted at this time of the year.

A sampling of the eleventh-century entries in the Annals of the Four Masters shows us several instances of festive violence: for instance, the Uí Crícháin from Monaghan travelled south to attack and burn the monastic settlement at Termonfeckin, Co. Louth, on Christmas night in 1025. About 30 years later one Eochaidh Ua Flaithen undertook a 'predatory excursion' into the territory of Magh-Itha (likely the region around Raphoe, Co. Donegal) on Christmas night. This raid resulted in the theft of some 500 cows and the deaths of dozens of people. In 1091 Muircheartach Ua Briain—king of Munster and a great-grandson of Brian Boru—launched a raid into Leinster territory. Clearly it was not unknown for Christmas celebrations across medieval Ireland to be disrupted by fire and blade.

Even a Christmas lull might not be lasting. Edward Bruce, earl of Carrick and younger brother of Robert I of Scotland, invaded Ireland in 1315. Having cut a swathe from Antrim south to Meath and then west, Edward seized the de Verdon manor of Loughsewdy (today Ballymore, Co. Westmeath) and spent Christmas there. Moreover, he then razed the site to the ground—surely making for a particularly bleak January for those left behind once Edward and his forces moved on.

And sometimes 'soft power' events such as feasting were used to remind guests who it was who held the sword. In 1171 Henry II of England held a lavish Christmas feast in Dublin, one attended by many Gaelic leaders who travelled there to make their submission to him. The feast took place in a specially constructed post-and-wattle palace, near the present-day College Green, and Henry surely hoped that the occasion would make a suitable display of his wealth and military power. While the historian Gerald of Wales assures us that the Gaelic lords 'greatly admired the sumptuous and plentiful fare' and 'the most elegant service', he goes on to say that 'in obedience to the king's wishes, they began to eat the flesh of the crane, which they had hitherto loathed'. Crane is a bird not often eaten because of its unpleasant taste and tough texture. Deliberately serving up something that he knew his guests would choke down demonstrates that, like many others who celebrated Christmas in medieval Ireland, Henry knew what made for an effective festive power play.

SOURCES AND FURTHER READING

The Annals of the Four Masters and the *Journey of Viscount Ramon de Perellós* are online at CELT: Corpus of Electronic Texts (celt.ucc.ie). Gerald of Wales's *Conquest of Ireland* and the Annals of Clonmacnoise are online at the Internet Archive (archive.org). For Thomas Bodenham, James Butler, William Roughead and Stephen Scrope, see CIRCLE: A Calendar of Irish Chancery Letters (chancery.tcd.ie).

CHRISTMAS IN LATE MEDIEVAL IRELAND: FEASTING, LORDSHIP AND WARFARE

Sparky Booker

Christmas was a festival of great religious importance across the medieval world, but it was also, then as now, a time for secular celebrations and feasts in households across Ireland. Later medieval English and European sources show that many of the customs we now associate with the holiday—like bringing evergreen branches into the house, decorating trees and even eating mince pies—may date from this period, and some of these customs likely made their way to Ireland. But what can the surviving sources from late medieval Ireland tell us more specifically about how the holiday was celebrated on this island some 600 or 700 years ago?

A range of literary sources and administrative records from the colonial administration in Ireland provide hints. Christmas appears most often in administrative records as a temporal marker to help structure the accounting, judicial, legislative and financial year. Typical mentions of Christmas in the records of the colony were that a certain rent was due annually at that time; that letters of protection or an appointment as a justice in one of the colony's courts might last from one Christmas to the next; or that a new piece of legislation might be enforced from the next Christmas onwards. Other feasts, often Michaelmas and Easter, as well as lesser feasts such as those of St Patrick, SS Philip and James and a multitude of other feast-days, were also used to mark time in this way, but Christmas was one of the most frequently mentioned.

As elsewhere in Europe, Christmas was the longest holiday each year, and the calendar in the Dublin Chain Book records double feasts (an honour given to the most important religious days) occurring each day between 25 and 29 December, as well as on the feast of the Epiphany on 6 January. The Christmas period thus lasted for the 'twelve days of Christmas' between 25 December and 6 January, but sometimes was extended even further until Candlemas (2 February). Just as today, Christmas was a time for food and feasting, music and entertainment (though unlike today this often included the recitation of bardic poems), showing off new clothes and gift-giving. If the rents paid by tenants living on monastic lands in Laois, Meath and Dublin are any indication, the consumption of beer was also an important aspect of the holiday, since rents due at Christmas and likely to have been consumed during feasting at that time included quantities of beer. Some tenants had to provide as much as 48 gallons!

Although feasting and gift-giving at Christmas are familiar to us, their significance for many medieval people was quite different. For lords, Christmas was of great seigniorial importance—a time to demonstrate and reinforce their lordship and their ties with their retainers and clients. Gifts from social superiors to their inferiors, including the food and entertainment at a feast, were used to demonstrate beneficence and to cement the seigniorial bond. The seigniorial and even political use of Christmas feasts is known from the English royal context—notably in Matthew Paris's descriptions of Henry III's Christmas feasts—but it is equally apparent in Ireland. Niall Óg Ó Néill's feast in 1397, examined in this volume by Tara Shields, is just one example, as Ó Néill's 'great court' at Christmas was attended by 'all his clergy and knights and bishops and abbots and other great lords'. William (Uilliam) Ó Ceallaigh's extravagant Christmas feast in 1351, mentioned elsewhere in this volume by Yvonne Seale and Pádraig Ó Macháin, included a general invitation to all the poets of Ireland and Scotland. Gofraidh Fionn Ó Dálaigh's praise-poem for Ó Ceallaigh to commemorate the occasion claims that his generosity in inviting, housing and feeding all these poets meant that all other Irish lords were deprived of poetry at their own holiday feasts:

> Because of the summons we have received, their own poets—I expect—will not remain with the tribe of Niall during this Christmastide.
> From the amount that will go to his royal fort during this coming Christmastide, when the nimble folk of Munster feast it will be a feasting without a man of art.

This feast was thus, in part, an exercise in one-upmanship, in which Ó Ceallaigh sought to embarrass other Irish lords while increasing his own prestige.

King Henry II's famous Christmas feast in 1171 at his purpose-built palace just outside the walls of Dublin, discussed by Regina Sexton elsewhere in this volume, also had clear political purposes. Gerald of Wales's *Conquest of Ireland* describes the feast as follows [in Scott and Martin's translation]:

> As the solemn festival of our lord's birth drew near, the princes of that land [Ireland] came to Dublin in great numbers to view the king's court. There they greatly admired the sumptuous and plentiful fare of the English table and the most elegant service by the royal domestics. Through the great hall, in obedience to the king's wishes, they began to eat the flesh of the crane, which they had hitherto loathed.

This Christmas celebration provided an ideal opportunity for Henry to display his wealth and power—through the sumptuousness of his table—and to demonstrate his supremacy over his English subjects in Ireland as well as the Irish kings who attended. If Gerald of Wales is to be believed, he reinforced the political submission of the Irish kings with a gustatory submission, forcing them to eat cranes, which, though now rarely found in Ireland, were (again according to Gerald) numerous in the late twelfth century.

A letter on behalf of the justiciar, James Butler, earl of Ormond, regarding his plans for Christmas in 1393 tells us about the menu for these Christmas feasts. The letter ordered the provision of '60 good bullocks, 4 boars, 80 large pigs, 60 small pigs, 100 geese, 100 ducks, 200 pairs of rabbits … 6 lambs, 5 meases of herrings, 100 cod and ling fish … and 100 salted salmons' to feed the justiciar's household over Christmas. It is difficult to draw conclusions about how many people Ormond was planning to feed, but what is clear is that he was planning over a month in advance for Christmas, and he intended to feed a large party with plentiful and varied food. This use of food as a way of displaying status was well recognised in the Middle Ages, and laws were passed (though not in Ireland) specifying the number of dishes that people could serve at their feasts according to their social status.

In keeping with this use of Christmas feasts as opportunities to strengthen seigniorial relationships, they were sometimes occasions for knighting a lord's more important retainers. Friar John Clyn notes that John FitzThomas made three men knights, including Nicholas FitzMaurice of Kerry, at his 'great, sumptuous and peaceful feast at Adare', and that 'the following Christmas, lord Maurice FitzThomas married Katherine, daughter of the earl of Ulster and there Edmund Butler made two knights'. These knighting ceremonies in the Christmas season sometimes occurred while campaigning, as in the case of Maurice FitzThomas's knighting of seven men while conducting a campaign against Brian Ó Briain on 3 January 1336. Clyn records other instances of fighting over the Christmas period, including punishing raids conducted by members of the St Albino/Tobin family on Compsey, Co. Tipperary, in 1344, the burning of Bordwell, Co. Laois, by the Irish of Slieve Bloom on the feast of the Innocents, 28 December 1345, and the destruction of Nenagh by Domnall Ó Ceinnéidigh and his allies during Christmas 1348.

The Irish annals confirm that there was considerable warfare and raiding around Christmastime. The holiday did not lead to a cessation of violence, in contrast to the exceptional but well-known examples of the brief lull in fighting at Christmas in 1914, or the less-famous medieval parallel of the suspension of the siege of Rouen at Christmas 1418. Some military activity took place on Christmas Day itself. John Mór Barry, described in the Annals of the Four Masters as 'the choicest of the English youth of Ireland', was killed during his attack on Donnchadh Óg Mac Carthaigh on Christmas Day 1486. Such campaigning also occurred during the wider Christmas period, as with the taking of the castle at Ballyshannon in 1496 by Aodh Ó Domnaill just after Christmas, or notable raids like the one led by Réamonn Mac Mathgamna in 1485 against the Taaffes of Louth and Meath 'shortly before Christmas'. In fact, an examination of warfare in Clyn's annals suggests that Christmas may have been a period of increased warfare. There were fewer raids and violent clashes in this period than during the high point of such activity in the spring/summer, but significantly more than in November and early December, and much more than occurred during the nadir of such activity from mid-January–March.

There are a number of possible reasons why Christmas celebrations could trigger armed conflict. The feasting and lordly display practised over the Christmas season led to the assembling of each lord's wider affinity. Once this affinity was gathered, and after lords had upheld their end of the seigniorial bargain by providing gifts and feasts to their retainers, these retainers may have sought or been encouraged to then show their willingness to provide the military service they owed. Alternatively, the stockpiles of food and goods to be used over the Christmas festival may have enticed lords and their retinues to raid their neighbours; the takings were particularly rich at Christmastime. Whatever the reason, it is clear that for many people in medieval Ireland Christmas was not just a time for relaxing, feasting, drinking and exchanging gifts; it was also a time for political manoeuvring, displays of lordship and, sometimes, violence.

SOURCES AND FURTHER READING

Peter Crooks (ed.), *A calendar of Irish chancery letters,* c. *1244–1509* (Dublin, 2023).

Peter Greenfield, 'Festive drama at Christmas in aristocratic households', in Meg Twycross (ed.), *Festive drama: papers from the Sixth Triennial Colloquium of the International Society for the Study of Medieval Theatre* (Cambridge, 1996), 34–40.

Lars Kjaer, 'Matthew Paris and the royal Christmas: ritualised communication in text and practice', *Thirteenth Century England* **14** (2013), 141–54.

Eleanor Knott, '*Filidh Éireann go haointeach*: William Ó Ceallaigh's Christmas feast to the poets of Ireland, A.D. 1351', *Ériu* **5** (1911), 50–69.

A.B. Scott and F.X. Martin (eds), *Expugnatio Hibernica: The Conquest of Ireland* (Dublin, 1978).

Bernadette Williams (ed.), *The Annals of Ireland by Friar John Clyn* (Dublin, 2007).

CHRISTMAS AND THE BARDIC POET

Pádraig Ó Macháin

Déanadh go subhach síol Ádhaimh:
san oidhche a-réir rug ar siúr
mac lér beanadh dhínn ar ndoirche,
leanabh cígh ó n-oighthe an t-iúl.

Tógbhaimne an lá-so, lá Nodlag,
nuachlann Éabha ó mhór go mion,
ar gcroidhe suas le méid meanma
don ghéig go gcnuas neamhdha a-niogh.

[Let the seed of Adam celebrate: last night our sister gave birth to a son who has taken our darkness from us, a suckling child to guide us.

Today, on this day, Christmas day, let us, the new children of Eve, great and small, raise our hearts in ecstasy to the branch with the heavenly fruit.]

The twin Church festivals of Christmas and Easter were busy times for the Irish master-poets, the *ollamhain*. These were occasions of celebration and feasting, as they are today. In medieval and early modern times poets could expect to receive Christmas invitations, either as a class or individually. Even after the passing of the era of the professional poets, their eighteenth- and nineteenth-century successors might still be invited to make up the company at a nobleman's feast. It was rare for a poet to refuse, as was the case in 1729, when a poet made his excuses in verse to Ó Súilleabháin Bhéarra on the grounds of his fear of being overcome by an excess of brandy—*ar eagla bheith treascartha ag an mbrannda thiar.*

Notable instances occur in the historical records of extravagant hospitality extended by patrons at Christmas time to the learned classes, poets included. As noted by Yvonne Seale, such an occasion was the famous festival convened by William (Uilliam) Ó Ceallaigh in 1351 at Galey, Co. Roscommon, which involved the building of an artists' village to accommodate everyone. The scale of the event was well captured in a famous poem by the Duhallow poet Gofraidh Fionn Ó Dálaigh, who describes the village laid out in streets, each street accommodating a particular branch of learning—and the houses, he says, arranged like letters on a line of a manuscript.

Over 200 years later, a Christmas festival hosted in 1577 by Toirdhealbhach Luineach Ó Néill at his castle near Coleraine was the subject of a poem by Tadhg Dall Ó hUiginn from south County Sligo. It is clear, from Tadhg Dall's list of the different varieties of poem that the poets had brought with them as Christmas gifts, that performances of poetry were expected on these occasions. The poet records, however, that none of these poems was of the type that appealed to the taste of the chieftain, who did not hesitate to let his guests know of his displeasure.

Despite the feasting and celebration, therefore, Christmas was a time of work for the poets and other members of the learned orders. In addition to the presentation and performance of poetry, manuscripts were written at this time. Sixteen leaves of the remarkable Book of Pottlerath were written on the Kilkenny–Tipperary border over the Christmas of 1454 by Giolla na Naomh Mac Aodhagáin—a member of a renowned legal family—for Éamonn mac Risteird Bhuitléir, nephew of Séamus, the 'White Earl' of Ormond. On Christmas Eve the colourist who was working on the lettering in the manuscript prayed for the protection of the Son of God for Éamonn. The following Saturday Giolla na Naomh records the completion of the copying of twin narratives: the discovery of the True Cross, and Charlemagne's search for the Crown of Thorns and the relics of the saints. These tales would have provided appropriately elevated entertainment and instruction at this time of year.

Poets were fascinated by the miracle of the virgin birth and made frequent reference to it in their religious poetry. Poems in celebration of the feast of Christmas itself are not plentiful, however. Two remarkable examples survive from the early seventeenth century, the first being the poem with which this piece began. It is attributed to a famous County Clare poet, Tadhg (mac Dáire) Mac Bruaideadha. As the opening verses state, Christmas is a time for celebration, and the poet sets out to explain why.

The core of the poem is the Nativity story, which, he tells us, is no exaggeration: *ní coiscéim ná léim tar líne* ('it is neither a step nor a jump beyond the line'). The narrative follows Luke Chapter 2 while incorporating the traditional, if apocryphal, ass and ox, who are the first to recognise the heavenly birth: *Tug an damh trá, tug an t-asal, / aithne ar an Rígh rugadh ann* ('The ox indeed, and the ass, recognised the King who was born there'). The birth is then announced by the angels, who sing a tune never heard before (*'aointiúin cheóil nach cuala cluas'*): *Glóir do Dhia sna diongnaibh arda … síodh do lucht daghthaile an domhain* ('Glory to God in the high places … peace to people of goodwill of the world').

The author lists the many blessings that accrued to the human race from the child who was born in the city of David, blessings which are reasons for rejoicing. In closing the poem he returns to the celebration mentioned at the very beginning:

> *I ló a bheirthe bíom go faoilidh,*
> *féasda 'na ainm dealbhthar dhúinn,*
> *bíodh gabháil uainn ris gach n-aoighidh*
> *d'anáir dá ghruaidh fhaoilidh úir.*

Canam molta don Mhac oirrdhearc,
éisdeam briathra beóil an Ríogh;
oircheas dúnn 'mun am-sa uile
rún almsa ag gach duine dhíonn.

[Let us rejoice on the day of His birth, let us make a feast in His name, let us embrace every stranger in honour of His radiant, happy face.

Let us sing praises for the noble Son, let us listen to words from the mouth of the King; it behoves us all at this time that each of us should be charitable.]

The better known of these two contemporary Christmas poems is attributed to Aodh Mac Aingil of County Down, a Franciscan theologian of the Louvain community. His poem, *Dia do bheatha, a naoidhe naoimh* ('Greetings, holy child'), discussed by Tadhg Ó Dúshláine in the essay following, is far removed from the sermon structure of Mac Bruaideadha's composition. It is much admired for its imaginative 'metaphysical' treatment of the Nativity, for its personal engagement with the infant Jesus, and especially for its core section, where the author asks Mary to admit him to the manger. There he will protect the child from the shepherds' dogs and see to it that neither the ass nor the cow intrudes—he will take their place: *asal mé is bó Mhic Dé Bhí* ('I will be the ass and the cow of the Son of the living God'). He then speaks of the domestic services that he will perform:

Do-bhéar uisge liom go moch,
sguabfad urlár bocht Mhic Dé,
do-ghéan teine im anum fhuar
's tréigfead tre dhúthracht mo chorp claon.

Nighfead a bhoichtbhréide dhó,

53

is dá dtuga, a Ógh, cead damh,
mo cheirt féin do bhainfinn díom
dá cur mar dhíon ar do Mhac.

Biad mar chócaire 'gan bhiadh
's im dhoirseóir do Dhia na ndúl,
's ó tá orthu go mór m'fheidhm,
iarfad fa mo dhéirc do thriúr.

[I will draw water early, I will sweep the humble floor of the Son of God, I will make a fire in my frozen soul and eagerly flee my perverse body.

I will wash His poor clothes for Him, and, if you permit me, Virgin, I will take off my own rags and put them on your Son to cover Him.

I will cook the food, I will be a doorkeeper for God of Creation, and, since they rely on me greatly, I will seek my alms on behalf of the three of them.]

SOURCES AND FURTHER READING

Eleanor Knott, 'Filidh Éireann go haointeach', *Ériu* **5** (1911), 50–69.
Eleanor Knott, *The bardic poems of Tadhg Dall Ó hUiginn 1550–1591* (2 vols, London, 1922, 1926).
Láimhbheartach Mac Cionnaith, *Dioghluim Dána* (Dublin 1938).
Cuthbert Mhág Craith, *Dán na mBráthar Mionúr* (2 vols, Dublin, 1967, 1980).

AODH MAC AINGIL'S NATIVITY HYMN (*C.* 1620): 'WELCOME, O HOLY CHILD'

Tadhg Ó Dúshláine

Dia do bheatha, a naoidhe naoimh ('Welcome, O Holy Child'), by the celebrated Franciscan theologian Aodh Mac Aingil (Hugh McCavill), is justifiably regarded as the finest Nativity poem in Irish, despite textual difficulties, less-than-satisfactory translations, editorial omissions and unhelpful comparisons which take from the work's significance and excellence. Cuthbert Mhág Craith OFM, editor of the scholarly edition of the Irish original (*Dán na mBráthar Mionúr, Cuid I* (1967)), admits to certain textual difficulties, which remained unresolved some thirteen years later when his translation was published (*Dán na mBráthar Mionúr, Cuid II* (1980): 'The translation, of course, is tentative').

The currently accepted authoritative version of the poem is found in *Nua-Dhuanaire, Cuid I*, edited by three distinguished professors of Scoil an Léinn Cheiltigh, Institiúid Ard-Léinn Bhaile Átha Cliath, first published in 1971 and frequently afterwards. Ten of the original verses have been excluded on the basis that 'they take from the unity of the poem, or because it is hard to make sense of them'. To put it mildly, this is a lame excuse. The textual difficulties can be addressed adequately by contextualisation with the theological and devotional tradition of the time, while even a cursory glance suggests that the omitted verses 10 and 11 are pivotal to the poem's unity, with the author declaring in the opening line of verse 12 ('Welcome again, O Holy Child') that he will *again* attempt to comprehend the mystery of the Incarnation by a different method of meditation than he employed at first.

The version produced by the cooperation of scholar and poet (Seán Ó Tuama and Thomas Kinsella) in the highly acclaimed *An Duanaire 1600–1900: poems of the dispossessed* (1981) would appear to take its cue from the editors of *Nua-Dhuanaire 1* in deciding to omit more than half (fourteen) of the 27 verses of the original; and while the joint effort of scholar and poet produces a reasonable partial translation, the accompanying introductory note is misleading:

> For an insight into the contrasting Irish and English literary traditions of the time, it is interesting to read the following Christmas hymn, with its great homeliness and simplicity, side by side with the *Ode on the Morning of Christ's Nativity* by Mac Aingil's contemporary, John Milton.

Louis Martz's seminal study *The poetry of meditation* (1954) points out that the difference is essentially that between contemporary Catholic and Protestant theological positions rather than that between Irish and English literary traditions, propagated by Daniel Corkery in his influential *The hidden Ireland* and elsewhere:

> Students of English Puritanism have often remarked upon the small part which the person and humanity of Christ played in Puritan writings of the sixteenth and seventeenth centuries ... numerous reasons for this difference in emphasis at once spring to mind ... Yet the fundamental reason surely lies in sacramental doctrine, in the emphasis on Incarnation which Catholic doctrine involves, and in the consequent sanctification of the sensory which flows from this.

The paradoxical awesome first section of Mac Aingil's composition (verses 1–9) has much in common with contemporary Catholic Nativity poems in English, particularly those of Robert Southwell and Richard Crashaw, featuring a fanfare of baroque wordplay. The genesis of this playful paradoxical reasoning stems from contemporary Catholic devotional practices, such as that, for example, in the English translation of Luis de la Puente's *Meditations upon the mysteries of our Holie Faith, with the practice of mental prayer touching the same* (St Omer, 1619):

> I will behold the person of that child, making a comparison between what he is, as he is almighty God, and between what he is there, as he is man; with an affection of admiration, and love the greatest that I am able: pondering how this child is that God of majesty, whose seat is in heaven … And on the other side, he is laid in a manger in the midst between two dull and lumpish beasts: And he that is the word of the eternal Father, by whom he created all things … is become a child not yet able to speak …

The following is a flavour of Mac Aingil's poetic version in the first section of the poem (verses 1–9):

> Welcome, Holy Child,
> In the manger reclining;
> Merry and rich tonight
> In your mansion above remaining …
>
> The Spirit of my everlasting God
> Incarnate I behold tonight
> the Word of God a dumbstruck child
> I am speechless at the sight.

In verses 10–11, the poet takes his cue from the *Adoro Te Devote* of Thomas Aquinas in rejecting the method of scholastic reasoning, and does so in similar fashion to that of Richard Crashaw's translation ('Down down, proud sense! Discourses die'):

Cease your reasoning and your sense
have faith and keep your tongue still
God alone this Child understands
you never did and never will.

Close your eyes for nature's blind
your knowledge here can't discern the way.
On the authority of the One who is truth itself
I believe what I say.

Verses 12–27 follow the second method of meditation recommended by de la Puente:

> … meditation runs from one thing to another, seeking out hidden verities, as hitherto hath been done: but contemplation is *a simple beholding of the truth* without variety of discourse, with *great affections of admiration, and love:* and as regularly it is obtained after meditation, so after we have meditated these mysteries of our Saviour Christ, it shall not be amiss to run over each of them again with this manner of affectuous contemplation.

This is how de la Puente explains 'affectuous contemplation':

> Beholding the heart of the child burning in love … I will join my heart onto his, that he may fasten onto it that love.

The paradoxical reasoning of Mac Aingil's first meditation is replaced here by the intimate motif of the 'kiss':

Outside, with your permission I remain, O King,
But what if I were to enter in,
With thousands and thousands of kisses then
I'd shower you with all my will.

I'd kiss your mouth in brotherly love,
Kiss your feet as Father above,
Kiss your hand as King and Son,
You're my God, thy will be done.

Behind the apparent 'great homeliness and simplicity' of this baroque sensory engagement is a metaphysical profundity, best described by T.S. Eliot as 'a tough reasonableness under the slight lyric grace'. Even the simple adjectives 'poor' and 'cold' in verse 20 are, in fact, transferred epithets, raising the concrete homely picture to the metaphysical spiritual level, the fire of God's love in his soul:

I'll carry water with me at morn
Sweep the poor floor of the Son of God,
Kindle a fire in my own cold heart
And from my bodily desires depart.

Baroque bears the hallmark of the Council of Trent, entailing an amalgam of Franciscan humility and Dominican rationality evident in the methodology of the *Spiritual Exercises* of Ignatius Loyola, where Aquinas's abstract reasoning in the *Summa Theologica* is grounded in concrete dramatic imagery. Such is the context that makes Aodh Mac Aingil's Nativity poem a masterly artistic presentation of baroque sensibility, as immediately captivating, and equally thought-provoking, as the homely and heavenly grace surrounding Rembrandt's *Nativity*.

SOURCES AND FURTHER READING

John D. Lyons (ed.), *The Oxford handbook of the baroque* (Oxford, 2019).
Louis L. Martz, *The poetry of meditation: a study in English religious literature* (New Haven, 1954).

THE ART OF GRIFT AND (RE)GIFTING: THE EARL OF CORK'S NEW YEAR PRESENTS

Clodagh Tait

Richard Boyle arrived in Ireland from Kent in 1588 with 27 pounds in his pocket, some jewellery, significant personal charm (it didn't work on everyone) and a brass neck. In the 1590s he cannily married an heiress, Joan Apsley; though Joan died giving birth to their child, he kept his newly extended Munster family close, and hung on to her dowry. His second marriage, to the very young Catherine Fenton, daughter of Geoffrey Fenton, principal secretary of state in Dublin, acquired him connections and an even more generous 'portion'. Catherine went on to have fifteen children, twelve of whom survived into adulthood; only the youngest, the scientist Robert, avoided the marriages that Boyle arranged to further extend his networks.

By 1603 his grifting as an escheator (an official managing aspects of the monarch's land interests) was beginning to pay off, and he had already begun to build up his own landholdings. He took advantage of the aftermath of the Nine Years War, which left many Munster Plantation landowners wary or ruined. Over the subsequent four decades he hoovered up much more property, although encountering some opposition, especially to his absorption of large chunks of church lands. Having bought first the title of baron and then an earldom from James I, Boyle made sure to present himself in a manner appropriate to his new standing. He acquired and expanded homes in Lismore, Youghal, Dublin and Dorset. He bought fine clothes, good horses, a coach, tombs celebrating him and his 'posterity', and plenty of silver tableware. He knew the value (monetary and social) of things. Boyle used hospitality and gift-giving to keep his friends (and enemies) close, and they acknowledged and courted his support in similar kind. In the diary of his day-to-day financial transactions he noted the gifts he received as well as those he gave.

For Boyle, Christmas was a time when debts might be paid, and when he might take stock of debts owed to him. For example, on 1 January 1616 he made a list in his diary of 'such debts as ar duely owing to me'. In 1627 he itemised his debts to others. The earlier diaries usually are silent between about 24 and 27 December, indicating that it was his custom to spend time with his family and that he did not expect his secretaries to be at work, though by the 1630s pressing business increasingly intruded. Card/dice-playing seems to have been part of the entertainment: in 1633 he recorded lending Boyle Smyth five shillings 'to play this Xmas when he had no money'. He did record some more notable Christmas events, such as the quiet wedding of his sixteen-year-old (widowed) daughter Sarah to Robert Digby in his chapel at Lismore Castle on Christmas Day 1626. The more boisterous wedding at Whitehall of his son Lewis, Viscount Kinalmeaky, on 26 December 1639 was attended by King Charles I and the queen.

In the 1620s and '30s Christmas, or rather New Year, increasingly appears in Boyle's diary as an occasion of gifting. In the first half of the seventeenth century, 25 March was still technically the start of the new year, but the first day of January was popularly recognised as New Year's Day (with additional confusion for historians deriving from the slow official adoption of the Gregorian calendar in the Irish and British Isles).

Some of the gifts that Boyle and his wife received at New Year are noted in the diary. His December and January entries record costly items given by and to a range of people, as well as occasional smaller gifts to servants, friends and young relations, such as 30 shillings given to Ned Boyle and ten shillings to his brother on 2 January 1623, and money sent to some associates imprisoned in the Dublin Marshalsea in 1632. In 1627 Sarah Boyle's new mother-in-law, Lady Offaly, 'gaue me for my new yeares guifte a fayr Bealt and girdle, all laced over with ritch silver lace, with massiv Spanish buckles and furniture of gold smythes work, worth 20 marks ster[ling] which I afterwards sent as a present to thearle of Castlehaven' (a friend of Boyle's to whose son he was hoping to marry another of his daughters). In return, Castlehaven 'sent me a tables diamond Ring to bestow on one of my daughters from his son, and I gave it Lettice'. The canny Boyle was a regular re-gifter of valuable items.

Boyle was fond of fine clothing, and regularly gifted and received clothes. I like the sound of the gold and silver girdle and hanger (a sword-belt) and peach silk stockings that he was given by Arthur Loftus in 1632, the nightcap and pantables (slippers) embroidered with gold thread received in 1639, and the fashionable beaver hat and embroidered gloves that he got from his children in 1640. In 1617 Boyle paid £13 for a 'murrey' (a dark red-purple or red-brown) satin petticoat 'that is embroidered' and an apron for his wife 'for her new years guifte'. The New Year of 1633 set Boyle up with a range of practical but elegant linens and accessories:

> thearle of Kildare sent me 6 fyne holland laced shirts; the L. digby a night capp wrought with silck & gowld; his Lady a Ruff band, and 2 pair of cuffs laced; my daughter Kildare a Ruffband and 2 pair of cuffes laced; my daughter Loftus 6 laced handkerchers; & my neec crow a purse of silck & silver, of her own worcking, for my new yeares guiftes; my daughter Kate 12 laced handkercheifs; Mrs Mary Jones a brave purse.

Gifts like the hand-worked purses demonstrated skill and industry and might be personalised, augmenting their symbolic value.

Boyle was a sentimental man, and he placed great personal value on certain items. After his wife's death, her possessions were gifted to others, and Boyle records presenting his daughter, the countess of Barrymore, with a purple velvet gown (a magnificent item that had cost over £50) for New Year 1634 'to wear for her mother's sake'. A 1631 presentation to his son Richard also invoked both the past and the future. Boyle had been given a gold chain with a medallion of the king of Denmark's image in gratitude for aid that he had rendered to a Danish ship forced into Youghal harbour by inclement weather. He instructed his son never to part with the chain, 'he to leave it to his heir, to be ever continued to the howse of thearles of Corke; which howse in unspotted Honnor & integrity I desire thalmighty for ever to uphold with his grace'.

Some other family gifts may have been more pointed, such as the bible that Boyle was given in 1634 by his troublesome son-in-law the earl of Kildare, three months after Lord Deputy Wentworth had intervened in a dispute between them. Whether Boyle took this as a conciliatory or a provocative gesture, he promptly passed the bible on to the wife of his nephew, Roger (Hodge) Power. Kildare gave him another bible in 1639.

The local politics of New Year's gifting is also hinted at. The mayor and corporation of Youghal, seeking to remain in Boyle's good books, regularly presented him with alcohol. In 1625 he got a butt (two hogs-heads) of sack, and in 1626 two hogsheads of new claret and a hogshead of white wine. In 1635 they gave him a tun of Bordeaux wine: his satis-faction with its quality is indicated by the twenty-shilling tip he gave to its bearer.

It is, however, Boyle's 'gifts' (read 'bribes') to members of the London court and privy council that especially reveal the politics of presents—and presentation. On 29 November 1615 he dispatched Peter Whaer to Mr Ball in London with 'a great Beaser stoan' in a needlework purse. Ball was instructed to deliver Boyle's letters to his fellow Kentishman George Abbot, archbishop of Canterbury, and 'to present the purse and stoan in it as a new years gufte from me to his grace'. Bezoar stones, formed in the stomachs of certain animals, were rare and valuable, believed to protect against poison and to treat other illnesses. Boyle had previously met Abbot, and he and his friends had been lobbying the archbishop since 1613 on the matter of regularising his possession of the embezzled church lands.

The 1st of January 1629 was particularly expensive. Boyle was in London, seeking favours from the council. He expressed his gratitude in New Year's goodies, handing out extravagant items of silver gilt and silver worth £216 10s. to fourteen individuals, as well as re-gifting several other items, including a rundlet (small barrel or cask) of whiskey and some agate-handled knives. The following day, Boyle 'was before the Lords at the councell table to gett their lettres signed, for staying all sutes [suspending legal actions] against me in Ireland'. To top off his expenses, he had to pay tips to a variety of minor officials. In 1640, back in court, Boyle was obliged to pay £20 in New Year's tips demanded by the king's guard and footmen.

From the exotic bezoar stone to the gold-embroidered slippers, the items gifted to and by Richard Boyle at New Year can tell us about taste, fashion and the conviviality of the Christmas period in early seventeenth-century Ireland. They hint at affection and care (and dis- agreements) within extended families, while also revealing the broader role of gifting in maintaining and rewarding 'friendship' of other kinds. Boyle understood that grift and gifts went hand in hand.

SOURCES AND FURTHER READING

I.K. Ben-Amos, *The culture of giving: informal support and gift-exchange in early modern England* (Cambridge, 2011).

Jane Fenlon, 'Acquiring magnificence: luxury goods in the material world of Richard Boyle, first earl of Cork', in David Edwards and Colin Rynne (eds), *The colonial world of Richard Boyle, first earl of Cork* (Dublin, 2017).

A.B. Grosart, *The Lismore Papers* (10 volumes, London, 1886–8).

Dorothea B. Townshend, *The life and letters of the Great Earl of Cork* (London, 1904).

LUKE WADDINGE'S CHRISTMAS SONGS AND THE WEXFORD CAROL TRADITION

Ciarán Mac Murchaidh

Many people of all faiths—and none—enjoy the tradition of carol-singing at Christmas. In fact, it's hard to avoid it, as so many TV and radio programmes feature carol services from all parts of the world. We Irish are used to hearing childhood favourites such as 'Away in a manger', 'Silent night' and 'An oíche úd i mBeithil', as well as classics such as 'In the bleak midwinter', sung in the lead-up to Christmas, and we're generally well disposed to the tradition and its practice. What many of us may not be so aware of is an ancient collection of carols deeply rooted in the Irish tradition, carols that are closely associated with Wexford and still celebrated there.

The story begins with a man called Luke Waddinge, who was born in Ballycogly in the barony of Bargy, Co. Wexford, in 1628. He was ordained a priest possibly sometime in the late 1650s, was appointed Catholic bishop of Ferns in 1683 and remained in that office until his death in 1687. The Waddinge family belonged to the prosperous merchant class and were descended from Old English Catholic roots. This prosperity was not destined to last, however, as Luke Waddinge's father was killed in Cromwell's attack on Wexford town in 1649 and the family's estates were lost under the Cromwellian confiscation. The whole experience was to have a lifelong effect on him. Shortly after, Waddinge left Wexford and moved to Paris, where in late 1651 he enrolled in the Irish College to study for the priesthood.

In 1672 he returned to Ireland and settled in Wexford town, where he concentrated on rebuilding church structures. It was during a period of five or six years from 1678 onwards that he wrote several carols and poems. These were published in Ghent, Belgium, in 1684 as *A smale garland of pious and godly songs composed by a devout man for the solace of his friends and neighbours in their afflictions*. In many of the texts Waddinge drew parallels between the suffering of Christ and that of the Catholic people under the religious restrictions of the Cromwellian regime. He greatly resented these restrictions on worship and wrote about them in his poem 'On Christmas Day, the Yeare 1678', in which the opening verse gives us a real sense of his frustration:

> This is our Christmas day,
> The day of Christ's birth,
> Yet we are far from joy
> And far from Christmas mirth.
> On Christmas to have no mass
> Is our great discontent,
> That without mass this day should pass
> Doth cause us to lament.

In spite of the tone of despondency that marks the poem, Waddinge adopts a more upbeat attitude in his other 'Christmas songs', in which he presents aspects of the story of Christmas and the birth of Christ, in particular, as a message of hope for all Christians. A good example of this is his carol 'First on Christ's Nativity', where he writes:

> Here's all the hopes of earth
> And the delights of heaven,
> The joy of all the angels,
> And the great price of men.

The ransom of all sinners,
All captives to set free;
How can we but rejoice,
and all must merry be.

Waddinge's text very quickly became popular and, despite the restrictions on printed Catholic material associated with the Penal Laws, his *Smale garland* was reprinted in London in 1728 and again in 1731 for Drogheda bookseller James Connor. Around that time an unexpected development helped to encourage further the singing of carols in Wexford. Father William Devereux, who had been in the Irish College in Salamanca, returned home to the county in 1728 as parish priest of Drinagh. He composed several carols and gathered them together in a manuscript entitled *A new garland containing songs for Christmas*. The manuscript included three of Waddinge's carols, and Diarmaid Ó Muirithe has shown that at least another of them was of English origin, although he accepts the local tradition that Devereux composed the rest.

Father Joseph Ranson, who in 1949 produced an edition of Devereux's collection of carols in the journal *The Past*, claimed that they were first sung in a little chapel at Killiane. The practice spread to other parishes and the carols were sung for many years in Ballymore, Lady's Island, Mayglass, Piercestown, Rathangan and Tacumshane. The tradition died out in those parishes, however, owing primarily to lack of support from various clergymen, and the tradition now survives only in the parish of Kilmore. Ó Muirithe concurred with Ranson's assertion that they were sung in churches in south Wexford in the eighteenth century and even into the nineteenth century but that not all clergy approved of them. The fact that the carol tradition belonged to the people rather than the institutional church may have been one reason why some clergy disliked them, as there was a strong sense within the Catholic church at the time that the liturgy was the preserve of the clergy and not of the people. In any event, the popularity of the carols among the people led to their frequently being copied by hand, and Ó Muirithe noted that this was still happening in the early 1980s as part of the long-established tradition around the singing and preservation of the carols.

Members of the Devereux family, who have been involved in singing the carols for many years in Kilmore, were interviewed as part of an *Irish Times* article in December 1998. They remarked that parish priests in Kilmore had largely been supportive of the singers. This was likely due to a growing appreciation for lay involvement in church ritual following the liturgical revisions of Vatican II, as well as a sense of the importance of preserving this long-established and venerable tradition. In the interview, however, Johnny Devereux recalled one priest who did not want them: 'They say if he'd ha' lived there'd be no carols. He gave us to understand it was our last year singing. Carols had always been sung during the collection or during communion but this priest changed that. He told us it was our last year. Then he died in November—just before Christmas!'

Father Ranson also explained that, traditionally, the choir consisted of six men. The practice for many years was that the six would divide into two groups of three and sing alternate stanzas of each carol. Harmonies or accompaniment are not used, and individual singers are free to ornament the melodies in their own way, as long as they don't stray too far from the others. Each song is initiated by a single voice and the others join in after a line or two. Johnny Devereux noted that the approach had evolved from the mid-1990s: the six no longer split into two trios, and all six now sing each verse.

The tradition of carol-singing in Kilmore, south Wexford, can trace its roots back to Luke Waddinge and his *Smale garland* of 1684. It's a celebration of a rich tradition that has survived through the centuries owing to the input and dedication of those who came after him—Fr Devereux initially and the men who initiated that amazing line of succession whereby the carols and the Christmas message itself were preserved not only in manuscript form but in an ongoing act of oral worship and celebration. The carol sung on Christmas Day, Devereux's 'On Christ's Nativity', illustrates this very succinctly:

The darkest night in December,
Snow nor hail nor winter's storm

Shall not hinder us for to remember
The babe that on this night was born.
With shepherds we are come to see
This lovely infant's glorious charms,
Born of a maid as prophets said,
The God of love in Mary's arms.

These Wexford carols not only act as a form of remembrance of the past—especially of those who sang them annually and thereby kept the tradition alive—but also speak to each new generation about the great Christian mystery of redemption and salvation through the birth and suffering of Christ as Saviour of mankind. The brief video clips included in the reading list below will provide readers with a real sense of this, as we see examples of the traditional style of singing and of more modern interpretation. While the sentiments in some of the carols reflect the dark and challenging times in which they were composed, the central Christian message of faith and hope permeates them all. In that respect, it is appropriate to leave the last word to Fr Devereux in his 'Carol for Twelfth Day':

Farewell, good Christians, farewell too,
Many a happy Christmas I wish you,
With a blessed end hence to ensue,
Through the merits of sweet Jesu.

SOURCES AND FURTHER READING

William Devereux, 'A Carol for Twelfth Day', performed by Giovanna Feeley (https://www.youtube.com/watch?v=8mMEgdYpTxk).
William Devereux, 'On Christ's Nativity', performed by the Kilmore Carollers (https://www.youtube.com/watch?v=qV52t75mxWQ).

Diarmaid Ó Muirithe, *The Wexford Carols assembled and edited* (Port Laoise, 1982).

Diarmaid Ó Muirithe provides the voice-over on a 1977 clip of the Kilmore Carollers (https://www.rte.ie/archives/exhibitions/922-christmas-tv-past/287756-kilmore-carols/).

'The Kilmore Carollers', *The Irish Times*, 2 December 1998 (https://www.irishtimes.com/culture/the-kilmore-carollers-1.228070).

Joseph Ranson, 'The Kilmore Carols', *The Past* **5** (1949), 61–102.

Thomas Wall, *The Christmas songs of Luke Wadding (Bishop of Ferns, 1683–1688)* (Dublin, 1960).

Kilmore Quay. Photo credit: Patrick Comerford.

THE 'WEXFORD CAROL' AND THE MYSTERY SURROUNDING SOME OLD AND POPULAR CHRISTMAS CAROLS

Patrick Comerford

The 'Wexford Carol' is said to date from the twelfth century. It is one of the oldest Irish carols and also one of the oldest surviving Christmas carols in the European tradition. Many musicians and listeners consider this carol to be unique and believe that it has a distinctly Irish character.

The carol is thought to have originated in County Wexford, although there are many traditions about this poem and song. For many years it was said that only men should sing it, but many popular female artists have also recorded it since it gained a new popularity from the 1990s onward.

The Wexford Carol attracted new attention in the early twentieth century owing to the work of Dr William Henry Grattan Flood (1857–1928), who was the organist and musical director at St Aidan's Cathedral, Enniscorthy, Co. Wexford, and the author of *The history of the diocese of Ferns* (1916). According to Revd Joseph Ranson in a paper in *The Past*

(1949), Grattan Flood discovered this carol in County Wexford. He transcribed it from a local singer and it was published in 1928, the year of his death, as No. 14 in the *Oxford Book of Carols*, edited by Percy Dearmer, Martin Shaw and Ralph Vaughan Williams.

The carol was quickly included in collections of carols and Christmas poems around the world. It is sometimes known as the 'Enniscorthy Carol' and was recorded under that title by the choir of Christ Church Cathedral, Dublin, on a Christmas recording in 1997. It is also known by its first line, 'Good people all this Christmas time'.

The *New Oxford Book of Carols*, in a detailed footnote, says that Grattan Flood 'lived in Enniscorthy from 1895 until his death, and […] took down the words and tune from a local singer; after revising the text, he sent the carol to the editors of *The Oxford Book of Carols*, who printed it as the "Wexford Carol".' The note continues, however, with more detail showing the text to be English in origin, and verses 1, 2, 4 and 5 are from William Henry Shawcross's *Old Castleton Christmas carols*. Certainly, the Irish-language version seems to be a translation from English, as it is unlikely that any carol was written in Irish in English-speaking County Wexford.

The Wexford Carol is often associated with the Kilmore carols from Kilmore, Co. Wexford, and is often attributed to Bishop Luke Waddinge and his collection of carols, first published in Ghent in 1684 and discussed by Ciarán Mac Murchaidh in the previous article. Waddinge's little book had the lengthy title *A small garland of pious and godly songs composed by a devout man, for the solace of his friends and neighbours in their afflictions. The sweet and the sower, the nettle and the flower, the thorne and the rose, this garland compose.*

Luke Waddinge (not to be confused with his kinsman, the seventeenth-century Franciscan theologian from Waterford of the same name), whose family came from Ballycogly Castle, Co. Wexford, was the Catholic bishop of Ferns (1683–92) and lived in Wexford town while holding that office. His book contains some religious 'posies' or poems written for the disinherited gentry of County Wexford as well as eleven Christmas songs, two of which are sung to this day in Kilmore.

A similar carol is found in Revd William Devereux's *A new garland containing songs for Christmas* (1728). Father William Devereux (1696–1771), from Tacumshane, was parish priest of Drinagh, near Wexford, in 1730–71 and wrote several carols.

The Wexford Carol is sometimes confused, too, with the 'Sussex Carol', also referred to by its first line, 'On Christmas night all Christians sing'. It is said that the words of this carol were first published by Bishop Luke Waddinge in *A small garland* (1684), but it is not clear whether he wrote the song or was recording an earlier composition. Edward Darling and Donald Davison, in their *Companion to Church Hymnal*, say that the words are from a traditional English source, that they were adapted by Luke Waddinge and that they were reintroduced to English use through later editions of Waddinge's carols, published in London in the early eighteenth century, subsequently undergoing considerable modification.

Both the text and the tune to which it is now sung were discovered and written down quite independently by Cecil Sharp in Buckland, Gloucestershire, and by Ralph Vaughan Williams, who heard it being sung by a Harriet Verrall of Monk's Gate, near Horsham, Sussex—hence its name, the 'Sussex Carol'. Vaughan Williams published the tune to which it is generally sung today in 1919. Several years earlier, he included the carol in his *Fantasia on Christmas carols*, first performed at the Three Carols Festival in Hereford Cathedral in 1912.

The Sussex Carol often features in the Festival of Nine Lessons and Carols in the chapel of King's College, Cambridge, on Christmas Eve, broadcast around the world by the BBC. A version of the Sussex Carol also appears in the Church of Ireland's *Church Hymnal* (5th edn, 2004) as Hymn No. 176.

THE WEXFORD CAROL

Good people all, this Christmas time,
Consider well and bear in mind

What our good God for us has done,
In sending His beloved Son.
With Mary holy we should pray
To God with love this Christmas Day:
In Bethlehem upon that morn
There was a blessed Messiah born.

The night before that happy tide
The noble Virgin and her guide
Were long time seeking up and down
To find a lodging in the town.
But mark how all things came to pass;
From every door repelled, alas!
As long foretold, their refuge all
Was but an humble ox's stall.

There were three wise men from afar
Directed by a glorious star,
And on they wandered night and day
Until they came where Jesus lay.
And when they came unto that place
Where our beloved Messiah was,
They humbly cast them at his feet,
With gifts of gold and incense sweet.

Near Bethlehem did shepherds keep
Their flocks of lambs and feeding sheep;
To whom God's angels did appear,
Which put the shepherds in great fear.
'Prepare and go,' the angels said,
'To Bethlehem, be not afraid;
For there you'll find, this happy morn,
A princely Babe, sweet Jesus born.'

With thankful heart and joyful mind,
The shepherds went the Babe to find,
And as God's angel had foretold,
They did our Saviour Christ behold.
Within a manger He was laid,
And by his side the Virgin Maid,
Attending on the Lord of Life,
Who came on earth to end all strife.

THE SUSSEX CAROL, BY RALPH VAUGHAN WILLIAMS

On Christmas night all Christians sing
To hear the news the angels bring.
News of great joy, news of great mirth,
News of our merciful King's birth.

Then why should men on earth be so sad,
Since our Redeemer made us glad,
When from our sin he set us free,
All for to gain our liberty?

When sin departs before His grace,
Then life and health come in its place.
Angels and men with joy may sing
All for to see the new-born King.

All out of darkness we have light,
Which made the angels sing this night:
'Glory to God and peace to men,
Now and for evermore, Amen!'

SOURCES AND FURTHER READING

Edward Darling and Donald Davison (eds), *Companion to Church Hymnal* (Dublin, 2005).

Hugh Keyte and Andrew Parrott (eds), *The New Oxford Book of Carols* (Oxford, 1992).

A 'DISSENTER'S' CHRISTMAS IN BELTURBET, 1693

Brendan Scott

On 26 April 1694 William Hansard, the Church of Ireland vicar of Lurgan and Munterconnaught in the diocese of Kilmore, wrote to Bishop William Smyth of Kilmore, informing him of a man called Magan (we do not have his first name), an especially troublesome resident of Belturbet, Co. Cavan, whom Hansard in his letter described at various times as a 'verry insolent fellow' and an 'infamous fellow'. Hansard related how Magan:

> was presented by the subsheriff for plowing nigh the church on Xmas day, & when he was desired to go to Church impudently replyed he was better employed. He plowed two or three fur[row]s in land not fitt to be broke up, & has not ploughed in that field since. When the Aparat cited him he threatened him severely & protested … he cared not a fart of his arse for yo[r] L[or]dship or the Church & never apeared tho frequently cited.

Hansard went on to relate how Magan 'has made aplication to some in Dublin but to no purpose. Mr Russell [a Belturbet parishioner] … declares he never saw him at church but once at a vestry, where he vigorously opos'd an aplotm[t] in order to repair the church'. Magan did not seem adept at either keeping old friends in Dublin or making new ones in Belturbet.

Richard Weaver, in a further letter to Bishop Smyth two days later, on 28 April 1694, gave a similar account of Magan and his actions:

> Upon Chrismas day as the people was goeing to service, he was asked by some of them if he would come to Church, to wch he replyed he would goe to his owne, and imediately in a contemptious manner yoked his plow in ffeild neer the Church, and plowed all the time of divine service, wch being noe sooner done, but he left off his plowing.

William Hansard and Richard Weaver clearly believed that Magan had chosen Christmas Day deliberately to make a point. Then, as now, Christmas was an important date in the Christian calendar—a time to cease work, to rest, to make merry and, of course, to celebrate the birth of Christ. That he had only ploughed while the service was ongoing, and had not returned to the field in the four months following, only confirmed Hansard and Weaver's suspicions that Magan had ploughed on Christmas Day deliberately to offend those attending service that day. Whether the point being made by Magan was anti-Church or anti-government, or a mixture of both, was not entirely relevant. What did matter, however, was that Magan was publicly defying, and in a quite egregious manner, the societal mores of the time. This plainly would not do.

Originally intending to charge Magan as a dissenter, the Church court instead brought a charge of contempt against him, possibly wishing to avoid further controversy and publicity. It seems from his actions and crude expressions that Magan had undertaken specifically to antagonise the local members of the Church or to make his mark as a dissenter, something which the Church was at pains not to recognise as such, as we can see in the reason given for his excommunication. Hansard wrote that 'He was not troubled as being a Dissenter but for a contempt'.

Weaver went on to counsel Bishop Smyth to take firm action, as Magan had refused to listen to the local minister, Robert Maxwell, informing the bishop that:

most of the Gentlemen hereabouts, declared that unless he was punished for the contempt he offered our Church they could not be obleidged to take notice of yoᵣ L'dshipp jurisdiction, so that it was for his contempt … he was excommunicated, and not for his plowing on Chrismas Day. [He] openly Braggs it was not the first time he was Excomunicated … and certainly my lord unless he be punished I am afraid none will take notice of yoᵣ Lordshipp jurisdiction.

So why was Magan taking this stand on Christmas Day, treating it like any other day, and why was he suspected of being a dissenter? Many Puritan Protestants disapproved of the holiday, as they regarded such celebrations as being Catholic in nature with no relevance to the Bible, where Christmas celebrations are not mentioned. Puritans also viewed with distaste the debauchery and drunkenness often associated with Christmas.

Attempts to cancel Christmas had been made in England and the wider Stuart kingdoms, including Ireland, particularly just preceding and during the interregnum period (1649–60). This was a time when England, Scotland, Wales and Ireland were without a monarch, and instead were ruled by Oliver Cromwell, the lord protector, and latterly— and unsuccessfully—by his son, Richard. These attempts to outlaw Christmas were unpopular among many of the laity and clergy, however, and in 1654 one group of zealous ministers in England complained that they had been 'much abused' by their parishioners for 'refusing customary and promiscuous communions … at Christmas'.

The first Christmas ban in England had taken place in 1644, as part of parliament's monthly day of fasting and prayers towards ending the civil war there, although it is likely that it was mostly ignored, as it was issued very close to Christmas during the chaos of a civil war. The following year, with the introduction of a new Directory of Public Worship, which was intended as a replacement for the Anglican Book of Common Prayer, parliament again attempted to end the observance not only of

Christmas but of Easter as well. These were prevaricating steps, however, and in June 1647 parliament banned Christmas outright, along with Easter and Whitsun celebrations. Nor could you observe these feasts in private, with those failing to regard the latest ordinances being fined. In many cases and in many parts of the country this ban was unenforceable, and all it served to do was to rile up a population exhausted by war who wished to observe a traditional holiday and forget their woes for a day.

Similar attempts to outlaw Christmas never took place in Ireland, but it may be that Magan's actions were an attempt to highlight his anti-Christmas position. We do not know what, if anything, happened to Magan following the stand he took in Belturbet on Christmas Day 1693, but tensions between the local Church of Ireland and a growing Presbyterian congregation in the town continued to grow apace, culminating by 1712–13 in a national controversy between both groups. It seems that this stand-off on Christmas Day 1693 between Magan and the Church of Ireland population in Belturbet was the first shot across the bows in this simmering dispute. Christmas was not ever to be cancelled in Ireland but, even so, there seems to have been little festive good will in Belturbet on Christmas Day in 1693.

SOURCES AND FURTHER READING

Robert Armstrong, 'Cavan and the Presbyterian frontier in the early eighteenth century', in Jonathan Cherry and Brendan Scott (eds), *Cavan: history and society* (Dublin, 2014), 217–40.

Ronald Hutton, *Rise and fall of Merry England* (Oxford, 1994).

Brendan Scott, *Belturbet, County Cavan, 1610–1714: the origins of an Ulster Plantation town* (Dublin, 2020).

COME ALL YOU FAITHFUL ...?
BISHOP FRANCIS MOYLAN'S
PASTORAL LETTER,
CHRISTMAS DAY 1796

Victoria Anne Pearson

Christmas can be a stressful time. When Francis Moylan, bishop of Cork, mounted the pulpit on Christmas Day 1796 he was under pressure. In front of him sat a snapshot of Catholic Ireland: the remnants of the Gaelic aristocracy, middle-class *nouveaux riches* and ordinary Cork people, who went about their daily lives amid the hustle and bustle of a burgeoning port city. Yet this established order was shifting, and awareness of this shift rippled through the congregation. The French were anchored in Bantry Bay. They brought the hypnotic message of *liberté, égalité, fraternité* and carried Wolfe Tone and military reinforcements for the United Irishmen, who sought to bond Catholic, Protestant and Dissenter in a rebellion that would sweep away the old order. This new dawn was a catalyst; the time had come for every citizen to choose a side, to stand up or be swept away. As the Christmas bells rang out over Cork, however, not all were enthusiastic for revolution. Moylan believed that the Catholic community now found itself embroiled in an all-or-nothing struggle, with their very existence hanging in the balance. The days of the Penal Laws and operating in the shadows had passed, but now Catholics faced a new and more insidious enemy in French republicanism. As he surveyed his flock, Moylan had an unequivocal answer to revolution: there was no room at the inn.

The prelate had followed French political events in the 1790s intently. France was not a distant country to Cork Catholics. There were close trading networks and long-established family ties between Munster and continental Europe. News of the storming of the Bastille or the October march on Versailles was not conveyed only in newspapers and pamphlets. Many Irish émigrés in France witnessed these events firsthand. Their relatives at home in Ireland worried about them, assisted them to return home and tried desperately to remain in contact. The psychological impact of the revolution and its impact on the Irish perception of events should not be underestimated. Indeed, the bulk of the surviving letters between Moylan and Abbé Henry Essex Edgeworth, his childhood friend, date from this period. In them Edgeworth gives an explicit account of the disintegration of the *ancien régime* and the devastation that he witnessed. Though the descriptions of danger and escape were sometimes thrilling, they also revealed the levels of jeopardy, vulnerability and menace faced by those caught up in the unfolding events of revolutionary France. In these letters, Moylan read of the closure and destruction of the Irish College at Toulouse, his Alma Mater; the seminary life that he knew as a young man was now lost forever. These reports became very real when the last superior of Toulouse, Cork-born Dr Robert McCarthy, was marked for death during the revolutionary massacres in the city but escaped back to Cork. He was not the only refugee to return. Moylan also housed Abbé Gauthier, a French refugee priest. This was not only an act of goodwill; Moylan was very aware of the threat to clerics in France. James Roche, from an established Munster Catholic banking family, had witnessed a Catholic priest guillotined while he was detained in France and imprisoned during the revolution.

Roche's testimony was remarkably similar to the account of Capuchin priest Fr John Donovan, who stood trial before the revolutionary court and was found guilty of treason. While he was awaiting his fate, an Irish officer approached the scaffold and saved seven Irish expatriates from among those sentenced to death. In later life, Fr Donovan made light of this daring escape by commenting that 'my pate was never any great thing of beauty, but I would have felt mighty awkward without it!' Despite this levity, Donovan's account described the terror of execution: the despair of those condemned, the *fait accompli* of the revolutionary show trials and the blood-lust that had gripped the Parisian citizenry. This horror was further confirmed in a letter to Moylan from Edgeworth which depicted in harrowing detail the incarceration of the French royal family and the execution of Louis XVI. As the king's confessor, Edgeworth accompanied Louis to his death, where he narrowly escaped the guillotine himself. Stained with the king's blood, he fled the scaffold among the huge crowd that had gathered to watch the spectacle. Indeed, it must have been a cause of sore annoyance to Moylan that the Sheares brothers, leading luminaries of the United Irish leadership in Cork city, boasted a handkerchief soaked in the king's blood—a grisly souvenir of his execution.

Moylan felt that his world was burning. Previous attempts to remind Cork's Catholic community of their obligations of loyalty and good order had not been enough. Dr Florence MacCarthy, his coadjutor bishop, had preached a funeral sermon on the French king's death in February 1793. Later that same year, he also publicly mourned the execution of Marie Antoinette in a sermon delivered in the chapel of SS Peter and Paul in Cork city centre. Now, on Christmas Day, when the Saviour was born to the world, the bishop, as a good shepherd, addressed his flock. He laid out in no uncertain terms the destructive nature of these 'impious invaders' who sought to unleash anarchy and untold evils, stating that, if the French landed during Christmas, the people's sense of seasonal comradeship and pastoral giving would be snatched from them. He warned his flock of 'the lure of equalising property … for the poor instead of getting any part of the spoil of the rich were robbed of their own little pittance'. He decried the atheistic principles of French fraternity and stressed that, if these interlopers 'were here established, you would not, my beloved people, enjoy the comfort of celebrating this auspicious day'. Christmas celebrations had not been restricted since Cromwell's time.

Despite all the fire and brimstone, Moylan knew that an appeal to his congregation's pockets or to their faith was not enough. Ultimately, he had to convince a people born and bred in a Jacobite tradition that their old French allies, who had sheltered the Stuart kings and the Gaelic Catholic aristocracy, were not the men in Bantry Bay and could no longer be relied on. Instead, Moylan asserted that the Irish Catholic nation did not need to be rescued; it had navigated, survived but also crucially resisted discrimination, recrimination and exclusion in eighteenth-century Ireland. Catholic agency had started to gain momentum, and the congregation sitting before him were 'no longer strangers in our native land'. Radicals and republicans, 'domestic enemies and unnatural children', could only destroy all that had been regained.

Nevertheless, a deep sense of grievance resonated among Cork Catholics, and throughout Munster celebrated Gaelic poets popularised a transition from Jacobite to Jacobin. Having witnessed injustice as a young boy growing up and as a priest ministering to his parishioners in the city, the prelate appreciated the potency of this message. Still, Moylan believed that he had the antidote to 'the French disease'. He looked to another Christmas Day in Cork, in 1775, when Honora 'Nano' Nagle, Moylan's close friend and collaborator, founded the Society of Charitable Instruction of the Sacred Heart of Jesus, which would later become the Presentation Order. A daughter of a prominent and influential Irish Jacobite family, Nagle had discarded a life of privilege and devoted herself and her fortune to the education of Cork's Catholic poor in defiance of the Penal Laws and their prohibition on Irish Catholic education. Since her death in 1784, the bishop had dedicated himself to the survival of her mission. Now, as the Yuletide bells rang out, joyful and triumphant, Moylan called on all Cork Catholics to stand with him and keep the faith that Nagle inspired.

SOURCES AND FURTHER READING

Evelyn Bolster, *A history of the diocese of Cork from the penal era to the Famine* (Cork, 1989).

David Dickson, *Old World colony: Cork and south Munster, 1630–1830* (Cork, 2005).

J.A. Murphy (ed.), *The French are in the bay: the expedition to Bantry Bay 1796* (Cork and Dublin, 1997).

CHRISTMAS IN THE POORHOUSE

Ciarán McCabe

In 1823, poor children in Dublin were treated by one of the city's most prominent charities, the Mendicity Association, to a festive dinner 'of beef beer & bread ... on Christmas Day'. Eight years later, the same charity's managing committee was continuing the tradition and resolved that 'the Superintendent be empowered to purchase the requisite quantity of Bread, Meat & Beer for the children's dinner on Christmas Day'. Established in 1818 to rid the city of street beggars, the Mendicity quickly established itself as a leading player within Dublin's crowded and competitive welfare landscape. The charity operated a poorhouse, originally at Hawkins Street before moving to Usher's Island, and in the early years of its existence the Mendicity ran a number of schools for poor children at Fleet Street, a stone's throw from Hawkins Street, where they were taught skills in straw-plaiting and lacework and were prepared for apprenticeships. The standard diet provided to the Mendicity's paupers was a mixture of vegetables, potatoes and offcuts of meat and bones collected from Dublin householders in what was termed the 'broken meat' cart, described by the charity as 'a diet at once cheap and nutritious'. As such, the provision of the Christmas allowance was something of a treat for the city's mendicants. It is worth noting that the 'beer' that accompanied the children's dinners was, most certainly, weak beer (or 'small beer'), which was not unknown in the dietary regimes of nineteenth-century institutions in Ireland and Britain.

Christmas was a significant time of year in Dublin's charitable landscape, when persons of means were reminded of their moral and Christian responsibilities to those worse off than themselves. In its Christmas Eve issue in 1803, the *Freeman's Journal* urged 'all who consider themselves Christians and good subjects ... the affluent and well-circumstanced' to actively ease the burdens of the 'poor and distressed, and by their humanity and liberality enable them to partake of comfort by ministering to their wants and necessities'. The wealthy were also urged to settle their bills with shopkeepers and tradesmen, so as not to leave these creditors 'embarrassed or distressed' over the Christmas season. Among those who did not forget those Dubliners who found themselves in straitened circumstances was a gentleman named Mr Powel, whose financial decline landed him in a debtor's prison one particular Christmas; upon his release and subsequent return to financial affluence, he bequeathed in his will the interest on the principal sum of £1,000 to be distributed annually in the form of 'a piece of beef, a loaf, and a piece of money' to each debtor confined in the Four Courts and City Marshalseas; the actual distribution of this festive bounty was conducted by the mayor and high sheriff, as reported in 1806. Powel had the ignominious firsthand experience of confinement in a debtor's prison without a Christmas dinner, and his empathy with those in a similar situation drove this particular act of benevolence.

The provision of Christmas dinners by charities in Irish towns and cities, such as the Mendicity Association in Dublin, was funded through either a special once-off subscription drive or the generosity of a particular benefactor. On Christmas Day 1842, 250 paupers were provided with a Christmas dinner at the Mendicity Association's premises at Usher's Island, the cost being borne by the lord lieutenant, Thomas Philip de Grey, 2nd earl de Grey. This practice continued into the later decades of the century; for instance, the 1874 Christmas dinner, provided to 500 paupers, was the personal gift of the lord lieutenant, James Hamilton, the 1st duke of Abercorn, while the following year's dinner catered for an estimated 600 persons.

Despite these charities' appeal to the generosity of the season, their benevolence was conditional and the poor persons in receipt of their bounty were required to conform to expected behavioural norms. These charities were, largely, founded and run by middle-class male élites— bankers, legal practitioners, merchants—and they espoused the values of these philanthropic yet moralising and paternalistic men: an aversion to idleness and licentiousness, and a championing of industry and restraint. In a century when disease epidemics, most notably typhus and cholera, were all too common, the capability of the poorer classes to spread disease through the entire community was realised and feared. As such, being attentive to one's personal cleanliness was insisted upon by the philanthropic élite. At Christmas 1820, a dinner was provided to poor children at the Mendicity Association's premises, while 5d. and free rations were provided to 'every Mendicant attending *clean* on Christmas day' (emphasis added): poverty did not, in the eyes of the managing committee, negate the need for propriety. Notions of deservedness shaped societal views towards poverty and the poor, even at Christmastime. In Dungannon, Co. Tyrone, in the 1820s/30s, collections taken up at the Church of Ireland service were 'divided among *the most deserving* Protestant poor at Easter and Christmas' (emphasis added).

The experience of voluntary charities in providing a special festive dinner for paupers contrasted sharply, it seems, with the attempts of Poor Law Union workhouses (established on foot of the 1838 Irish Poor Law) to offer similar allowances for their inmates. In the instance of the rates-funded workhouses, the public's tolerance for paupers receiving a decent meat dinner was diminished, especially when the expense for such generosity fell on ratepayers. For example, at Christmas 1841 the *Freeman's Journal* editorialised that the two Dublin city Poor Law Unions (South and North Dublin Unions) should not levy ratepayers with the expense of a meat dinner for the workhouse inmates but should instead fall back on voluntary subscriptions from the well-off. A year later, the matter arose again when the North Dublin Union board of guardians debated whether to provide a meat dinner to the workhouse paupers. A Dr Gray asserted the view that many families liable for the poor rate would themselves not have a meat dinner on Christmas Day—perhaps a reference to the impact on Dubliners of the UK-wide economic depression of 1839–41—while another contributor to the discussion countered that paupers within the institution's walls suffered considerably greater discomforts than the rate-paying families and, as such, were deserving of this once-off gesture.

Similar sentiments were expressed at a meeting of the Middleton Poor Law Union in Co. Cork in December 1842. When one guardian tabled a motion for the paupers to receive a meat dinner on Christmas Day, another board member, a Mr Adams, objected: 'I for one will not vote for it. This is not to be a house of luxury.' When put to a vote, the motion was passed by fourteen to eleven votes, showing that the board was far from unanimous on this matter. It was agreed that each pauper would receive 1½lb. of meat, at which the chairman quipped 'I think we had better give them plum-pudding', a comment that was met with laughter from those present. The Middleton exchange reveals, aside from patronising attitudes towards the poor, the conflicting opinions and priorities of those in charge of relieving destitution in their locality: one cohort prioritised the provision of a festive allowance to the destitute, while the other group gave precedence to the avoidance of what they saw as superfluous expenditure of the money of ratepayers, to whom they were answerable.

Among the most jarring features of the workhouses was the separation of families: men, women, boys and girls were divided into different areas, for sleeping, labouring and eating, and rarely got to see each other. This separation, directed by centralised rules from the Poor Law Commissioners, as well as being built into the very design of these institutions, undoubtedly proved upsetting for families already experiencing considerable distress; as workhouse inmates did not leave behind their own records, we can only make assumptions about how stressful they found this feature of workhouse life. Christmas could provide some relief, however, and one instance where this occurred was in the South Dublin Union at Christmas 1841, when the board of guardians resolved 'That the separation[*sic*] of families be not enforced in the workhouse on Christmas Day, but that for a considerable portion of the day, and as far as may be consistent with orders, the different members of families may be allowed to spend their time together'. Even within the grey walls of the nineteenth-century workhouse, Christmas was a time when normal rules could be suspended.

SOURCES AND FURTHER READING

Virginia Crossman, *Poverty and the Poor Law in Ireland 1850–1914* (Liverpool, 2013).

Ciarán McCabe, *Begging, charity and religion in pre-Famine Ireland* (Liverpool, 2018).

Audrey Woods, *Dublin outsiders: a history of the Mendicity Institution, 1818–1998* (Dublin, 1998).

IRISH CHRISTMAS FOOD: SHAPING AND ENCODING TRADITIONS

Regina Sexton

In December 1805 the *Dublin Journal* newspaper advertised as 'a useful Christmas gift for Young House Keepers' Hannah Glasse's *The art of cookery made plain and easy*. This Dublin-printed edition for publisher Gilbert and Hodges contained 'all the modern improvements'—an important advertising note, as the first edition of this best-known cookery book of the eighteenth century was first printed for the author in London in 1747. Glasse's book was a best-seller for nearly 100 years, and editions for Dublin publishers had been printed in the city since 1748. These publishing-history details are significant, as they indicate the increase in the inward movement of food fashions and their diffusion amongst certain social groups throughout the eighteenth century.

The transmission of new foods and culinary trends should not come as a surprise. The development built on Ireland's late medieval and early modern colonial status, which brought the island into direct and deeper contact with food and culinary cultures and the mercantile trading activities of the empire. These dynamic connections of cultural exchange gave those of means access to an array of ingredients that made possible the recipe-based dishes promoted in cookery books. Sugar above all other ingredients would revolutionise what and how people ate. By 1700 it was the most traded international commodity and, in a demand–supply effect, a decline in the price of sugar saw an upsurge in the importation and use of all grades of sugar, which facilitated its prime role in shaping sweet Christmas dishes, confections and baked goods.

The case of the Glasse cookbook is one illustrative example of how Ireland aligned itself to a very British way with food and, over time, came to accept a very British package of typical Christmas foods. Glasse's inclusion of recipes designated as festal foods—Christmas plum porridge and Yorkshire Christmas pie—reveals a certain degree of formality and custom around food preparations, marking a continuation of sixteenth- and seventeenth-century evidence linking specific ingredients and dishes to the festive period. Increased commercialisation of the food industry throughout the nineteenth century and associated developments in retail and advertising promoted a standard set of food items as quintessential to Christmas. In both the domestic and commercial domains, Christmas foods were characterised by the use of expensive ingredients like sugar, spice, dried and candied fruits and nuts. When used in the preparation of Christmas dishes, these ingredients embellished and elevated the every-day to special status. Dishes that were sweet, spiced, highly seasoned, and rich in meat and fat defined Christmas foods and gave them a distinctive taste profile. Nevertheless, interpretations of how Christmas was celebrated through food and ingredient combinations differed greatly with location, outlook and economic standing, and with the nature and material culture of kitchens and standards of cooking competencies.

The food and culinary culture of the aristocratic, gentry and wealthy sectors of Irish society are well represented in manuscript collections created by women from the mid- to late seventeenth century. Handwritten recipe collections borrow heavily from printed cookery books, including typical traditional British foods such as sweet and savoury puddings and pies, sugar-rich and highly flavoured dairy-based dishes and highly seasoned meat and fish dishes, together with select inclusions of foreign dishes adjusted to meet British sensibilities of taste and household economy. A simplification of these grand foodways reduced British food identity to pudding and meat. 'Pudding is so necessary a part of an Englishman's food, that it and beef are accounted the victuals they most love', says the English agricultural, domestic economy and cookery writer William Ellis in his *The country housewife's family companion* (1750).

Although reductionist, the pie, pudding and meat combination came to define occasions of celebratory eating and feasting. For instance, in the mid-eighteenth century, stewards and servants in the Carton household of James Fitzgerald, marquis of Kildare, were served mutton or beef pie once a week, and roast beef and plum pudding on Sundays. Meat and minced meat pies were commonplace, and recipes for them in manuscript collections from Irish estates are numerous and various, depending on the choice and array of ingredients used in their preparation, while plum pudding was a seasonal dish from late winter into spring. Embellished versions of pies and puddings, boosted with higher-than-usual volumes of fruit, spices, eggs, ground nuts, animal fats and alcohol, were stitched into Christmas menus as essential components of celebratory dining. As vital elements in idealised festive eating, conforming to the beef and pudding pairing unified the different social grades, from the wealthiest to the recipients of charity support. Donations and bequests to the poor and destitute at Christmastime financed meals of roast beef and plum pudding organised by charitable agencies and church parishes throughout the nineteenth century, with the meal serving as a means to include the most socially excluded.

Luxury and ingredient-rich items also became central to the activities of commercial specialist traders and provisioners at Christmastime. Extensive advertising by grocers, bakers, confectioners and cooked-food provisioners throughout the nineteenth century highlights the popularity of and demand for élite and exotic goods and traditional specialities, particularly Christmas beef, Christmas pies and Twelfth Night cakes. An extensive range and variety of exotic goods and cooked foods was offered by businesses like those of Peter Tharel and E. Hayes, both of Clarendon

Street in Dublin. These providers offered seasonal, regional and festive specialities for the Christmas period. Typical of their extensive offerings were Christmas pies; mince pies; chicken, pigeon, beef steak, mutton and veal pies; spiced red rounds of beef; spiced potted beef; hams; boars' heads; ox and sheep tongues; meat collars; German and Irish sausages; made dishes; brown, white and portable soups; real and mock turtle soups; branded pickles and relishes; pickled and smoked salmon; and jellies, pastries and Savoy cakes. A range of specialist quality-assured goods linked to a region of production included Kerry beef; hams (Westphalia, Cumberland, Belfast, Dublin, Limerick, Yorkshire and Wicklow); cheeses (Gloucestershire and Stilton); and Cork and Wicklow butter rolls. Dishes like beef à la mode (similar to spiced beef) set in aspic could be made to order, while bespoke pies were made for home consumption or sent to any part of Ireland and Britain.

In 1827 the Old Established Fruit and Foreign Warehouses on Grafton Street had the following seasonal fruit and specialities on offer for Christmas: sweet pot oranges; sweet raspberry oranges; muscatel raisins; sultanas; new Zante currants; new lemons; Turkey figs; walnuts; Spanish grapes; Spanish onions; chestnuts; candied oranges and lemons; West India tamarinds; Indian arrow root; Scotch marmalade; brandy fruits; and liqueurs and whiskey. Andrews and Company of Dame Street, agents to the (1862 International Exhibition) award-winning London provisioners J. McCall, sold luxury hampers at different price points with Limerick hams; mixed Yorkshire game pies; the finest Eleme figs; dessert raisins; Rahat Lacoum (Turkish delight); mixed crystallised fruit; Tafilalt dates; Andrews' celebrated mixed tea; Jordan almonds; and bottles of Imperial French plums.

The commercialisation of sophisticated and class-distinctive recipe-based cooking, with its emphasis on pies, puddings, made dishes and elaborate confectionery work and baked goods, gave to those of means access to the foodways of élite groups. Tactics to set distinctiveness and quality are evident in advertising notes from purveyors begging 'to inform the Nobility, and Gentry' of their offerings and setting out their professional pedigree, as in the case of E. Hayes, who advertised his role as cook to the lord chancellor. These specialist purveyors defined expectations and popular imaginings of the ideal array of Christmas foods. A dilution of these ideals was promoted by the grocers' shops that were increasing in both urban and rural settings in the second half of the nineteenth century, with even the most modest enterprise offering special food items for Christmas: dried fruits; sugar of different grades; branded cocoas, biscuits and chocolates; mineral waters and cordials; alcohol; and a wide range of puddings and Christmas cakes—iced and plain fruit cakes; Madeira, sultana and seed (caraway) cakes; gingerbreads; and barmbracks.

At its most basic, the Christmas meal contained a meat element, with commercial goods bringing additional celebratory gloss. As seen above, a template of what constituted Christmas fare, although variable and flexible, was formed by the nineteenth century, and it became more uniform and standardised by the early decades of the twentieth century. A 1920 Christmas Day three-course menu in the *Belfast Newsletter* with clear soup, roast turkey, sausage stuffing, bread sauce, brown gravy, boiled ox tongue, boiled cauliflower and sauce, boiled sprouts and baked potatoes, plum pudding and hard sauce, mince pies, trifles and jellies, is one that had spun together an array of inherited elements from the past.

This multi-layered and inherited construct of Christmas fare is one that we continue to transmit, prepare and perform as traditional practice. Its strictures give structure, security and identity to our engagement with Christmas food culture. And although we might perceive the nature and range of typical Christmas foods to be immutable, they are open and receptive to additions and adaptions that reflect wider social realities and accompanying tastes. Mince pies without meat, salted caramel and chocolate puddings beside heavier plum ones, and nut roasts in place of turkey do not rupture traditions, but rather their inclusion makes the endless cycle of living tradition relevant and a reflection of our dynamic relationship with Christmas food.

SOURCES AND FURTHER READING

Louis Cullen, *The emergence of modern Ireland, 1600–1900* (London, 1981).

Terence Dooley, 'A copy of the marquis of Kildare's household book, 1758', *Archivium Hibernicum* **62** (2009), 183–220.

William Ellis, *The country housewife's family companion 1750* (Devon, 2000).

Hannah Glasse, *The art of cookery made plain and easy which far exceeds any thing of the kind yet published* (Dublin, 1796).

Regina Sexton, 'Food and culinary cultures in pre-Famine Ireland', *Proceedings of the Royal Irish Academy* **115**C (2015), 257–306.

THE IRISH ORIGINS OF 'ONCE IN ROYAL DAVID'S CITY'

Nicole Gallagher

Often sung as a processional hymn at services of nine lessons and carols, 'Once in Royal David's City' has become one of the best-known, most-loved hymns of the traditional Christmas carol repertoire. Its original purpose was not, however, to be sung by full congregations or choirs but to act as an educational tool for Victorian children.

'Once in Royal' was written by the Irishwoman Cecil Frances Alexander, wife of Archbishop William Alexander and one of the foremost hymnists of the Victorian era. Born Fanny Humphries in Eccles Street, Dublin, in 1818, she enjoyed an upper-middle-class life of privilege. After moving with her family to a country estate near Rathdrum, Co. Wicklow, she developed a passion for writing poetry, and as a teenager she undertook the religious instruction of local children by reading the Bible to them and helping to prepare them for confirmation. This voluntary work continued after Fanny and her family moved to Strabane, Co. Tyrone, where she eventually came to the conclusion that the most effective way of teaching Christian beliefs to children was through simple, easy-to-memorise poetry. While in Strabane, Fanny and her sister began teaching the deaf and set up a small school for four or five deaf children, which eventually led to the establishment of the Derry and Raphoe Diocesan Institution for the Education of the Deaf and Dumb. By this time she had already published four collections of her writings, and the money received from them was put towards the upkeep of this school. One of these collections, *Hymns for little children* (1848), was designed to provide an accessible way of teaching various points of the Apostles' Creed to children, and it was within this collection that 'Once in Royal David's City' was first published, its purpose being to expand upon the lines 'who was conceived by the Holy Ghost, born of the Virgin Mary'. This collection also saw the inclusion of another well-known hymn by Mrs Alexander, 'There is a Green Hill Far Away', which was written to accompany the lines 'He suffered under Pontius Pilate, was crucified, died and was buried'.

'Once in Royal' is a classic example of the Victorian method of teaching morality and good behaviour to children through the medium of specially written children's hymnody. The Victorian era saw a resurgence of the seventeenth-century philosophy of John Locke, who was of the belief that children are born as blank slates and that it is the responsibility of both family and the community to turn them into upstanding citizens for the good of society. It was not long, therefore, before nineteenth-century religious societies saw an opportunity and began to produce books and hymnals on moral themes for children. Many of these hymns were written by women, who in the nineteenth century undertook the role of 'the Angel in the House' (a phrase taken from an 1875 poem of the same name by Coventry Patmore), taking on the responsibility of the moral instruction of both their children and their husbands. The writing of hymnody and other religious texts was a way in which the women of this era could extend their influence outside of the walls of their own homes at a time when they were treated as second-class citizens. The third and fourth verses of this hymn are prime examples of how Victorian hymnists such as Mrs Alexander used the medium of hymnody as an educational tool to teach good conduct to children. They remind children that Christ, too, was once a child and that they should model their behaviour on the young life of Jesus:

> And through all His wondrous childhood
> He would honour and obey,
> Love and watch the lowly maiden
> In whose gentle arms He lay;
> Christian children all must be
> Mild, obedient, good as He.
>
> For He is our childhood's Pattern,
> Day by day, like us, He grew,
> He was little, weak, and helpless,
> Tears and smiles like us he knew;
> And He feeleth for our sadness,
> And He shareth in our gladness.

It is particularly interesting that these verses portray the young Jesus as being a paragon of obedience and good behaviour: the ideal Victorian child. However, there is little evidence of this to be found in the Bible. In fact, an example of quite the opposite can be found in the second chapter of Luke's Gospel, when Jesus stayed behind in the temple in Jerusalem without the knowledge or consent of his parents. When Mary and Joseph found him and questioned his behaviour, Jesus responded almost with indignation, saying 'Didn't you know I'd be in my Father's house?' Therefore Mrs Alexander and, indeed, other hymnists of the time most certainly took liberties in their description of the conduct of the boy Jesus with the aim of the encouragement of good behaviour in children.

In 1849, a year after *Hymns for little children* was first published, the English organist and composer Henry John Gauntlett came across 'Once in Royal' and set it to music. This tune was to become synonymous with Mrs Alexander's hymn. It was first published in Gauntlett's *Christmas carols, four numbers* (1849) as a single line of melody with keyboard accompaniment, but Gauntlett himself rearranged it into a four-part setting for its inclusion in the 1868 Appendix of the English Anglican hymnal *Hymns ancient and modern*, where it was placed in the 'For the Young' section. It was in this hymnal that Gauntlett's tune was given the title 'Irby', by which it is still known today. The second, third and fourth editions of the Church of Ireland's *Church Hymnal* (published in 1873, 1915 and 1960 respectively) also included 'Once in Royal' in their children's hymns sections, and it was not until the publication of the current (fifth) edition of the *Church Hymnal* in 2000 that the hymn was moved into the Christmas section. This shows the transition of 'Once in Royal' from a Victorian children's hymn to a mainstream Christmas carol sung by children and adults alike.

Part of the reason for this transition, and for its enduring use and popularity amongst almost all English-speaking congregations, is its use in services of nine lessons and carols. This tradition of using 'Once in Royal' as a processional hymn began in 1919 at the chapel of King's College Cambridge, when the Chapel Choir used the organist's (Dr Arthur Henry Mann) arrangement of the music. As the choir processed, the first verse was sung as an unaccompanied solo by a boy soprano, who was joined by the choir and organ for the second verse and finally by the congregation from verse three. Throughout the course of the twentieth century, this arrangement by Mann became a popular way to begin festivals of nine lessons and carols throughout the British Isles and beyond.

Given the fact that 'Once in Royal' has achieved mainstream popularity partly through the very 'British' institution that is King's College Cambridge, it is important that its Irish origins are not overlooked or forgotten. This is a hymn that was written in Ireland by an Irishwoman, with the proceeds from its original publication going towards the upkeep of an Irish school. So perhaps, next time you hear 'Once in Royal David's City' broadcast live from the carol service at King's College Cambridge or you see it appear on the Christmas edition of the BBC's *Songs of Praise* programme, you will take a moment to remember that this hymn is one of Ireland's own, written by one of our finest hymn-writers.

SOURCES AND FURTHER READING

Edward Darling and Donald Davison, *Companion to the Church Hymnal* (Dublin, 2005).
Valerie Wallace, *A life of the hymn-writer Mrs Alexander 1818–1895* (Dublin, 1995).

'WE THREE KINGS OF ORIENT ARE': AN EPIPHANY CAROL WITH IRISH LINKS

Patrick Comerford

The Christmas or (more correctly) Epiphany carol 'We Three Kings of Orient are' ranks alongside 'O Little Town of Bethlehem' by Bishop Phillips Brooks as one of the best-known and popular American carols, but few people in Ireland realise that the author's father was born in Dublin and was one of the bishops who played a pivotal role in the formation of the Anglican Communion.

'We Three Kings of Orient are' was written in 1859 by the Revd John Henry Hopkins junior (1820–91). He was the rector of Christ Church in Williamsport, Pennsylvania, when he wrote this carol for a Christmas pageant in the General Theological Seminary, New York, although it did not appear in print for another six years. He was the son of John Henry Hopkins (1792–1868), an Irish-born Episcopal bishop who was the first bishop of Vermont and later the eighth presiding bishop of the Episcopal Church.

Bishop John Henry Hopkins was born in Dublin on 30 January 1792, the son of Thomas Hopkins and his wife Elizabeth (née Fitzackerly). In 1800 Thomas and Elizabeth emigrated from Dublin to Philadelphia. There, the young John Henry began his education at home with his mother, and he was reading Shakespeare before the age of nine. Elizabeth established a school for girls in Trenton, New Jersey, and eventually sent her son to a Baptist boys' school in Bordentown, and then to Princeton University. Because of his family's straitened circumstances, Hopkins took a job at a counting-house. At the time he was not particularly religious, and his parents' marriage was troubled. When his mother moved to Frederick, Maryland, to establish another school, he remained in Philadelphia with his father and friends.

Hopkins worked for an ironmaster in New Jersey and in Philadelphia before moving west to manage the ironworks at Bassenheim in Butler County. James O'Hara (1752–1819), an immigrant from County Mayo who became the wealthiest man in Pittsburgh, employed Hopkins to run the ironworks in the Ligonier Valley. There Hopkins got to know the Muller family, descended from a long line of German Lutheran ministers, and, after a religious awakening, he began studying the Bible and other religious books. He travelled back to Harmony, Pennsylvania, to marry Caspar Muller's daughter Melusina, and they settled at Hermitage Furnace. The iron business failed, however, and Hopkins returned to Pittsburgh, where he taught drawing and painting while studying law. He was called to the bar in 1819 and set up a legal practice in Pittsburgh.

John and Melusina attended the Presbyterian church, but he was also the organist and choirmaster at Trinity Church, the local Episcopal church. When the rector of Trinity Church moved to New Jersey and the next priest proved inadequate, Hopkins applied to be accepted for the priesthood, planning to combine his ministerial and legal vocations. He was licensed as a lay reader in 1823 by William White, bishop of Pennsylvania, was ordained deacon on 14 December and was ordained priest on 12 May 1824. He was placed in charge of Trinity Church, Pittsburgh, and he was professor of Rhetoric and *Belles-Lettres* in the Western University of Pennsylvania (now the University of Pittsburgh) in 1824–30. He read the works of the Church Fathers in the original Greek and Latin and, although in principle committed to high church liturgical practices, he opposed the introduction of the confessional to the Episcopal Church.

In 1827 he stepped back from the opportunity to become a coadjutor bishop to Bishop White, who was also the presiding bishop of the Episcopal Church. He realised that his own vote would have decided the election in his favour, and he lost by one vote. Later he told his son that if he had voted for himself he would have wondered for the rest of his life whether his will or God's had been done.

In 1831 he moved to Trinity Church, Boston, where his vision was to establish a diocesan seminary. In 1832 he was elected the first bishop of Vermont, and was consecrated in St Paul's Church, New York, on 31 October. At the same time, he became the rector of St Paul's, Burlington. While he was bishop of Vermont, the diocese faced financial depressions, mass migration to the west, which was opening up, personal bankruptcy and controversies.

Hopkins is credited with introducing Gothic architecture to the Episcopal Church and was the architect of Trinity Church, Rutland, where he was the rector in 1860–1. In 1861 he published a controversial pamphlet, *A scriptural, ecclesiastical, and historical view of slavery*, in which he argued that slavery was not a sin *per se* but an institution that was objectionable and should be abrogated by agreement. His dream of a diocesan seminary was realised in 1860 with the opening of the Vermont Episcopal Institute near Burlington. For a time he was also the chancellor of the University of Vermont.

He was elected the presiding bishop of the Episcopal Church in January 1865, and presided that October at the general convention in Philadelphia. Largely through his friendship with Bishop Stephen Elliott of Georgia, the presiding bishop of the breakaway Protestant Episcopal Church in the Confederate States of America, the Northern and Southern branches of the Episcopal Church were reunited in 1866 after the end of the American Civil War.

Hopkins took a leading role in the first Lambeth Conference in 1867, bringing together all bishops in the Anglican Communion. He survived only two months after his return to Burlington and died on 9 January 1868, aged 75. His funeral took place in St Paul's Church, Burlington, and he was buried beside the seminary that he founded.

John and Melusina Hopkins had thirteen children. In 1866 most of their large family gathered at the family home to celebrate their Golden Wedding anniversary. The University of Vermont and Harvard University hold many of the family papers.

The bishop's son, the Revd John Henry Hopkins junior, the author of 'We Three Kings of Orient are', was born on 28 October 1820 in Pittsburgh. He graduated from the University of Vermont with an AB in 1839, and received his master's degree in 1845. He worked for some time as a journalist before entering the General Theological Seminary, New York. After ordination, he was the seminary's first music teacher (1855–7), composed several hymns and edited the *Church Journal*. As the rector of Christ Church in Williamsport, Pennsylvania (1876–87), he delivered the eulogy at the funeral of President Ulysses S. Grant in 1885. He died in Hudson, New York, on 14 August 1891 and is buried beside his father.

Hopkins wrote the words and music of 'We Three Kings of Orient are' for a Christmas pageant in 1859 when he was visiting his father's home in Vermont, although it did not appear in print until his *Carols, hymns and songs* was published in New York in 1863. The carol is based on the story of the Visit of the Magi (Matthew 2:1–12). Three male voices each sing a single verse on their own, corresponding with the three kings. The first and last stanzas are sung together by all three as 'verses of praise,' while the intermediate stanzas are sung individually, with each king describing his gift and revealing the sacramental nature of the gifts offered to the Christ Child. The refrain praises the beauty of the Star of Bethlehem.

This is the first Christmas carol from the US to win widespread popularity, and it was included in Bramley and Stainer's *Christmas carols old and new* in London in 1871. In 1916 it was published in the hymnal for the Episcopal Church. When it was included in the *Oxford Book of Carols* (1928), it was described as 'one of the most successful of modern composed carols'.

SOURCE AND FURTHER READING

John Henry Hopkins III, 'The Rev. John Henry Hopkins, Jr.', *Historical Magazine of the Protestant Episcopal Church* **4** (4) (December 1935), 267–80.

TRANSPORTED TO FAIRYLAND: THE IRISH BRIGADES CELEBRATE CHRISTMAS DURING THE AMERICAN CIVIL WAR

Damian Shiels

Near one of the huge fires a kind of arbor was nicely constructed of the branches of trees, which were so interwoven on one another as to form a kind of wall. Inside this, some were seated on logs, some reclining in true Turkish style. Seated near the fire was Johnny Flaherty, discoursing sweet music from his violin … beside him sat his father, fingering the chanters of a bagpipe in elegant style … it was Christmas Eve, and home-thoughts and home-longings were crowding on them …

This was how Tipperary native David Power Conyngham recalled the Irish Brigade's first Christmas of the American Civil War, sitting around Virginia campfires in 1861. Together with St Patrick's Day, the celebration of Christmas—particularly early in the conflict—marked an important occasion for ethnic Irish units in the US military to celebrate both their cultural identity and their American service. For Irish soldiers, however, Christmas could bring both joy and melancholy.

Conyngham marked it as a time of year when 'the exile feels a longing desire … for the pleasant, genial firesides and loving hearts of home'. Just as many men's thoughts were filled with memories of times past that December in Virginia, Christmas 1861 would in its turn come to hold a special place in the remembrance of Irish Brigade veterans. Fate decreed that it would be the last Christmas they celebrated together before war tore their ranks asunder. In later years, the recollection of that pleasant festive scene conjured up other sorrowful memories for Conyngham: 'How many of the group will, ere another Christmas comes round, sleep in a bloody and nameless grave!' By 25 December 1862, battlefields with names like Malvern Hill, Antietam and Fredericksburg had all but destroyed the Irish Brigade, leading one officer to comment that the year would witness 'a sad, sad Christmas by many an Irish hearthstone in New York, Pennsylvania and Massachusetts'.

Christmas 1862 may have been a bittersweet occasion for the men of the Irish Brigade, but it was an altogether different story in the Union's only other ethnic Irish brigade, the Irish Legion. The Christmas of 1862 was their first in the field and, like the Irish Brigade before them, most had yet to experience the real horrors that the war held in store. In 1862 the Legion spared no effort in making the occasion at their camp in Newport News, Virginia, one to remember. The Irishmen started by hauling copious quantities of trees into their camp, creating bowers of greenery between their tents and constructing 'triumphal arches' of vegetation, some up to 30ft high, which they decorated with giant holly stars. Each company spelt out their designations using green and red berries, while different coloured clays were used to add a range of motifs and adornments, including mottoes such as 'Erin-go-Bragh'. One of the awed visitors to the Christmas camp solemnly declared that 'without exaggeration I believe such a camp and such a fairylike scene were never seen before and may never be again'. As was intended, the efforts of the Legion drew sightseers and admirers from many other units—not only promoting the celebration of Christmas but also showcasing the ingenuity of Irish America.

Aside from their decorative endeavours, we have also been left with a detailed account of how the Irish Legion celebrated Christmas Day itself. For those lucky enough to receive them, enjoyment of the occasion was greatly enhanced by Christmas boxes from family in New York, bringing treats and tipples from home. The formal proceedings began at midnight on Christmas Eve, when all the officers attended Mass. Singing and music accompanied Father Dillon's service, which naturally enough was followed by a glass of imported Irish whiskey for each of the participants. Christmas Day likewise began with a 10am Mass, this time for all the regiments of the Legion. After that the 'amusements' began. First up was one of the great staples of wartime Irish celebrations—the horserace. Officers donned their colours and mounted animals sporting names such as 'Bull Run', 'George Washington', 'Pontius Pilate' and 'Sweepstakes' for the three one-mile-long heats. At 11am the enlisted men lined the specially prepared course to take in the spectacle, which netted the winner a silver cup but brought the owner of the slowest horse the forfeit of paying for a basket of wine.

While the officers indulged in the Sport of Kings, the programme of events for the enlisted men of the Legion was somewhat less exalted in nature—as with other units, Irish regiments were not without their class distinctions. Soldiers of the 155th New York Volunteers were the first to bring home laurels, though not before numerous 'falls and tumbles', as they finished victorious in the sack race. Next up was the turn of the unfortunate 'Mr Porky', a shaved pig which the men of the Legion pursued in a wild chase as they sought to catch it by the tail. Blindfolded wheelbarrow races and foot races rounded off what by all accounts was a fantastic day for all who participated. Intended to be exciting, enjoyable and humorous, these distractions not only fostered comradeship within the group but also undoubtedly helped many soldiers through what might otherwise have been a difficult day, far from home.

The arrival of evening saw officers and men again separate into their respective groups to continue the festive celebrations. The Legion's 'Monks of the Screw'—a brigade social organisation named for an eighteenth-century Irish drinking club—took charge of the officer's Christmas dinner, slated for 9pm. It was attended by Brigadier-General Michael Corcoran and 80 of his officers, together with six US Navy officers and a number of ladies. The bill of fare for their shindig has survived:

Oyster Soup
Raw Oysters
Turkey, Chicken, Tongue
Roast Beef

Dessert
Plum Pudding
English Cheese

Fruit
Raisins, Almonds, Apples

Liquors
Bourbon, Brandy

Wine
Champagne, Sherry

As at all formal nineteenth-century Irish-American dinners, toasts abounded. Glasses were raised to General Corcoran, to the 'Monks of the Screw', to comrades in the Irish Brigade and to many others. Even the Confederate President Jefferson Davis was included, mocked by a silent toast with empty glasses. The party—and the drinking—rolled on until four in the morning. When the night finally did draw to a close, proceedings were ended with a rendition of the 'Star-Spangled Banner'.

The impressive Yuletide exertions of the Irish Legion well illustrate the marrying of Irish and American identities that were a hallmark of ethnic Irish units during the Civil War. They wanted to celebrate—and to be seen to celebrate—both their Irish cultural identity (which included music and drink) and their identities as proud and patriotic Americans. This was further exemplified in the words of the song 'Hurrah for the Sixty-Ninth, My Boys', composed especially for Christmas 1862 by Dr John Dwyer. Its lyrics also highlight the strong Fenian sentiment which ran especially deep among the Irish Legion's officers:

HURRAH FOR THE SIXTY-NINTH, MY BOYS
Air—The Young May Moon

Hurrah for the 69th, my boys,
The brave old 69th, my boys,
Once more we all meet,
Our old friends to greet,
And present our campaign laurels, boys.

We've proved our Celtic blood, my boys,
And fought by field and flood, my boys,
Let no one then dare
To say that we fear,
'Tis not in our language at all, my boys.

Chorus:
Hurrah for the flag of green, my boys,
The richest that ever was seen, my boys,
Long, long may it wave,
The Union to save,
Entwined with the Stars and Stripes, my boys.

And when we have done with the South, my boys,
With our regiment gallant and stout, my boys,
We'll be off to the East
To give England a taste

Of fighting on our own hook, my boys.

For now that we've handled the gun, my boys,
We'll make the Saxon churls run, my boys,
Then over the sea
To set Ireland free,
We'll do it by hook or by crook, my boys.

[Chorus]

For our General brave let us shout, my boys,
And now that we have him about, my boys,
To take the command,
We're all here on hand
To conquer or die for our country, boys.

And here on this jovial night, my boys,
We'll drink to that Isle so bright, my boys,
Where the shamrock so green
For ever is seen,
The emblem of Irishmen true, my boys.

[Chorus]

As with the Irish Brigade in 1861, the Irish Legion's 1862 Christmas festivities would be the last they enjoyed free from the spectre of loss wrought by the war. Although they had faced only minor combat by December 1863, that Christmas was nonetheless marred by the death of their beloved General Corcoran, lost on 22 December following a fall from his horse. By Christmas 1864 the horrors of the Overland Campaign had inflicted staggering losses, consigning many of the men who had created the Christmas 1862 fairyland to 'a bloody and nameless grave'.

SOURCES AND FURTHER READING

David Power Conyngham, *The Irish Brigade and its campaigns* (New York, 1867).

New York *Irish American Weekly*, 10 January and 17 January 1863.

WILLIAM O'BRIEN'S 'CHRISTMAS ON THE GALTEES', 1877

Felix M. Larkin

In the days after Christmas 1877, the *Freeman's Journal* published a series of five articles that are generally acknowledged to be the earliest piece of investigative journalism in Ireland. Entitled 'Christmas on the Galtees', they were written by William O'Brien, then only in his mid-twenties but already the *Freeman*'s star reporter. He was later an Irish Party MP at Westminster and a prominent agrarian leader in the Land War in the 1880s.

The articles were described by O'Brien as 'the investigation of a historic agrarian struggle on an estate around the Galtee mountains'. The estate in question was 'a poor mountainous estate' in County Tipperary that had been acquired by a wealthy English manufacturer, Nathaniel Buckley. He raised the rents—in most instances by a factor of two or three—and resistance to this impossible burden escalated to the point where a bailiff was killed, and the estate agent and a policeman wounded, in a gun attack.

The plight of the tenants on the estate was first highlighted in letters from a prominent local Fenian, John Sarsfield Casey, published in the *Freeman* and in the *Cork Examiner*. This resulted in a libel suit against Casey. When the suit failed and Casey was vindicated, the

Freeman decided to pursue the matter further. O'Brien was dispatched to Tipperary with, in his own words, instructions 'to see for myself; to avoid heated and exaggerated language; and to tell the plain truth, whatever it might be, without fear or favour'. The first of his articles was dated Christmas Eve and appeared in the *Freeman* on 27 December. The remaining articles were published at intervals between 29 December and 5 January. All five articles were gathered together in a pamphlet soon afterwards.

The *Freeman's Journal* was owned at this time by Edmund Dwyer Gray, and the Buckley estate was located in the constituency for which Gray had recently been elected MP. The candidate that he defeated was the same John Sarsfield Casey who had drawn attention to conditions on the estate. In his *Recollections*, O'Brien recalls that Gray personally gave him the commission to write the 'Christmas on the Galtees' articles. In doing so, Gray was clearly taking steps to avoid being outflanked in his political backyard.

What makes O'Brien's articles extraordinary is the quality of the analysis that underpinned his exposition of the wretched circumstances of the tenants—'the shameful scenes which passed under my own eyes', to quote O'Brien—and its focus on the experience of individual tenants. In this regard, O'Brien writes:

> The inquiry was original in this sense, that it was, so far as I know, the first time when, in place of general statements, there was substituted a house-to-house visitation, telling in detail the story of every family—their crops, their stock, their debts, their struggle for life—from documents examined on the premises, and in words taken down in shorthand from the peasants' own lips.

A good example of O'Brien's approach is his account of visiting the farm of Johanna Fitzgerald, one of the tenants on the estate. O'Brien remarks upon 'her bare feet and coarse petticoat', and he tells us that her 'husband has gone to England as a labourer to earn bread for her four children'. He continues:

> A mess of Indian meal was in the pot for dinner. The family, of course, slept in one room [...]. Mrs Fitzgerald said she had not heard from her husband these five weeks, and a shilling was all the money she had in the world. Her rent was raised from £2 10s 4d to £4 4s. Her stock of potatoes was out this month past, 'except a handful of seed', and from this to August yellow stirabout must be bought on credit. [...] Two geese and some hens made a total of her live stock.

This woman's husband was a great-uncle of the late taoiseach Garret FitzGerald.

Of another tenant, the Widow Condon, O'Brien says that she 'had eight children feeding on dry Indian meal stirabout when I entered her cabin, and the floor was pounded into a gelid mass of filth quite six inches in depth; the rain streaming through the thatch, the out-offices tumbling to ruin; the whole furniture miserable and scanty beyond description'. He adds: 'Within this desolate rookery, Widow Condon spent her Christmas night, having begged a meal of bread and tea from her neighbours as her Christmas dinner—not the poorest scrap of meat even then'.

In the second article in the series, part of which was dated Christmas Day, O'Brien recalls that 'not a sprig of holly was to be seen in any house I visited'. He observes:

> It would be almost a levity to speak of the ordinary Christmas adjuncts of merry making. [...] As I drove past the base of the hill after nightfall, when no cheerful twinkle lighted the cabin windows, and when a snowstorm breaking over the Galtees overspread it like a shroud, there seemed to be few spots in Christendom that had less business with a happy Christmas.

O'Brien visited a total of 226 holdings during his sojourn in County Tipperary. His precise and vivid reporting of the results of his investigations makes the 'Christmas on the Galtees' articles a perfect specimen of the new genre of journalism—the so-called 'New Journalism'—just emerging in Britain and associated with the legendary W.T. Stead. The articles also display the passionate advocacy that was so much a part of the New Journalism. The final one thus concludes with an appeal to public opinion, which, with its implicit assumption that the articles would galvanise public opinion, is characteristic of the New Journalism:

> One wave of that English opinion, before which Cabinets have fallen and nationalities been raised up—one generous impulse, such as was at the call of undeserved human misery in Bulgaria—would either end this unhappy strife or sweep away for ever the law that allows it.

'Two Christmas Hearths', by John Fergus O'Hea. This cartoon, which appeared in the *Weekly Freeman* on 18 December 1886, contrasts in very stark terms the plight of an evicted family at Christmastime with the good fortune of their former landlord and his family enjoying the festive season snug inside the Big House in the distance.

W.T. Stead, as editor of the Darlington *Northern Echo*, had played a central role in publicising atrocities in Bulgaria in 1876. By linking his exposé of conditions on the Buckley estate with that controversy, O'Brien was very deliberately identifying himself with the New Journalism.

O'Brien notes in his *Recollections* that the publication of his articles was 'not without perils for the proprietor of a great newspaper'—specifically, the risk of a libel action. Edmund Dwyer Gray showed great courage in publishing the articles in the *Freeman*. He was also extraordinarily prescient in bringing the land question to public attention at this early stage; the articles appeared almost twenty months before the founding of the Land League by Michael Davitt. Moreover, they set the tone—a crusading tone—for the later press coverage of the Land War. Courting public opinion through the press would be an integral part of the strategy adopted first by the Land League and later, in 1886, in the Plan of Campaign. Indeed, the Plan's manifesto stated that 'the fullest publicity should be given to evictions', and accounts and pictures of evictions and other outrages were used quite explicitly for propaganda purposes both at home and abroad. O'Brien's 'Christmas on the Galtees' articles blazed a trail in this regard.

But did the articles have any effect? O'Brien concedes in his *Recollections* that they did not. He states that 'no relief came to the Galtee estate, or to any other, until, a couple of years later, the Land League Revolution shook the earth'. The failure of his ground-breaking journalistic effort leads him to ask this awkward, somewhat despondent question: 'who can be surprised if, in the cabins among the Galtee Mountains, there was sometimes a weary suspicion that the only effective force of public opinion lay in the crack of Ryan's blunderbuss?' Ryan was the name of the man who had killed the bailiff on the Buckley estate.

SOURCES AND FURTHER READING

John Sarsfield Casey, *The Galtee Boy* (ed. Mairead Maume, Patrick Maume and Mary Casey) (Dublin, 2005).

Felix M. Larkin, '"Green shoots" of the New Journalism in the *Freeman's Journal*, 1877–1890', in Karen Steele and Michael de Nie (eds), *Ireland and the New Journalism* (New York, 2014).

William O'Brien, *Recollections* (London, 1905).

CHRISTMAS AND THE BRETHREN

Crawford Gribben

The Brethren were not initially a very festive bunch. Emerging during the crisis of the Anglo-Irish establishment in the run-up to the repeal of the Test Act (1828), Catholic Emancipation (1829) and the Reform Act (1832), those who became known as 'Brethren' withdrew from denominations in order to bear witness to the unity of Christians and to prepare for the second coming of Christ. But they were also preoccupied by Christ's first coming. As their numbers, geographical range and print culture expanded, Brethren became embroiled in the debates about Christology that shook large sections of early nineteenth-century evangelicalism. Speculative questions were exhumed from antiquity: in what way was the Word made flesh? Did Christ have a mortal body? Could he have died of old age? As these debates continued, and as the movement divided into 'open' and 'exclusive' networks, no one defended Christian orthodoxy more forcefully than John Nelson Darby (1800–82). Formerly the Church of Ireland curate of Calary, Co. Wicklow, Darby became the most important leader among the exclusive Brethren, and one of the century's most widely published individuals. And yet, in his millions of published words, for all that he defended the orthodox view of the Incarnation, he hardly ever referred to Christmas.

For their eccentricity, the Brethren certainly caught the public imagination. In the 1830s and 1840s the movement attracted adherents from the higher ranks of Irish society, including Lady Theodosia Powerscourt, who hosted large conferences for the discussion of biblical prophecy on her Wicklow estate. Only after the evangelical revival of 1859 did the appeal of the Brethren extend into the working classes—a fact recognised by the Irish novelist George Moore, whose account of *Esther Waters* (1894), a Brethren woman struggling to make her way through poverty, was regarded by James Joyce as one of the finest novels of the century.

For the Brethren made a very distinctive offer. As adherents of one of the period's most remarkable religious movements, they promoted an often extremely controversial argument about ecclesiastical 'ruin'. This was the idea that the Church had begun to fail before the close of the New Testament canon, and that no effort to restore apostolic purity—including the Protestant reformation—could possibly succeed.

These arguments were influential. So, while valuing the ecumenical creeds, and speaking most highly of the Athanasian, Darby and his brethren met for worship without clergy, liturgy or any order of service. The central feature of their meetings for worship was the Eucharist. While their preaching and writing covered the breadth of Christian theology, their hymnody developed around reflection on the humiliation and exaltation of Christ—his incarnation, sufferings, death, resurrection, ascension and return. And these themes for worship were developed without any attention to the Church calendar, so that Christ's birth would be considered at Easter just as much as his death would form suitable meditations for Christmas.

Darby did not approve of Christmas, even in its very respectable Victorian guise. 'The feast now celebrated at Christmas (the very evergreens are pagan)' was 'the expression of one of the worst principles of heathenism', he worried. The festival celebrated the

> reproductive power of nature, celebrated at the return of the sun from the winter solstice. The Hindoos celebrate their Uttarayana at this time—have their twelve days, sending presents, and wishing many happy returns: so the heathen nations, so the Teutonic nations.

As Christianity expanded, and adapted whatever among the pagans it could not control, the Church had taken over the 'worst of heathen festivals, to celebrate the return of the sun from the winter solstice, without a pretence that Christ was born on that day, but as they could not stop the revelry, they put Christ's birth there'—a decision that for Darby represented a 'return to heathenism'. In his mind, the celebration of Christmas reflected the ruin of the Church.

It was this rigorous commitment to scriptural precedent that made Brethren, in Ireland and elsewhere, so suspicious of festive fun. In London, Edmund Gosse, the future literary critic, remembered how his father, the distinguished naturalist Philip Henry Gosse, held views on the 'feasts of the Church' with an 'almost grotesque peculiarity':

> The keeping of Christmas appeared to him by far the most hateful, and nothing less than an act of idolatry. 'The very word is Popish', he used to exclaim, 'Christ's Mass!' pursing up his lips with the gesture of one who tastes asafoetida by accident. Then he would adduce the antiquity of the so-called feast, adapted from horrible heathen rites, and itself a soiled relic of the abominable Yule-Tide. He would denounce the horrors of Christmas until it almost made me blush to look at a holly-berry.

At Christmas 1857, however, young Edmund could no longer resist the festive temptation. His father had given the servants the 'strictest charge that no difference whatever was to be made in our meals on that day; the dinner was to be neither more copious than usual nor less so'. But the servants made a small plum pudding for themselves and shared a slice with Edmund. He was consumed with guilt: 'At length I could bear my spiritual anguish no longer, and bursting into the study I called out: "Oh! Papa, Papa, I have eaten of flesh offered to idols!"'

By the end of the nineteenth century, of course, Christmas had become a powerful symbol of Victorian sentimentality—and it was Prince Albert who had introduced to England the evergreens that Darby had mourned.

Still, the festival occupied little space in the movement's print culture. A tiny number of Brethren attempted to take advantage of the evangelistic opportunities it represented, circulating a sixteen-page pamphlet, *The Word was made flesh and dwelt among us: a tract for Christmas* ([1865]). To put this work into perspective, however, the Christian Brethren Archive at the John Rylands University Library, Manchester, which holds almost 18,000 printed items related to the movement, includes only four items with 'Christmas' in their title—and three of these are critiques.

Of course, this rejection of Christmas was extremely hard to maintain, especially as the movement internationalised. American Brethren leaders were particularly concerned by believers' changing habits. F.C. Jennings remembered that, 'when in 1877 I first came into fellowship with those called Brethren, they were practically a unit in abstaining from all complicity with the observance of Christmas and similar abominations ... tracts were written against it'. As that generation of leaders passed away, however, 'other generations have come upon the scene'; younger Brethren no longer regarded Christmas with appropriate 'abhorrence', as the 'climax of heinous wickedness'. Others developed the theme. In 1900 E.S. Lyman argued that the celebration of Christmas involved 'setting aside God's word which, as an evil principle at work, has wrought confusion and corruption far and wide in the Church's history ... If we do this, where shall we stop?'

It was a pertinent question. After all, the celebration of Christmas struck at the very heart of the movement's understanding of the Church's 'ruin'. Many Brethren did eventually come to celebrate Christmas, but at the cost of their most distinctive ecclesiastical claim.

SOURCES AND FURTHER READING

J.N. Darby, *Collected writings* (ed. William Kelly) (34 vols, London, 1866–83).

Edmund Gosse, *Father and son* (ed. Michael Newton) (1907; repr. Oxford, 2009).

F.C. Jennings, *An open letter* (privately printed).

E.S. Lyman, 'The observance of Christmas', *Help and Food for the Household of Faith* **18** (1900), 341–3.

'FESTIVAL-DAYS … ARE NOT TO BE CONTINUED': IRISH PRESBYTERIANS AND CHRISTMAS DAY

Laurence Kirkpatrick

Christmas cards, like many of our traditional Christmas routines, were popularised in the Victorian era. English civil servant Sir Henry Cole, who had helped establish the Post Office in England in 1840, organised distribution of a pre-printed seasonal greeting card in December 1843, and the idea caught on rapidly and became increasingly popular. In the same year, Charles Dickens published 'A Christmas Carol' and introduced the world to the memorable Ebenezer Scrooge. Carol services became popular some years later, in the 1880s, as epitomised by the annual seasonal performances by the choir of King's College Cambridge. Henry Cole's first Christmas card depicted a family celebrating around a dining table, but not everyone was pleased. He ran afoul of the emerging temperance movement, which criticised the presence of children and alcohol in the same image. Is this an early example of 'Bah! Humbug!'?

I was intrigued in 2021 to note that the Irish Presbyterian moderator, Revd David Bruce, announced a photographic competition to help him select an appropriate image for his Christmas card. His chosen title for his card was 'Hope at Christmas', but what to portray by way of illustration? Over 200 photographs were submitted, and the successful image was by talented Belfast freelance photographer Bill Corr. It featured a bleak winter scene, depicting two foreground figures walking away from camera along a snow-covered path on the Cave Hill above Belfast.

There were no obvious Christmas symbols in the image; the observer is invited to contemplate the purpose or destination of the travellers and make some sort of esoteric connection with the journey that we all make from one year into the next. Announcing the winning photograph, Revd Bruce stated:

> I am looking forward to being able to send out my Christmas cards this year with Bill's evocative photograph on the front. God takes us on a journey through life, walking with us. Sometimes the way is easy, but at other times, it is bleak and harsh. However, His promise of hope at journey's end puts a spring in our step, as His warm hospitality awaits.

The Moderator was, perhaps subliminally, illustrating the historic Irish Presbyterian discomfort with traditional Christmas expressions of celebration.

Irish Presbyterians are no different from any other church in Ireland in struggling to proclaim a sacred message in an increasingly secular society, but Presbyterians have always had something of a problem with Christmas and have fought a dogged and increasingly futile battle against popular societal norms. Irish Presbyterians trace their spiritual lineage through John Knox and the Scottish Mother Church to John Calvin's Geneva. The Scottish Presbyterians were heavily involved in the Westminster Assembly of Divines, which produced a programme for national reform of Christianity throughout Britain during the 1640s. The resultant documents included a *Directory of public worship* and *Appendix* that stated: 'There is no day commanded in scripture to be kept holy under the gospel but the Lord's Day, which is the Christian Sabbath. Festival-days, vulgarly called Holy-days, having no warrant in the word of God, are not to be continued.' Undergirded by this theological apparatus, the English parliament famously banned Christmas between 1647 and the Restoration in 1660.

While the English ultimately rejected the Westminster Assembly recommendations, the Established Scottish Presbyterian Church accepted them. The Scots were much more interested in celebrating Hogmanay, and it is no accident that Christmas Day was not declared a national holiday there until 1958, and Boxing Day was only added as an additional official holiday in 1974.

The Anglican ascendancy in Ireland led to problems for the dissenting Presbyterian community. Irate Anglican bishops occasionally fined Presbyterians for going about their ordinary business on Christmas Day in defiance of episcopal declaration that the day should be observed as a holy day. Irish Presbyterians, like their Catholic neighbours, rejected the State-sanctioned imposition of Anglican beliefs and practice. Congregational records preserve examples of ordinary Presbyterians who ran afoul of the local bishop for mundane activity such as using a wheelbarrow on the holy day. While some Presbyterian ministers did organise a religious service on Christmas Day, this was very much the exception; common Presbyterians were much more likely to indulge in local amusements than in any religious activity at Christmas. The term 'Christ-mass' was a pejorative term to Presbyterians; it was popularly regarded as having a polluting influence on them and so meriting avoidance.

The religious ideal of reserving Christmas Day as an opportunity for sacred activities was always contested. While Martin Luther, perhaps exhibiting his German Saxony stock, fully enjoyed the festivities associated with the entire Christmas season and the Lutherans generally embraced Christmas, John Calvin was a more reluctant celebrant and consistently pointed out in his sermons that Jesus Christ was certainly not born in December. His followers, including the Presbyterians, reacted against the imposition of this holy day by Anglican and Catholic authorities—hence the aforementioned Westminster pronouncements, to which Irish Presbyterians still adhere.

While the Presbyterians have historically downgraded Christmas and Christ's incarnation in favour of emphasising the importance of Easter and Christ's death, they cannot deny that the former was a prerequisite for the latter. Early insistence that Christmas Day is just an ordinary day unless it falls on a Sunday was always going to be impossible to maintain. The natural Irish propensity to celebrate the midwinter solstice proved impossible to insulate themselves against. As with other clerical demands for such practices as total abstinence, Sabbatarianism and attendance at additional midweek and evening services, in which ordinary Presbyterians have voted with their feet, so the Irish Presbyterian Church has had to accommodate the popular demand for Christmas festivities.

There are still occasional protest actions. I recall an assistant minister a few years ago who unilaterally absented himself from the church building while the Christmas tree, 'that pagan symbol', was *in situ* within. In reality, he withdrew his labour for about three weeks at one of the busiest times in the church calendar. Such stands are rare, however. Most Presbyterian congregations today accommodate a tree, stage a carol service and have a special informal service on Christmas morning. To do otherwise would surely be to confirm their irrelevance to an increasingly sceptical population.

Most Presbyterian leaders realise that they must ride the seasonal Advent wave. Ministers increasingly encourage children to bring a new toy to church on Christmas morning. By swimming with the natural elation of the day, they hope to exhibit relevance and secure a meaningful sacred slot among the many seasonal demands to feast and indulge and relax with friends and family. For many people Christmas is the only time in a year when they will attend a church service, possibly a candlelit carol service or the Christmas Day jamboree.

Of course, the traditionalists are not happy. Ministers are easily accused of pandering to secular behaviour patterns and focusing on the gifts that children receive at Christmas as a crude enticement for parents and their children to attend church on Christmas Day. But any attempt to make a church relevant to ordinary people at Christmas is no more than a re-enactment of Constantine's adoption of the pagan festival of *natalis solis invicti*, the cult of the sun, celebrating the rebirth of the sun after the shortest day, 22 December. The battle to lace our midwinter festivities with spiritual reflection is not new; the earliest evidence of Christians celebrating Christmas on 25 December is from AD 336. The biggest difference in contemporary Ireland is that we live in a free society and are not ruled by an absolute emperor who favours Christianity.

The reality for Irish Presbyterians today is that their church, like others, is experiencing an unprecedented shrinkage problem that demands serious attention. Presbyterian membership in Belfast has fallen by 40% in the past ten years, and by 20% across the whole church in the same period. The moderator's Christmas card might just as easily depict a glimpse into a cold and lonely future for traditional churches with little relevance at Christmas or any other season on this island.

Bill Corr, *Hope at Christmas*. With thanks to Bill Corr for permission to use this image.

SOURCES AND FURTHER READING

A.R. Holmes, *The shaping of Ulster Presbyterian belief and practice, 1770–1840* (Oxford, 2006).

A.R. Holmes, *The Irish Presbyterian mind* (Oxford, 2018).

CRIMES OF CHRISTMAS PAST

Pauline Murphy

Some of us tend to view Christmas of times past through rose-tinted glasses. In our minds, we venture back to an era of old-world charm when Christmas had a spiritual rather than a consumerist meaning. We think of a time of 'peace and goodwill to all men'. This article takes a step back from the glitter and into a more gritty reality. A simple browse through newspapers and court reports will produce Christmases brimming with lawbreaking antics—a Yuletide of thieves, drunks, vandals and outlawed snowballers!

The *Cork Examiner* of 23 December 1878 carried a report on excessive festive fun. That year saw snow blanket the city by the River Lee. When it snowed at Christmas it was often said that the falling snow was the feathers of geese being plucked in heaven, but for Mr J.F. Barber and Mr Robert Beresford the falling snow represented a less than heavenly way to pass the time. The two men were engaged in a snowball fight when a constable came upon them in the street, and Mr Barber and Mr Beresford were arrested and charged with disorderly conduct. For simply throwing snowballs, the merry gentlemen were fined ten shillings each.

Throwing snowballs was not the only crime reported at Christmas 1878. The *Cavan Weekly News* of 20 December detailed how sixteen children were arrested by a constable for sliding on the street. The young offenders were hauled before a frosty judge, who fined them a shilling each.

In Myshall, Co. Carlow, a young lad took festive drinking to the extreme when he drank six glasses of whiskey. The *Cork Examiner* of 1845 reported how one under-age drinker, twelve-year-old James Loughlan, ventured into a public house during Christmas week to partake in the season of good swill. Sadly, the young lad dropped dead after downing his sixth glass of whiskey.

Christmas can be a stressful time for many people, and the 27 December issue of the *Cork Examiner* in 1888 carried a story about a furious festive encounter between two firemen. On Christmas Day, the firemen of Cork city were called to a chimney fire at a premises on Patrick Street. The firemen dashed from their station on Sullivan's Quay to the scene of the emergency on the city's main thoroughfare and successfully dealt with the fire. As the firemen were preparing to head back to their station, however, two of them got into a heated argument. Fireman Patrick Ellard told Fireman John Sullivan to carry the hand-pump. Sullivan told Ellard to carry it himself, and Ellard responded by throwing an axe in Sullivan's direction. The axe struck Sullivan's head and fractured his skull. The newspaper reported that 'Sullivan, naturally, became maddened by the pain he felt, and as the blood flowed profusely from the wound he turned on Ellard and struck him several times'. The police were soon on the scene and the fighting firemen were pulled apart. Sullivan spent Christmas night in the hospital, and Ellard spent it in the Bridewell.

Fireman Ellard was not alone in the Bridewell. Christmas 1888 saw record numbers of people detained in Cork city cells owing to the excesses of Christmas libations. Court reports inform us that 30 people were held in the Bridewell on charges of drunkenness, while one poor woman who wanted to indulge in a finer Christmas was charged with stealing wine and cheese.

The Galway petty sessions of Christmas 1860 saw a number of people charged with brewing *poitín* for the festive period. This was a favourite tipple at Christmastime, but stills were often discovered by police. While illegal distilling was happening inland, illegal activity was also occurring at sea. A week before Christmas 1860, the authorities proclaimed victory in the war against snuff when a large quantity of it, destined for the Christmas black market in the west of Ireland, was discovered and seized in Galway Bay aboard a steamer from New York.

Meanwhile, in County Carlow during the Christmas of 1899, Patrick Byrne, known locally in Bagenalstown as 'the Ass Byrne', was arrested for conducting Indian warfare on his wife. 'The Ass Byrne' was gifted a tomahawk for Christmas and was very proud of his new weapon. On Christmas night he invited neighbours around for some festive fun. He showed them his Indian weapon of war and decided that the best way to demonstrate it was to throw it at his wife. It being late in the evening, after a day of indulging in festive port 'the Ass Byrne' was not so steady on his feet and his throwing arm was not so firm. Nevertheless, he flung the tomahawk and it struck his wife on her face. Mrs Byrne lost her right eye and 'the Ass' was sent to jail for three months.

At Killadysert, Co. Clare, in 1876, Christmas Mass was disturbed by a man named Scanlon who sang songs of a patriotic nature. Appearing at the Killadysert petty sessions, Mr Scanlon, who was a former national school teacher, could not explain his outburst in the middle of the religious service, and he was committed to a week's jail time for his sins.

The *Cavan Weekly News* of 1877 reported a case of Christmas fowl-stealing in Cavan town. Charges were brought against Matthew Saddler and William Walsh after two constables on Christmas Eve patrol came upon the men acting suspiciously on Wesley Street. Mr Saddler and Mr Walsh were carrying bundles under their arms, and when they were startled by the constables they ran off. Mr Saddler was the slowest of the two and he was caught, but not before he had disposed of the bundle he was carrying. One of the eagle-eyed constables spotted the bundle thrown in a doorway. He picked it up, and on opening it he found a goose and ducks. Mr Walsh did not enjoy his liberty for long; constables found him hiding under a cart. His bundle also contained fowl. The men had stolen the birds from a neighbour, who would have been denied Christmas dinner if the constables had not caught the foul thieves.

During Christmas week 1891 a marching band caused annoyance on the streets of Armagh city. Sixteen members of the O'Brien Fife and Drum Band were charged with causing an obstruction from Irish Street to the Shambles. The band ignored calls from constables to cease playing. They continued to belt out festive tunes, and for this each band member was fined ten shillings.

Also in Armagh, just a few days after the band incident, constables stopped Samuel Warren, who was walking along the street in a rather odd fashion wearing an oversized coat. The constables asked Mr Warren what he was carrying inside his coat, to which Mr Warren replied 'Just a Christmas duck!' Not believing him, the constables ordered Mr Warren to open his coat, and when he did they discovered that he was concealing a hare. When questioned, Mr Warren changed his story and declared that the hare was simply a Christmas present, but he was nonetheless charged under the Prevention of Poaching Act.

On St Stephen's Night 1891 in Armagh, Peter McKee was charged with being drunk and disorderly. He was standing on top of a cart shouting 'Parnell forever!' His devotion to the 'uncrowned king of Ireland' cost Mr McKee a 40-shilling fine.

SOURCES

This article has drawn its material from contemporary newspaper accounts.

CHRISTMAS AND THE DOMESTICATION OF THE ROYAL IRISH CONSTABULARY

Brian Griffin

If one were looking for a location in which to hold a Christmas celebration in the nineteenth century, the constabulary's Phoenix Park depot would probably not have sprung immediately to mind. Established in 1842 as a headquarters for training the recruits of the Irish Constabulary (renamed the Royal Irish Constabulary (RIC) in 1867), the depot was run along the lines of an infantry regiment base. Recruits lived in austere barrack-like dormitories that overlooked a large parade-ground, where the men spent a considerable amount of their four to six months of training in practising drill. Discipline was strict, with an emphasis on order and cleanliness. Every room in the depot was ritually disinfected once a week, and bed sheets were changed twice weekly. The rooms were inspected each morning and, as one recruit remarked, 'woe betide the man who had left even a handkerchief out of place'. According to one RIC officer, the strict regime was aimed at 'turning country louts into smart infantry men in a short time'.

Sir Andrew Reed, appointed inspector-general in 1885, was the first officer to command the RIC without having previously served in the military. He wanted to mould the force along civil rather than martial lines—in essence, to 'domesticate' the force. While high standards of discipline continued to be maintained during Reed's tenure, some of the more onerous elements of the RIC regulations were softened: simple admonitions replaced many punitive fines, and there was a marked reduction in the force's dismissal rate. Reed encouraged the ordinary policeman to view his barracks not merely as a police station but also as his home. Pets were allowed in barracks for the first time in 1891. Libraries were established in many barracks. The men were encouraged to participate in sports as much as possible. A wide variety of RIC sports clubs were established in the 1890s, and policemen were also often prominent members of local civilian sports clubs.

Promoting Christmas celebrations played an important role in Reed's domestication of the RIC. Each year, the inspector-general and his wife, Lady Elizabeth Mary Reed (née Lyster), organised a party at the Phoenix Park depot for the hundreds of wives and children of the Reserve force who resided there. The rooms where the entertainment took place were decorated lavishly with holly, ivy, mistletoe and other evergreens, as well as festoons of coloured paper, paper chains and Japanese lanterns, transforming the otherwise bleak rooms into veritable 'fairylands'. Cakes and other treats were provided. Policemen sang comic songs, and the depot string band performed as well. The children were also treated to a comic entertainment. In 1889 and 1890, for example, a 'Professor Como' entertained the children with 'some really clever feats in the way of thought-transmission, which were much applauded', while an amusing 'waxwork exhibition' formed part of the entertainment in 1891. This consisted of various officers, lower-ranking policemen and members of their families representing such characters as Jack the Giant-Killer, Sleeping Beauty, the Dirty Boy and the Little Old Woman Who Lived in a Shoe, amongst others. In 1896 a conjuror was the star performer, while in 1897 the children were entertained by a series of magic-lantern slides. As far as the children were concerned, the main attraction was probably the immense Christmas tree which the Reeds provided each year. On this hung hundreds of presents, 'prettily-dressed dolls, toy guns, helmets, swords, and other innumerable toys', all of which the Reeds purchased.

The Christmas celebrations also alleviated the monotony of depot life for the hundreds of recruits and the unmarried men of the Reserve force who were permanently stationed at the Phoenix Park. Their bleak quarters and mess-rooms were decorated in a similar manner to the rooms in which the children's entertainment took place, and they also erected mottoes that were made out of plants or written on banners, conveying such messages as 'God Save Our Gracious Queen', 'Long Life to the Inspector-General' or 'Ceade Mille Failthe'. A special dinner was laid on for them; they amused themselves with singsongs, concerts or games, and they were given a few extra days as holidays by the depot commandant. In the first decade of the twentieth century, the commandant also permitted large numbers of Reserve men to attend Leopardstown races over the festive season. The homesick 'youngsters', as the recruits are often described in contemporary publications, were treated with special kindness by their superiors, as their Christmas at the depot was usually the first that they had spent away from their parental home. Reed and his successor as inspector-general in 1900, Sir Neville Chamberlain, were also solicitous of the welfare of RIC patients in Steevens's Hospital, whom they visited over the Christmas period. The patients were given special dinners and in some years were treated to phonograph or gramophone concerts.

Christmas celebrations also brightened the lives of the men who were stationed in the hundreds of RIC barracks that were dotted throughout Ireland. The *Meath Chronicle* reported that the Navan constabulary spent Christmas 'in right merry style' in 1897, when 'Good cheer abounded, and songs and toasts went round' as they celebrated the holiday. Similar scenes took place in police barracks throughout Reed's and Chamberlain's stewardship of the RIC. Christmas was the only time of the year when barracks' whitewashed day-room walls, which were usually utterly devoid of ornamentation, were decorated. The men in some barracks, such as Mohill and Musgrave Street in Belfast, regularly hosted dances over the Christmas period. The Musgrave Street dance was a particularly impressive affair, as its day-room—Ireland's biggest—accommodated around 50 dancing couples. Jeremiah Mee records that in Kesh, Co. Sligo, in 1911 and 1912 ordinary patrol duty was suspended during Christmas week: the station diary and patrol books were completed to give the impression that the men were diligently performing their duties, but their main focus was on their dances and card-playing parties. Christmas in hundreds of barracks was further enlivened by the presence of the children who resided in them with their parents. Some of these children wrote accounts of their Christmases for the *Weekly Irish Times*'s children's column, 'Granny's Corner'. These show that games such as ludo, tiddly-winks and La Brosse were popular, and that the children put on entertainments including recitations, singing, step-dancing and plays, such as 'Babes in the Wood', which May Johnstone and her siblings and friends performed in Clones barracks around 1905.

Men who lived in barracks where there were no children probably indulged in alcohol a bit more freely than those who shared their barracks with policemen's families. The unwritten rule that officers' inspections would not be conducted over the Christmas period facilitated this. Jeremiah Mee records how on one Christmas Eve, just as he and his comrades were settling down to enjoy their Christmas drinks—four cases of stout and several bottles of whiskey from publican friends—their peace was disturbed by an old man named Horan, who was returning home drunk from a local pub and repeatedly shouted for the police to come out of their barracks, presumably to fight him. Rather than arresting him, two constables escorted Horan home and watched over him for around two hours until he fell asleep. One of them left a bottle of whiskey in a chair beside Horan's bed, with a note 'From the R.I.C. with the compliments of the season. Call at the barracks first thing in the morning.' On Christmas morning, instead of a summons for being drunk and disorderly, Hogan was given another glass of whiskey and 'a good breakfast of turkey and ham', with an invitation to return later for his Christmas dinner, which he did. This heart-warming vignette illustrates Christmas's importance in the domestication of the Royal Irish Constabulary.

SOURCES AND FURTHER READING

G. Garrow Green, *In the Royal Irish Constabulary* (London and Dublin, 1905).

J. Anthony Gaughan (ed.), *The memoirs of Jeremiah Mee, RIC* (Dublin, 1975).

W.J. Lowe and Elizabeth Malcolm, 'The domestication of the Royal Irish Constabulary, 1836–1922', *Irish Economic and Social History* **19** (1992), 27–48.

A policeman and three children on the RIC depot parade-ground. Lawrence Photograph Collection, L_ROY_05560. Image courtesy of the National Library of Ireland.

CHRISTMAS AND THE BIG HOUSE

Ian d'Alton

The Big House. For many, as alien as a Klingon. For some, an identity. For most, difficult to ignore. Mysterious as a stranger, romantic, Gothic. And also a set, a backdrop, a screen onto which the everyday tiny dramas of the Irish gentry's and aristocracy's lives could be projected—a 'representative if miniature theatre', as Anglo-Irish novelist Elizabeth Bowen wrote of her house in County Cork, Bowen's Court. Containing the 'vestigia of generations', the Big House is 'a receptacle of illusion … a richly evocative symbol of its occupants' encapsulation in the past'. Pervading damp, dry rot and a faint aroma of boiled cabbage build atmosphere—Danielstown in Bowen's 1920 novel *The last September* has a 'pellucid silence … distilled from a hundred and fifty years of conversation'. Here in introverted miniature worlds the landed classes weave an intricate social filigree, indulging in a variant of Freud's narcissism of small differences. Christmas—the festival of champagne and chatter and 'small differences'—would seem to suit the Big House.

Whether the House suits Christmas is another matter. The Big House is a touchy character, sure of its dominance over the family that occupies it. At Christmas, though, 'the house does defer, as it does to no individual son or daughter'. It can be a much darker thing, too—a lowering behemoth, Virginia Woolf's great stone box, out of scale and sympathy with the landscape's 'unwilling bosom' within which it is set. Here be ghosts, and ghosts of ghosts. 'It is at Christmas that the place looks oldest,' writes Bowen: 'its bony under-structure stands out. The accumulated character of the house seems as inevitable as the lie of the land. All who have ever lived here are to be felt.' Glittering windows in summer, but book-darkened corners and shadowlands in winter. And so we approach the Big House in this longest of seasons and shortest of days, travelling along 'white high-hedged damply glimmering roads' where the gentry's and aristocracy's grand and not-so-grand tragedies fuse into a Christmas pudding of the lively and the decayed.

The Irish aristocracy and gentry always lived lavishly, often well beyond their (and their tenants') means. Hospitality was their middle name. The life of the country house revolved around these visitors—why they were there, what they did, how they fitted in. Or not, as the case may be. Homan Potterton's father wasn't fond of guests; 'no one was ever asked to stay the night' at Rathcormick, Co. Meath. This introvert appears to have been exceptional, however. What was more likely was an excess of guests rather than a deficiency. Even in the revolutionary and evolutionary period of the early 1920s, 45 guests on average stayed each year with the Bruens at Oakpark, Carlow. Between 1860 and 1900 the Lords Portarlington entertained an impressive total of 1,327 guests at Emo Court, Queen's County. Such patterns were a function of class rather than anything else—the well-off Catholic Grehans of Clonmeen had 266 overnight visitors between 1887 and 1893.

The House was a swan—calm on the surface, furious activity below, in this hub of commercial, social and familial busyness. Christmas was no different. The hospitality of the season was just another in the endless loop of shooting and tennis parties, balls and coming-of-age celebrations that characterised the gentry's social year, fending off the inherent ennui of a perpetual Protestant afternoon tea. Elizabeth Bowen's grandfather had seating for 24 in his capacious dining room, 'few of which, at Christmas, my grandfather expected to see unoccupied. Subsidiary relatives were bidden; respectful neighbours also could claim a place.' If in December 1907 a gossip sheet recorded a 'socially dull time in Dublin', with no festivities in the viceregal or chief secretary's lodges, it wrote of a homely return of the great and good—the Ernes to Crom Castle, the Waterfords to Curraghmore, the Dunsanys back in Meath, Lord Westmeath at Pallas, and the Inchiquins at Dromoland with a shooting party. The Fingalls, though, had to slum Christmas in Killeen Glebe, the castle having been let out to an American for the hunting season. Doubtless most were conventional Protestant Christmases; few would have embraced the *Irish Homestead*'s 'A Celtic Christmas' as enthusiastically as Coole's Lady Gregory.

Elizabeth Bowen wrote that the Big House was more 'an effect rather than a reality'. That reading, too, mirrors Christmas, itself an act of imagination, from Santa Claus to the Christmas story. It is a time of fantasy and the fantastical. At Oatlands, Surrey, in the 1820s the duchess of York converted the great dining room into an imitation of a German fair, with booths and an early version of a Christmas tree with oranges, gingerbread and cakes. It was then, as now, a 'child-fest' if children were to be had—'On Christmas Eve, I thought, as a child, even the furniture looks different!' At Bantry House, maid Nora O'Connor was an observer of an Edwardian festival with 'a Christmas ball' where the orchestra came from Cork city. Ice cream—which also came all the way from the city—was served to the guests. The servants had a Christmas ball too, also held in the grand ballroom. They invited all their friends, a supper was served, and Nora got a new dress for the occasion. Perhaps only the grimy and grim Christmas poor were real: 'Beggars, whose status with us is almost sacred, come one by one up the steps to stand at the door. Many but not all of them are women: stately, draped in their rusty black shawls they bless the house before and after receiving alms.'

Our Christmases are elongated, commercialised, wearisome marathons. Christmas in the Big House was much more focused on the day itself, captured so evocatively in the twelve-year-old Sarah Bowen's diary entries for Christmas Eve, Christmas Day and St Stephen's Day 1876:

December 24ᵗʰ. Sunday.

We drove to Church, as the ground was covered with snow. When we were returning we were obliged to get out of the car, as the avenue was too slippery for the horse.

Christmas Day.

A bright frosty day, and the ground covered with snow. We wished everybody a merry Christmas, then Mama called us all up to the Lobby where we received many pretty presents from our Aunts … We did our usual Christmas pieces for Papa and Mama, also a drawing of Black Rock Castle … We all went to Church, it was very prettily decorated. The text was Gal. iii.16, 'God was manifested in the flesh.' We had late dinner with Papa and Mama and plum pudding. After dinner we had great fun playing consequences and with some crackers Aunt Mary sent us. Nurse had a bad night and did not enjoy her Christmas much.

December 26ᵗʰ.

A very wet day. We had music and scripture lessons only. We painted texts and played in the long room.

Christmas, though, can be dangerous. Christmas can be *murder*. It is one of the miracles of the season that, fired by drink, boredom and over-indulgence, there aren't more of them. John Banville's novel *Snow*, set in 1957, has, unusually, a Protestant Garda inspector investigating the gruesome mutilation and killing of a Catholic priest in a decaying Big House in Wexford; his superiors think that he would be suitable for the job. It's a clever take on a genre nearly as old as Christmas itself. The Big House is snowed in as Christmas approaches; no one can escape. Here is the House as ocean liner, desert island, Orient Express, the theatre for this play of the damned. This is the Big House as Anti-Christmas—a startling contrast to the near-sentimental images of Elizabeth Bowen or the fond humour of Somerville and Ross.

Murder aside, at the last maybe Big House Christmases weren't that much different to any other Christmases anywhere. Arriving at the sanctuary of Bowen's Court from London, Bowen wrote: 'balm—the sense of fret, of crisis which one has come to associate with one's own identity slips away. In that moment, one becomes simply another wanderer back for Christmas.' Big House, little house—the universality of the emotional return to home is independent of everything except the humanity of those who experience it.

SOURCES AND FURTHER READING

J. Banville, *Snow* (London, 2020).

M. Bence-Jones, *Twilight of the Ascendancy* (London, 1987).

E. Bowen, *Bowen's Court and seven winters* (London, 1984).

A. Hepburn (ed.), *People, places, things—essays by Elizabeth Bowen* (Edinburgh, 2008).

NOLLAIG NA MBAN ('WOMEN'S CHRISTMAS') AND JOYCE'S 'THE DEAD'

Mary M. Burke

The Western Christian liturgical calendar celebrates 6 January as the Feast of the Epiphany, a commemoration of the visit of the Magi to the Christ Child. In Ireland, however, an alternate folk calendar observed that date as 'Women's Christmas' (*Nollaig na mBan*). Traditionally, it was the day on which housewives took a break from the Christmas season's chores and ate their preferred foods together in what was a woman-only celebration. Furthermore, it was the custom in certain regions for men to take over 'women's work' on the day. In a 1998 *Irish Times* article on *Nollaig na mBan* published on the day itself, Rosita Boland mused that the tradition was not strictly formal but was one that passed from mother to daughter: 'It's a custom which seems to have been passed on orally and informally, drifting down like feathers from one generation to the next. Few women spoken to for this article had read anything about Nollaig na mBan, but all had heard about it from other women or female family members—grandmothers, mothers, aunts.'

James Joyce's 'The Dead', the culminating story of *Dubliners* (1914), is set in the Irish capital on 6 January 1904. It centres on Gabriel Conroy, who attends a formal and large dinner-dance in the all-female household of his two Morkan aunts, Julia and Kate, their niece, Mary Jane, and their maid, Lily. Gabriel's lack of deep appreciation for his aunts' labour in preparing the meal on what would have been their day of rest in a more folkloric Ireland comes into view once the date's traditional significance for women is remembered. Joyce de-emphasises the Christian significance of 6 January, auditing instead, with his finely detailed attention to the busyness of the household's women, the lost rural and oral cultural associations of that date. James Joyce's father, John Stanislaus Joyce, was born in July 1849 in Cork, a location in which Women's Christmas has traditionally been strongly celebrated, and the last region in which it still thrived before its popularity exploded throughout Ireland in recent years. As the observant son of a Cork father, Joyce was likely aware of the folkloric and perhaps even familial 6 January traditions concerning women and their role as food-preparers.

The fact that *Nollaig na mBan* has often been translated as 'Little Christmas' rather than its literal meaning of 'Women's Christmas' suggests that its association with female revelries was diluted with the transition from oral, Irish-language culture: speaking to Boland, Alan Titley suggested that the custom faded with the widespread use of Irish. Stiofán Ó Cadhla similarly suggests that the contemporary 'girls' night out' celebrated under the English-language title of 'Women's Christmas' may be more accurately termed a *revival* rather than a *survival* of *Nollaig na mBan*, which was, by contrast, a home-based event. (The custom is also returning in cosmopolitan Irish America: the Irish American Partnership has hosted a *Nollaig na mBan* women's leadership breakfast fund-raiser in Boston over the past few years.) In an increasingly Anglophone post-Famine Ireland, the Catholic Church generally refrained from engaging with worshippers in the native tongue. The work of Cork folklorist Gearóid Ó Crualaoich suggests that Gaelic culture retained traces of a 'female' and even pre-Christian calendar beneath the 'male' liturgical year. As such, the association of the Epiphany with a vaguely 'pagan' women's celebration was, arguably, more liable to re-emerge in Irish-language literature such as Seán Ó Ríordáin's 1952 poem 'Oíche Nollaig na mBan', discussed by Ríona Ní Churtáin elsewhere in this volume.

Women's Christmas was associated with specific foods. Kevin Danaher notes that 'Christmas Day was marked by beef, and whiskey, men's fare, while on Little Christmas Day the dainties preferred by women—cake, tea, wine, were more in evidence'. This gendering of the season's food into 'hearty' (male) and 'delicate' (female) is reflected in a variant on a saying in Irish collected from a rather chauvinistic Kerryman in 1936 for the National Folklore Collection to the effect that '*Nollaig na bhfear*' ('Men's Christmas' or 25 December) 'is a fine big Christmas', but Women's Christmas 'is no good' (*Nollaig na bhfear—an Nollaig mhuar mhath / Nollaig na mban—a Nollaig [gan] mheath*).

In contrast to the women's revelries of the traditional 6 January, the female party guests in 'The Dead' are noticeably abstemious, and the heavy fare on offer is, according to the folkloric classification just described, more to male than to female taste. While the male party-goers refill their own drinks repeatedly, Joyce pointedly has the young women in attendance refuse punch and large helpings. Moreover, the guests perform conventional waltzes and quadrilles, a forgetting of the subversive Irish dance named for Women's Christmas in which females took the lead: Connecticut Irish-dance teacher Kathy Mulkerin Carew has told me that in the 'Women's Christmas Dance' performed on 6 January female participants enact the day's house visits and topsy-turvy tone by taking the active 'male' role of switching from partner to partner. (Kathy's Galway-born mother, Kathleen Mulkerin, learned the dance from a Connecticut-based Kerry teacher in the 1930s.) Altogether, Joyce's details reveal that the female party-goers of 'The Dead' are prim, middle-class Edwardians, entirely unaware of the ancestral tradition that would have allowed them to let loose on 6 January.

A Cork housewife interviewed in 1938 for the National Folklore Collection listed the huge preparation that Christmas required of women, concluding, 'An' the men, if you killed 'em, they couldn't spare time to sweep the chimney for us [women]'. When read with an eye for the work that the season entailed for women, Danaher's description of the rural Irish Christmas suggests that it carried a heavy burden for the housewife and her daughters:

[Preparations involved] [...] sweeping, washing and cleaning. A major laundering operation included all washable garments and household linen. Tables and chairs were scrubbed with sand, while pots, pans, and delf [*sic*] were scoured [...]. Christmas Eve was spent mainly on the last preparations for the festival, in the final sweeping and cleaning and, especially, in preparing the festive food for the next day's dinner [...]. On returning from church [on Christmas Day] the womenfolk busied themselves with cooking the Christmas dinner while the men and boys remained out of doors, usually taking part in some sport or pastime. [...] The Christmas dinner was the biggest and most elaborate meal of the year and the housewife took pride in setting a generous table before appetites sharpened by hurling or hunting.

In the light of the efforts required during the season, the necessity of its last day being reserved for women's own fun is thrown into relief. The opening of 'The Dead' stresses that Lily, the Morkans' maid, was 'run off her feet', underlining how distanced the Dublin party is from the folkloric 6 January. Kate and Julia Morkan proffer an astounding array of foods to their many guests; as an example of the degree of preparation involved, one might consider that spiced beef, just *one* of the party's numerous dishes, takes up to nineteen days to make, and requires attention almost every day of that period.

As goose-carver and speech-maker during the evening's dinner, Gabriel volubly enacts the ceremonial role of patriarchal dispenser of the largesse prepared by women, the centre of attention in contrast to the women's silent doling out of pudding during the dessert course. It is ironic that Gabriel refers in his speech to a party made possible by the work of women as a reprieve from 'the bustle and rush of our everyday routine', since the unobserved *Nollaig na mBan* was precisely such a celebration. Far from being restful, this is the busiest day of the Christmas season for the Morkan household. Altogether, 'The Dead' underlines Gabriel's seeming obliviousness to the discounted traditions of women. Such were acknowledged by feminist Mary Robinson, Ireland's first woman president, who made the radical gesture of attending Mass with women prisoners on 6 January 1991, shortly after her inauguration. That event may well have been a beginning point in *Nollaig na mBan*'s subsequent comeback in Irish and Irish-American culture.

SOURCES AND FURTHER READING

Mary Burke, 'Forgotten remembrances', *James Joyce Quarterly* **54** (3–4) (2017), 241–74.

Kevin Danaher, *The year in Ireland* (Dublin, 1972).

Stiofán Ó Cadhla, 'Women's Christmas', *Encyclopedia of Ireland* (New Haven, 2003), 1150.

MOLLY BLOOM'S CHRISTMAS CARD: WHERE JOYCEAN FICTION MEETS A REAL-LIFE FAMILY

Patrick Comerford

The centenary of the 1922 publication of *Ulysses* was celebrated in Dublin with a style and gusto in 2022 that James Joyce undoubtedly would have found endearing and entertaining. One of the many places that attracted attention is 52 Upper Clanbrassil Street, where a plaque claims that the house is the birthplace of Leopold Bloom.

In Episode 17 ('Ithaca') of *Ulysses*, Molly Bloom is searching through the contents of Leopold's locked drawers when she finds the document that places the Bloom family at 52 Clanbrassil Street at the time of her husband's birth. She also finds 'a Yuletide card, bearing on it a pictorial representation of a parasitic plant, the legend *Mizpah*, the date Xmas 1892, the name of the senders: from Mr + Mrs M. Comerford, the versicle: *May this Yuletide bring to thee, Joy and peace and welcome glee.*'

But who were the Comerfords who sent a Christmas card to Molly Bloom? With a hint of self-interest, I have wondered why Joyce chose a couple named Comerford to send that card in 1892.

The card reveals a recognition by the Comerfords of Bloom's Jewish background, though by 1892 he had been baptised on three occasions.

Christmas is abbreviated to 'Xmas' and the name of the season is not spelt out. There is a reference to 'Yuletide'; instead of a Nativity scene there is a depiction of mistletoe, and the word *Mizpah* was a common alternative greeting for Jews sending cards in the late Victorian period.

In her soliloquy, Molly Bloom has good reason to remember Christmas 1892–3: it was a harsh winter, and the Grand Canal, separating Clanbrassil Street from Harold's Cross, had frozen over in February 1893. Molly and Leopold were invited to a party at the Comerfords' that winter, and she recalls how she had too many oranges and too much orange and lemonade at a party in the Comerford home in Clanbrassil Street. She was caught short on the way home that night and had to use the men's toilets in a pub, with great personal discomfort.

Any pub between Upper Clanbrassil Street and Lombard Street, where the Blooms then lived, would have been at Leonard's Corner, the junction of Clanbrassil Street and the South Circular Road, the main crossroads in the area that became known as 'Little Jerusalem'. She recalls: 'O and the stink of those rotten places the night coming home with Poldy after the Comerfords party oranges and lemonade to make you feel nice and watery I went into 1 of them it was so biting cold I couldn't keep it when was that 93 the canal was frozen' ('Penelope').

Why did James Joyce choose the name Comerford for the Blooms' friends in *Ulysses*? Apart from coming across my grandfather's brother, James Comerford, at 62 Lower Clanbrassil Street in *Thom's Directory*, was there another reason why the family name caught his imagination?

John Henry Raleigh suggests in *The chronicle of Leopold and Molly Bloom: Ulysses as narrative* that 'This Anglo, somewhat toffish name, is meant to suggest, I believe, that the Blooms had some friends rather higher on the social scale than previous or subsequent to their Lombard Street West days'. The Comerford name may also have attracted Joyce's attention because he claimed that some family portraits had been painted by the Kilkenny-born miniaturist John Comerford (1771–1832).

What had the Comerfords of Clanbrassil Street to celebrate in early 1893, just after Christmas? In 1893 my great-grandfather James

Comerford (1817–1902), a stucco plasterer, his sons James (1853–1915), Stephen Edward (1867–1921) and Robert (1868–1902), and his nephews James Comerford (1839–1903) and Robert Comerford (1855–1925) were founding members of the Regular Stucco Plasterers' Trade Union of the City of Dublin. His nephew James Comerford later lived at 50 Upper Clanbrassil Street, and he and his wife had much to celebrate in 1893 with the birth of their youngest child, Robert Thomas Comerford (1893–1958), at 62 Lower Clanbrassil Street. Perhaps, however, this was a little too late for Molly's post-Christmas party, as Bob was born on 27 April 1893.

Joyce's choice of 52 Clanbrassil Street as the birthplace of Leopold Bloom has led to the presumption that he was referring to Upper Clanbrassil Street rather than Lower Clanbrassil Street, which is actually at the heart of Little Jerusalem. Two doors away from No. 52 Upper Clanbrassil Street, a Comerford family was living at No. 50 in 1904, the year in which Joyce sets Bloomsday. My grandfather's cousin, James Comerford, lived at this No. 50, and this may have prompted placing the plaque at No. 52, claiming this as Bloom's birthplace.

Although members of the Comerford family were living at No. 50 Upper Clanbrassil Street on the first Bloomsday on Thursday 16 June 1904, my grandfather's cousin, James Comerford, had died the previous year, 1903, and his widow Ellen was living in the house in 1904.

But what if Leopold Bloom was born not at No. 52 *Upper* Clanbrassil Street but at No. 52 *Lower* Clanbrassil Street and the plaque was erected on the wrong house? It is more credible to suggest that at Christmas 1892 Joyce is asking us to imagine that the Comerford and Bloom families were actually living in Lower Clanbrassil Street, which was then at the heart of the Jewish community in Dublin.

If Joyce actually intended to place Leopold Bloom's birth at No. 52 Lower Clanbrassil Street, then who are the Comerfords referred to in *Ulysses*? In the short space of a half-century or so, immediate members of this one branch of the Comerford family had addresses in at least fifteen houses in Lower and Upper Clanbrassil Street, and many more lived in the warren of streets off Clanbrassil Street, in Little Jerusalem, in Portobello and around Charlemont Street.

If I add their in-laws, their cousins and their nieces and nephews, it must have been impossible then to walk along Clanbrassil Street without meeting and greeting a member of the Comerford family. Family lore recalls that it seemed that every second person on Lower Clanbrassil Street then was either a Jew or a Comerford.

Joyce used the 1904 edition of *Thom's Directory* to locate key Dublin characters and figures in *Ulysses*. In the 1901 census, No. 62 Lower Clanbrassil Street was shared by three families: my grandfather's eldest brother James Comerford, his wife Lena and their five children; their cousin James Comerford and his wife Ellen; and the Keegan family.

Previously, this house had been the home of my grandfather's cousin Thomas Comerford, a plasterer, and his wife Mary Anne (Ludlow), who lived there in 1862–72, along with his sister Elizabeth and her husband Denis Cuddy. In 1874 it was the home of another family member, Thomas Comerford and his wife Mary Jane (Cusack). By the time of the 1904 edition of *Thom's Directory*, however, 62 Lower Clanbrassil Street was no longer divided into flats. Instead, the house stands out from all the tenements on the street as being occupied by only one family, being the home of my grandfather's brother James Comerford and his family.

By 1911 this James Comerford and his family were sharing 82 Lower Clanbrassil Street with his sister and brother-in-law, Mary and Francis Coleman, and their family, and with Isaac Joffe, a 58-year-old Jewish shopkeeper from Russia and his Russian-born Jewish wife, Hannah.

Therefore, if the Blooms got a Christmas card from the Comerfords in 1892, and Molly was at a party with the Comerford family two months later, it must have been Joyce's intention to refer to the Comerfords at No. 62 Lower Clanbrassil Street and not at No. 50 Upper Clanbrassil Street. Today, the site of 62 Lower Clanbrassil Street is the premises of Capital Glass.

As for Leopold Bloom's birthplace, it was more convenient to erect that plaque in Upper Clanbrassil Street because No. 52 Lower

Clanbrassil Street no longer exists: it has long since been demolished in road-widening schemes.

SOURCES AND FURTHER READING

James Joyce, *Ulysses* (various editions).
John Henry Raleigh, *The chronicle of Leopold and Molly Bloom: Ulysses as narrative* (Berkeley, 1977).

No. 52 Upper Clanbrassil Street, Dublin. Was this the birthplace of Leopold Bloom?
Photo credit: Patrick Comerford.

AN IRISH CHRISTMAS
IN JAIL

Melissa Melanephy

During the Irish revolutionary years in the early twentieth century, many Irish Volunteers went on the run, hiding out in safe houses and sheds, away from the comfort and warmth of their homes and families. Life on the run was particularly keenly felt over the Christmas season. Many more Volunteers were imprisoned, first in internment camps in Wales and then in jails around the country, during the War of Independence. The imprisonment was often eased by the kindness of strangers or of the religious orders who donated food parcels over Christmas. In some cases, however, relief could also come by way of their perceived enemies, such as the British soldier who winked at Garry Holohan, a senior officer of the Fianna Éireann, who was arrested on Christmas Day. This soldier was from Belfast, and he later agreed to deliver a letter to the Holohan family letting them know of Garry's whereabouts. There was also the newly appointed RIC District Inspector Gallagher in Dundalk, who delayed ordering a raid on a house where a known IRA man was hiding out. By chance, a second man, James MacGuill, who had just arrived seeking refuge over Christmas, was caught by the Black and Tans. A surprised DI Gallagher arrived on the scene and escorted a lame MacGuill to the barracks, protecting him in his room overnight lest the men attack him.

Accounts from the Military Archives detail prison life at Christmas for some of the men and women involved in the revolution. After the Easter Rising in April 1916, members of the Irish Volunteers and Irish Citizen Army were interned in camps such as that at Frongoch in Wales. The camp was emptied in December 1916, with the men released just in time to arrive back in Ireland for Christmas. After Bloody Sunday 1920, Ballykinlar internment camp was established in County Down. It was the first such camp established by the British authorities in Ireland to suppress the War of Independence. Camp conditions were described as harsh, with five men dying owing to maltreatment, while three internees were shot dead.

When the camp opened in December 1920, the internees were transported on an open-deck boat into Belfast Lough. Thomas J. Meldon, a brigade musketry officer, was the prison quartermaster, and he recalled organising the cooking of Christmas dinner in the camp—not an easy request under the circumstances. Turkeys and hams were gifted to the camp by Cumann na mBan.

Meldon met with the British quartermaster and requested 'stuffing ingredients for the turkeys, twelve loaves, the rations for twenty-four men, onions, sage, thyme'. Smiling, the British quartermaster asked Meldon whether he knew where he was. A few days later, however, a sack with the ingredients was delivered. Meldon thanked the officer and wished him a happy Christmas. He found a poulterer to dress the turkeys. The next night, Christmas Eve, he found a few men to cook the turkeys and permission was granted by the authorities for the men to be locked into the cookhouse for the night. Meldon himself became locked out of his hut and the cookhouse by accident and spent Christmas Eve hiding between huts lest he would be caught as a potential escapee.

Meldon recounts that the Christmas dinner was a great success. A group of Longford men presented him with a couple of cigars in thanks. He retired to his hut that evening, lay on his mattress and lit a cigar, and 'allowed my mind to drift to the sound of surf on the shingled beach of Killiney, forgetting past troubles and future difficulties'.

In 1919 Bridget O'Mullane, an official organiser in Cumann na mBan, delivered a speech in Fermanagh encouraging a boycott of the members of the RIC. Two months later, when O'Mullane went to visit the governor of Sligo Gaol to advocate for her father to be given political prisoner status, she was arrested outside the jail. She was convicted and sentenced to two months' hard labour for giving the seditious speech.

O'Mullane served her sentence in Sligo Gaol, in solitary confinement over the Christmas period. She found herself entirely alone, with no other prisoners for company; not even the prison wardress stayed the night in the wing formerly used for those condemned to the gallows. O'Mullane was terrified of being alone in prison but did not want to make her fears known in case she was accused of cowardice. She slept on a plank for a bed and had nightmares, with every creak in the old prison waking her. She looked forward to Christmas Day in the hope that she would receive some extra food. At the dinner hour of 12.15pm, feeling faint with hunger, she heard the rattle of the cans brought to the criminal wing, but no food was delivered. Eventually, in the late afternoon, a Christmas dinner arrived from the Ursuline nuns, who also sent dinners for her father and the other political prisoners. 'That dinner stands out in my memory,' she later recalled, 'and my gratitude to the kind nuns was unbounded.'

By 1921 conditions appear to have improved for the male prisoners over the festive period in Sligo Gaol. Seán Mac Eoin, OC Longford Brigade IRA, stated that 'it was one of the most enjoyable Christmas Days I ever spent', with all the doors kept open during the Christmas season. Mac Eoin acknowledged, in particular, the support of Mother Cecilia from the Ursuline convent during his prison stay. He also tells of a soldier named Clements, whose English origins were shrouded in mystery. Corporal Clements—or Jordy, as he was known—was based in Longford Barracks, and he had agreed to steal arms and pass them on to the IRA in exchange for money. General Mac Eoin recounted how he lost track of Jordy until Christmas 1923, when it was reported that two hams and two turkeys had been stolen from the officers' mess in Custume Barracks, Athlone. A search was made, and Jordy was captured in possession of all four items. By then he had managed to reinvent himself in the Irish Free State Army as Sergeant-Major 'Cunningham' of the Defence Forces. Mac Eoin observed that he was 'as handy lifting a bird or a ham as he was lifting a gun or ammunition'.

Christmas in jail was not a very consoling thought for Captain Seán O'Neill, IRA flying column, Galway, in 1919. O'Neill lamented spending 'a damp depressing Christmas Eve' working as an assistant to Hartney, the trades' warder. For O'Neill, that Christmas was made up of bricks and mortar rather than his customary at-home celebration of 'mead and honey and sweet cake and a glass of wine'. His one consoling thought was that Hartney had promised to bring him a packet of Woodbines so that he might enjoy a smoke on Christmas Eve, but the handyman's promise proved 'as empty as O'Neill's cell was of champagne'. At the end of the shift, O'Neill was left crestfallen when Hartney did not produce the coveted cigarettes. This broken promise on Christmas Eve still stung O'Neill as keenly over 30 years later as it did on Christmas Eve 1919.

Later an ex-British soldier-cum-warder helped to lift O'Neill's spirits when he opened his cell door and pulled out a small orange from his greatcoat and gave it to him, warning him to be careful with the skins and smell in case anyone would find out. O'Neill wished the Englishman well for his kindly act.

SOURCES AND FURTHER READING

Witness Statements, Bureau of Military History (1913–21): Bureau of Military History—A collection of 1,773 witness statements; 334 sets of contemporary documents; 42 sets of photographs and 13 voice recordings (militaryarchives.ie).

THE BEST AND WORST OF TIMES: AN IRISH COLONIAL CHRISTMAS

Seán William Gannon

The last 25 years have seen the production of a large and ever-increasing body of research on Irish participation in the British imperial project. That Irishmen had swelled the ranks of the British Army since the turn of the nineteenth century was already well documented, yet their military service formed part of a wider Irish engagement with British empire-building through settlement, missionary work and, most significantly, civilian colonial service. By the early twentieth century, Irishmen could be found serving as colonial administrators, doctors, lawyers, engineers and (most numerously) policemen, and this remained the case until the closure of the Colonial Office in 1966. Together with compatriot soldiers, settlers and missionaries, they formed transient Irish diasporas throughout the British dependent empire.

For these 'imperial Irish' diasporas, St Patrick's Day was the central communal calendric event, but Christmas ran it a close second. December 25th was a red-letter day in the colonies which, as one Singapore newspaper noted in 1909, 'embraced all the [British expatriate] community' regardless of status or station. 'British' included Irish; minority status in alien lands forged a British communal identity amongst natives of the

United Kingdom and Ireland, while membership of the colonial services promoted a cohesive corporate/group culture, cultivating an *esprit de corps* that transcended ethnicity. Thus the 'imperial Irish' were an integral and generally indistinguishable part of the British colonial ruling class.

Irish personal testimonies (such as letters, diaries, memoirs and interviews), together with press reports, convey a sense of the experience of Christmas they enjoyed. In centres with significant British/Irish populations such as India, Kenya, Singapore, Palestine and Hong Kong, Christmas was celebrated communally in public buildings, clubs and hotels. In larger British Army and Colonial Police settings, barrack messes staged the event. British (largely Victorian) seasonal traditions were assiduously observed. Christmas lunches and dinners came complete with roast goose or turkey, mince pies and plum pudding—the latter a recognised imperial symbol by the mid-1930s thanks to the promotion of a recipe by London's Empire Marketing Board which sourced ingredients from around the empire, including 'eggs from the Irish Free State'. Entertainments such as carol-singing and Christmas concerts were commonplace, as were Christmas trees, decorations, presents and cards. Meanwhile, *en famille*, Santa brought gifts for children and Christmas 'boxes' were distributed to servants, while those with radio access tuned into the King's Christmas Message, instituted on the BBC's Empire Service in 1932. Some 'imperial Irish' did remark on what they saw as the incongruity of Christmas in what could be tropical climates and/or non-Christian environments. As one Indian civil servant reported home from Calcutta in 1929, 'Christmas doesn't seem real in this sunshine, nor does eating [plum] pudding on what is here just a week day'.

For some 'imperial Irish', the performance of traditional Christmas ritual created a simulacrum of home overseas which ameliorated the nostalgic impulse. For many others, however, it exacerbated the loneliness for family and friends that could form part of colonial life, particularly amongst single men serving in the military and police. As Patrick Tynan from Galway city, who served as a police constable in Palestine in the mid-1940s, put it, '[Christmas] was the time that you missed [them] the most'. His colleague John Power from Kilkenny agreed: 'Christmas in Palestine was really the best and worst of times. We enjoyed the celebration, the mess sergeant went all out. But it actually made us homesick … by evening, all you could think of was your loved ones back at home.' Christmas could also be an acutely lonely time for the many Irish colonial servants whose children were in boarding-schools in Britain and Ireland ('What is Christmas without the children?', as one Irish doctor in 1920s Nigeria lamented), and also for those who, like Maurice de Courcy Dodd (a colonial servant from Kerry), found themselves alone on the day. His letter of 25 December 1898 to his mother from Lokoja in the Royal Niger Protectorate expressed the loneliness typically felt by those serving in outstations and isolated border posts on Christmas Day:

> Here I am in the old spot this Holy Xmas day. Well I hope ye are all … enjoying it to the full, so far as I am myself concerned I don't think this is the very pleasantest Xmas Day I ever spent. I don't know a soul here now, all I did know are either up country or gone home. Then again, I wasn't able to get a fowl or even vegetables in the market yesterday. They were all snapped up by the officers who are having a big 'bust up' tonight so that … I shall probably have to be content with sardines and biscuits for dinner. But no matter—you can give Francis [his brother] my share of plum pudding.

So important did the traditional Christmas become that those denied it sometimes compensated when they could, a detachment of Irish Hussars on active service in North Africa during the Second World War providing the most idiosyncratic example. Having made do with bully beef, biscuits and water on Christmas Day 1940, they organised a belated roast Christmas dinner complete with plum pudding on the following St Patrick's Day.

Religion, of course, had a role in the colonial Christmas. The major Christian denominations (Anglican, Roman Catholic, Presbyterian and Methodist) in expatriate population centres advertised church services in the local press which were reportedly well attended. Midnight Mass proved a popular draw, most particularly, and unsurprisingly, in the

Palestine Mandate, where the Basilica of the Nativity and the adjoining parish church of St Catherine in Bethlehem were packed to capacity in peacetime, with significant overflow gathered outside. In letters home and in interview, the Irish amongst them describe an ornamented, awesome affair: the attendance of Palestine's Roman Catholic top brass, including the consular staff of Catholic countries; the procession of the Latin patriarch and other high Catholic clergy into the basilica from St Catherine's carrying a statue of the infant Jesus; their descent to the Holy Grotto downstairs and placing of the statue on the traditional Nativity spot there; the singing of the Gospel afterwards, and the continuous saying of Masses there until the afternoon of Christmas Day. The Irish policemen who attended in the mid- to late 1940s (who were officially required to wear their 'ceremonial' blue uniform to so do) described a service so spiritually uplifting that their non-Catholic colleagues often went along: as Constable Martin Moore from Dublin recalled, 'lots of chaps went up there [Bethlehem] for midnight mass—Church of England, Church of Scotland, Presbyterian … they wanted to have the experience'. For him, it was 'an experience like no other. I felt it the greatest privilege … to kneel upon the sacred spot where Christ was born on the day of his birth', while for Sergeant Patrick McGrath these midnight Masses would remain 'some of the most special experiences of my whole life'.

Palestine was, however, an exception in terms of the Nativity's central place in the colonial Christmas. Little mention of the religious dimension can be found in the personal testimonies of the Irish resident elsewhere in the dependent empire, suggesting that it was not fundamental in the same way. For them—and, indeed, for their British counterparts—the British colonial Christmas was less a celebration of Christ's birth than a celebration of Britain itself.

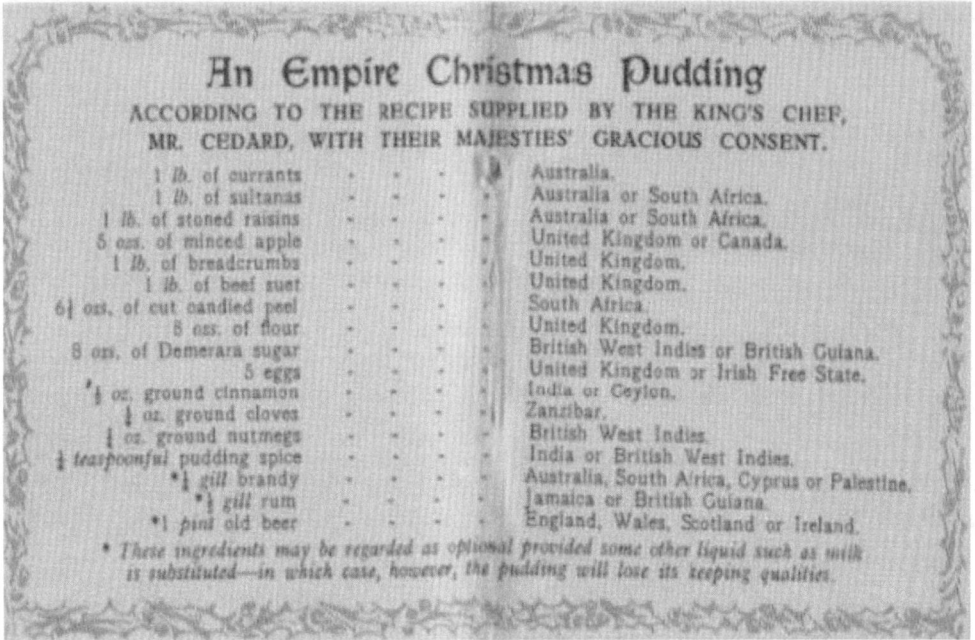

An Empire Christmas Pudding

ACCORDING TO THE RECIPE SUPPLIED BY THE KING'S CHEF,
MR. CEDARD, WITH THEIR MAJESTIES' GRACIOUS CONSENT.

1 *lb.* of currants	Australia.
1 *lb.* of sultanas	Australia or South Africa.
1 *lb.* of stoned raisins	Australia or South Africa.
5 *ozs.* of minced apple	United Kingdom or Canada.
1 *lb.* of breadcrumbs	United Kingdom.
1 *lb.* of beef suet	United Kingdom.
6½ *ozs.* of cut candied peel	South Africa.
8 *ozs.* of flour	United Kingdom.
8 *ozs.* of Demerara sugar	British West Indies or British Guiana.
5 eggs	United Kingdom or Irish Free State.
½ oz. ground cinnamon	India or Ceylon.
¼ *oz.* ground cloves	Zanzibar.
¼ *oz.* ground nutmegs	British West Indies.
½ *teaspoonful* pudding spice	India or British West Indies.
½ gill brandy	Australia, South Africa, Cyprus or Palestine.
½ gill rum	Jamaica or British Guiana.
1 pint old beer	England, Wales, Scotland or Ireland.

* *These ingredients may be regarded as optional provided some other liquid such as milk is substituted—in which case, however, the pudding will lose its keeping qualities.*

Opposite above: Police mess in Palestine decorated for Christmas lunch, c. 1923. Image owned by the author.

Opposite below: Irish members of the Palestine Police enjoying Christmas lunch at their billet, Jaffa 1947. Image owned by the author.

Above: The 'British Empire Christmas Pudding' recipe, 1932.

SOURCES AND FURTHER READING

Bodleian Library, University of Oxford: Commonwealth and African Studies collection.

Carl Bridge and Kent Fedorowich (eds), *The British world: diaspora, culture and identity* (London, 2003).

Middle East Centre Archive, St Antony's College, Oxford: Palestine Police Old Comrades Association papers.

IRISH CHRISTMAS PIE: 'A DAINTY DISH TO SET BEFORE THE KING'?

Sonja Tiernan

A surprising Irish Christmas tradition, established in the early nineteenth century, caused much controversy after the establishment of the Irish Free State. Charles Chetwynd-Talbot served as viceroy of Ireland from 1817 to 1821. As the British monarch's representative in Ireland, Lord Talbot sent a woodcock pie to King George III, who was particularly partial to game. Although now rarely eaten, woodcock was considered the highest quality of Irish game at the time. Taking his inspiration from the old children's rhyme 'Sing a Song of Sixpence' by Mother Goose, Talbot arranged for 24 woodcocks to be baked in a pie and sent to the king, to be eaten as part of the royal Christmas dinner:

Sing a song of sixpence,
A pocket full of rye,
Four and twenty blackbirds
Baked in a pie.

When the pie was opened
The birds began to sing—
Wasn't that a dainty dish
To set before the king?

Talbot established what became an annual tradition. For many years the pie was cooked in the kitchens of the viceregal lodge in the Phoenix Park, now Áras an Uachtaráin. It was sent by special courier to the monarch's residence, with a Christmas greeting. The Irish dish was served cold on Christmas Day and featured prominently on Queen Victoria's Christmas menu throughout her reign. In later years the Irish viceroy arranged for 24 woodcocks to be sent to London, where the pie was cooked locally.

In January 1922 the last viceroy, Edmund Bernard FitzAlan-Howard, officially handed over power to Michael Collins and the provisional Irish government. After the Free State was established in December 1922, the position of viceroy was formally abolished and replaced by that of governor-general of the Irish Free State. The requirement for a representative of the British monarch in Ireland was abhorrent to nationalists; this was a vivid reminder of the dominion status of the Irish Free State. An agreement was reached between the British and Irish Free State governments to appoint T.M. Healy to the position, as he was viewed as an elderly statesman who could fulfil the ceremonial duties of governor-general. Healy was sworn in on 6 December 1922 and he served in the post until January 1928. A governor-general of Northern Ireland was also created, who could no doubt have continued the tradition of sending a Christmas pie to the reigning monarch. Healy, however, continued the tradition. Woodcocks were duly sent every year to London, where the pie was baked and presented to the monarch at Christmastime on behalf of the governor-general of the Irish Free State.

After his term ended in 1928, Healy was replaced by James McNeill, an experienced diplomat. McNeill's term in office was relatively uneventful and he continued with the annual Christmas tradition, which did not seem to gain much public attention in Ireland. On 12 December 1931, however, John Brennan of 10 Belgrave Road, Rathmines, wrote a letter to the *Irish Press* newspaper signalling his disdain for this Christmas tradition. Brennan described how he had read reports that morning of starving children in Dublin. After reading the report, he had opened a copy of the *News-Chronicle*, a British newspaper, which reported that the king and queen would receive a present of four and twenty woodcocks baked in a pie from the Irish Free State governor-general. While it is not certain who John Brennan was, the address that he gave was that of prominent republicans Una and Robert Brennan. Belgrave Road had earned the moniker of 'Rebel Road' owing to the abundance of notable political activists among its occupants, including Hanna Sheehy Skeffington, Kathleen Lynn and Madeleine ffrench Mullen.

Brennan noted in his letter how governors-general in the Free State had simply continued the Christmas tradition. This would change, however, when Eamon de Valera came into power just weeks later. In February 1932 Fianna Fáil, under the leadership of de Valera, formed a government with the support of the Labour Party. De Valera set to work on dismantling symbols of British rule in Ireland, starting with the position of governor-general. Throughout 1932 de Valera ensured that McNeill was not granted any privileges by the government, and he was not invited to attend official functions. Most significantly, McNeill was excluded from State preparations for the Eucharistic Congress to be held in Dublin in June that year. This resulted in what historian Michael Kennedy has called a growing cold war between the governor-general and the Irish executive.

Matters came to a head in October 1932, when de Valera submitted a request to King George V for McNeill to be relieved of his post, which came into effect almost immediately. De Valera put forward a strong republican figure, Domhnall Ó Buachalla (Donal Buckley), as his replacement. Ó Buachalla, an Irish-speaker, refused to be addressed by the title of governor-general, insisting on using An Seanascal (chief steward) instead. The use of an Irish-language title was just the beginning of a systematic plan to devalue the office of governor-general in Ireland. Ó Buachalla did not reside in the official residence of the viceregal lodge, choosing instead to live in a modest house in the suburbs of Dublin. He rejected all ceremonial roles associated with the British monarch's representative in Ireland and was rarely even seen in public, let alone at official events.

Not surprisingly, Ó Buachalla abruptly ended the tradition of sending a Christmas pie to the king. The Tralee newspaper *The Liberator* reported the end of the tradition with glee, noting that this move was particularly welcomed by the people of Dublin, who had popularised a new verse in the 'Sing a Song of Sixpence' rhyme:

> When the pie was opened
> The birds began to sing:
> Three Cheers for Donal Buckley
> No pastry for the King.

The position of governor-general of the Irish Free State was abolished in 1936. As historian Marie Coleman notes, by that time the office had virtually ceased to exist.

SOURCES AND FURTHER READING

Marie Coleman, 'Ó Buachalla (Ua Buachalla), Domhnall (Donal/Daniel Richard Buckley)', in *Dictionary of Irish Biography* (www.dib.ie).
Michael Kennedy, 'McNeill, James', in *Dictionary of Irish Biography* (www.dib.ie).

CHRISTMAS IN NEWSPAPERS AND NOVELS IN IRELAND IN THE 1930S, '40S AND '50S

Caitriona Clear

At the beginning of John D. Sheridan's last novel, *God made little apples* (1962), the elderly Brother Bernard is irritated by Dublin city Christmas lights in mid-November. He prefers Christmas to be 'sharp and sudden' and to take him by surprise, as it did when he was a boy in Donegal. An early start to Christmas was not new even in the late 1950s, when the novel is set. On the front page of the *Irish Independent* on 17 November 1936, a cartoon Santa holding a megaphone called all good little boys and girls to come and see him in Clery's in Dublin. Nan Mahony told *Irish Press* readers on 11 November 1938 that the 'Christmas Clean-up was Now Due'. The same newspaper told readers on 19 November 1947 that it was 'Not Too Early To Make This Christmas Cake'. A year earlier, the *Independent* gave Christmas pudding recipes on 5 December. This *was* late, because cakes and puddings had to be made early to allow them to mature, as 'Lady Edith' in the *Belfast Newsletter* no doubt knew when she gave a Christmas cake recipe on 4 November 1938, and a plum pudding recipe just five days later. Recipes for festive cakes and puddings appeared as early as 4 November in the *Irish Press* in 1938, and on 7 November in 1956. The first of a three-part weekly Christmas cooking column by Monica Nevin in the *Irish Independent* on 13 November 1958 was 'Let's Begin With The Cake!'; the last in the series was 'Points in Preparing Poultry' on 27 November—nearly a month before the feast, but not too early to start planning what to order or kill for the festive board. Home-made toys also had to be started early, and thus 'A Leprecaun' in the *Irish Press* of 3 November 1938 gave tips on 'Home-Made Toys For Xmas Boxes'. Eight years later, the same paper reminded readers to start 'Knitting toys for Christmas' on 8 November 1946. Preparations for a good Christmas had to begin early. John D. Sheridan himself knew this, when in *My hat blew off* (1950) he described lending a hand in the strenuous pre-electric-mixer task of creaming the butter and the sugar for the Christmas cake: 'When it is in this condition it is known as "the batter", which is also what your husband goes on when he finally manages to escape'.

Christmas, then as now, was a good filler for newspapers, but when the festive season is introduced in novels and short stories it is to bring characters together, to highlight happiness or tension, to add texture, or simply to pause the action of the story. The bustle of the run-up to Christmas in a small town is relished in Patricia Lynch's *The mad O'Haras* (1948): Norrie and Sally, one working in a sweetshop, the other in a hairdressing salon, barely have time for a cup of tea in their hands on Christmas Eve. Urban Christmas was spectacle as well as bustle. When Nan Mahony gave *Irish Press* readers a glowing description of Dublin shop-window decorations on 25 November 1946 she was certainly pleasing advertisers, but she was also expressing a common reaction to the novelty and glow of Christmas decorations in public places. Going to look at the 'toy bazaars' in the big Dublin department stores is a great seasonal treat for tenement children in William Hand's *Fair city* (1946); despite seeing all the toys they cannot afford, they are thrilled with what they get from a shop Santa—a box of paints, a small clockwork train.

Private houses were decorated as well as public spaces. In the east Cork farmhouse where Margaret O'Leary's *Lightning flash* (1939) is set, complex decorations of holly and ivy are the father's job. The factory-working Montgomery family in Patricia O'Connor's *The mill in the north* (1939) decorate the kitchen with evergreens; chrysanthemums are the seasonal blooms, as also in the 1940s Dublin city described by M.L. Stewart in *The cliff-dwellers* (1946). Here, the basement-dwelling caretaker of a block of fancy apartments and his sister sit down to goose—the people for whom they work eat turkey—and a bottle of wine purchased from the grocer for 4/6, which neither of them like very much but consider an essential part of the Christmas fare. Lemonade, not wine, is the accompaniment to the Christmas dinner in one 1940s Kilkenny farmhouse described by Patrick Purcell in *A keeper of swans* (1944); the fare is soup in cups, turkey with breadcrumb stuffing, boiled beef, baked ham, potatoes in their jackets, trifle, tinned fruit and custard. In the east Cork farmhouse described above by O'Leary, there is a turkey on Christmas Day, another turkey on New Year's Day, and yet another on Little Christmas (the feast of the Epiphany)—no relaxing 'Women's Christmas' of tea and sweet cake here.

There is, however, some consideration for women's hectic work in Francis MacManus's short story 'Family Portrait' in *Pedlar's pack* (1944), when the men cut short their Christmas Day 'hunting' (with dogs, on foot) to come home and help the women, in an unspecified Leinster locale. Here, not only is turkey being prepared but also half a dozen small fowl are roasted with thin slices of bacon on top, a ham is roasted in a case of dough to keep the juices in, and there is roast beef, spiced beef, brawn, baked and boiled potatoes, and, to come after, baked apples in whipped cream, custards, jellies, a pie and plum pudding. The point of this story is the photographer who turns up just as the large extended family is about to sit down to this feast and assembles them in the yard. Declining politely to eat with the family, he goes about his business in such a leisurely fashion that the dinner is nearly ruined and the resulting photograph shows everybody grinning humourlessly. It is implied that Christmas visitors like this were not unknown in rural Ireland at that time. The photographer—described as tall and thin but not otherwise distinctive—was probably Jewish, someone for whom the feast held no significance. The photograph needed daylight, which suggests that this dinner, like the ones described by Purcell and Stewart, was taking place either in the middle of the day or in the very early afternoon.

The difficulties of Christmas are sometimes mentioned. Schoolmaster John Lee in Francis MacManus's *Flow on lovely river* (1941) dozes before the fire with his widowed father and brothers on the night of Christmas Day, 'and let words fall as uncertainly as leaves in breathless autumn weather'. They might have been a bit livelier had they heeded an advertisement like the one in the *Western People* on 5 December 1936 for a 'Radio for Xmas' (run on a battery, of course). Not all homes had in-house entertainers, and the seasonal atmosphere, then as now, was often helped along by broadcasters. After all, it cannot only have been in the tense middle-class Belfast family described in Janet McNeill's *Tea at four o'clock* (1956) that Christmas was 'a miracle of sustained civility which they were all glad to have done with'.

SOURCES AND FURTHER READING

William Hand, *Fair city* (Dublin, 1946).
Patricia Lynch, *The mad O'Haras* (London, 1948).
Michael McLaverty, *Call my brother back* (London, 1939).
Francis MacManus, *Flow on lovely river* (Dublin, 1941).
Francis MacManus, *Pedlar's pack* (Dublin, 1944).
Janet McNeill, *Tea at four o'clock* (London, 1956).
Patricia O'Connor, *The mill in the north* (Dublin, 1939).
Margaret O'Leary, *Lightning flash* (London, 1939).
Patrick Purcell, *A keeper of swans* (Dublin, 1944).
John D. Sheridan, *My hat blew off* (Dublin, 1950).
John D. Sheridan, *God made little apples* (Dublin, 1962).
M.L. Stewart, *The cliff-dwellers* (Dublin, 1946).

AN *NOLLAIG* IN POEMS BY
MÁIRTÍN Ó DIREÁIN

Marie Whelton

Máirtín Ó Direáin (1910–88) was an Irish-language poet from the Inishmore Gaeltacht, Aran. This short article discusses four of his Christmas poems composed between 1939 and 1949. Ó Direáin has written other poems about Christmas which could be included in this discussion, and some would argue that these poems should be assessed alongside his prose pieces about Christmas. Considered together, however, these four representative poems paint a picture of aspects of Christmas on Aran before, during and directly after the Second World War, and they also provide a microcosmic insight into the evolution of some of Ó Direáin's major poetic themes, particularly the theme of modern displacement.

In *Coinnle ar Lasadh* ('Candles lighting'), first published in 1942 but dated 1939, Ó Direáin tenderly describes, from afar, in colloquial Irish, the tradition in Aran of lighting twelve candles on the eve of the Epiphany. The poet's certainty that the age-old practice will be faithfully honoured and re-enacted on Aran emphasises the ritualistic nature of the community's Christmas traditions and, as a result, the recalled island of memory is presented as the real island of the present day. Instead of focusing on the exile's romantic nostalgia for past Christmases, the poem becomes part, rather, of the current year's symbolic candle-lighting ritual—a vehicle for a Christmas blessing-prayer uttered in faith, *in absentia*, for loved ones at home and especially for the poet's mother, to whom the verses are dedicated (Ó Direáin, 23; my translation):

In oileán beag i gcéin san Iarthar
(On a small island away in the West)
Beidh coinnle ar lasadh anocht,
(Candles will be lighting tonight,)
I dtithe ceann tuí, is i dtithe ceann slinne,
(In thatched and slated houses,)
Dhá cheann déag de choinnle geala a bheas ar lasadh anocht.
(Twelve bright candles will be lighting tonight.)

Mo chaoinbheannacht siar leis na coinnle geala
(My kind blessing west to the bright candles)
A bheas ar lasadh anocht,
(Which will be lighting tonight,)
Is céad beannacht faoi dhó
(And one hundred blessings doubled)
Le láimh amháin a lasfas coinnle anocht.
(To one hand which will light candles tonight.)

In *Oíche Chinn an Dá Lá Dhéag* ('Eve of the Twelfth Day') (Ó Direáin, 31), also written in January 1939, religious and political experience are fused to critique the modern abandonment of traditional Christian values. The imagery is binary throughout and the Three Wise Kings who travel from the Orient are juxtaposed with the leaders of Ó Direáin's own era, whom he wishes would emulate their biblical counterparts. This poem can be read as a precursor to Ó Direáin's later poems in which he satirises contemporary politicians for their failure to fulfil the ideals of early Irish nationalism. While, in the words of Louis de Paor, 'Ó Direáin has been criticised for his failure to develop beyond the primary contradiction articulated in his work between the communal values of traditional rural society and the deracinated individualism of the modern urban industrial world', and while some of his later poetry shows an acerbic disillusionment with contemporary politicians and leaders, Ó Direáin continues to hope that leaders will emerge in the future who will succeed in realising some of the social-justice goals of early nationalism. Consequently, Ó Direáin's poetry often champions the cause of the weakest, the smallest and the most vulnerable, and it is that element of the Magi's adoration of the Christ Child and the Christian values of generosity and humility which are explored here:

Ón domhan thoir anois do thriall
(From the eastern world now journeyed)
Triúr Rí onórach uasal eolach críonna:
(Three honourable, noble, knowledgeable, wise Kings:)
Bronntanais a thugadar leo go fial
(Gifts they brought with them generously)
Le toirbhirt go humhal do Íosa.
(To offer humbly to Jesus.)

Sa mainséar sínte, is É beag bídeach,
(Stretched in a manger, small and tiny,)
Bhí an tÉ a chruthaigh an domhan mór millteach,
(Was the One who created the huge world,)
I bhfianaise an naíonáin ar a nglúine dóibh
(On their knees before the infant they went)
Gur thugadar Dó ómós go huiríseal […]
(And humbly paid Him homage […])

Mo mhairg is mo bhrón géar,
(Alas and my bitter sorrow,)
Taoisigh an lae inniu go léir
(That all the leaders of today)
Nach ndéanann le hatuirse croí
(Don't with sincere heart)

Aithris orthu siúd do thriall anoir.
(Emulate those who journeyed from the east.)

Cuireadh do Mhuire (Ó Direáin, 47) was published in 1943 but is dated 'Nollaig 1942' by the poet. It is, perhaps, one of Ó Direáin's best-known poems and has experienced something of a revival of late thanks to a musical setting by Ronan McDonagh (2010) and a recent recording by Róisín Elsafty (2015). As in *Coinnle ar Lasadh*, the candle is its central image, but this time Ó Direáin draws on the rural tradition of putting a candle in the window on Christmas Eve to show Mary and Joseph that they will find welcome within the house. The custom itself, of course, witnesses to the Christian belief that each Christmas the Christian is offered a chance to rectify the rejection and exclusion experienced by the Holy Family on the first Christmas night when, being met with closed doors, they had to take refuge and shelter in a stable. It also alludes to the identification of the Holy Family in Bethlehem, and on their flight into Egypt, with all those who are rejected, excluded and displaced, meaning that the lighted candle, in this case, is a symbol of universal welcome for all. Ó Direáin speaks directly, in apostrophic form, to Mary and asks her whether she knows where she and her baby will sleep this year, as the human race has closed all doors to Christ:

An eol duit, a Mhuire,
(Do you know, Mary,)
Cá rachair i mbliana
(Where you will go this year?)
Ag iarraidh foscaidh
(Seeking shelter)
Do do Leanbh Naofa,
(For your Holy Child,)
Tráth a bhfuil gach doras
(At a time when each door is)
Dúnta ina éadan

(Closed against him)
Ag fuath is uabhar
(By the hate and pride)
An chine dhaonna?
(Of the human race?)

He then invites her to accept his invitation to shelter in Aran, where bright candles will be lighting in each window and where a turf fire will burn on each hearth:

Deonaigh glacadh
(Consent to accept)
Le cuireadh uaimse
(An invitation from me)
Go hoileán mara
(To an ocean island)
San Iarthar cianda:
(In the remote West:)
Beidh coinnle geala
(Bright candles will)
I ngach fuinneog lasta
(In each window be lighting)
Is tine mhóna
(And a turf fire)
Ar theallach adhainte.
(Ignited on the hearth.)

The simple binary oppositions and contrasts between darkness and light, war and peace, alienation and welcome are immediately apparent. Aran with its candles and fires is a symbol of light, peace and welcome, while the modern world is a place of darkness, war and alienation. Ó Direáin doesn't mention Ireland's neutrality during World War II, but some critics, such as Peter MacKay, suggest that the reference to a 'western island' could be read as Ireland 'offering a moral haven to the rest of Europe'. Whether Aran or Ireland, in this poem Ó Direáin undoubtedly sees the remote island in the west as a place of respite from war and of sanctuary for the displaced.

The three poems examined so far illustrate that the best of Ó Direáin's poetry celebrates the beauty of tradition and explores the tension between the traditional and the modern while retaining the dream to create a more just, egalitarian world. As Louis de Paor points out, however, 'Gradually, the poems become shadowed by doubt as the actual island changes over time and no longer provides a physical sanctuary to which he can retreat'. *Cuimhní Nollag* (Ó Direáin, 64), our final selected poem, which was published in 1949, gives the reader a taste of the darker side of Ó Direáin's experience of cultural dislocation in the modern city.

The poet begins each of the first three verses with *Is cuimhin liom* ('I remember') and goes on to describe the preparations which used to be made for Christmas on Aran—new sand and stones spread out in front of the house, holly and ivy on freshly whitewashed walls, and candles 'lighting the road for Christ'. There is an acknowledgement in the first verse, however, that those Christmases are in the past and will never return (*nach bhfillfidh ar ais choíche*). The memories that inspired a blessing-prayer in *Coinnle Geala* are now, as expressed in the final verse, the ghost of Christmas past tormenting him as he walks on unwelcoming urban streets. The poet's pain is so great that he would rather forget than remember:

Is cuimhin liomsa Nollaigí
(I remember Christmases)
Nach bhfillfidh ar ais choíche,
(Which will never return again,)
Nuair a bhínn ag tarraingt gainimh is mulláin bheaga chladaigh
(When I used to draw sand and little shore stones)
Is á scaradh os comhair an tí.
(To spread out in front of the house.)

Is cuimhin liom an t-eidheann
(I remember the ivy)
Is an cuileann lena thaobh
(And the holly by its side)
Thuas ar bhallaí geala
(Up on bright walls)
Is boladh cumhra an aoil.
(And the perfumed scent of lime whitewash.)

Is cuimhin liom na coinnle
(I remember the candles)
Lasta i bhfuinneoga,
(Lighting in windows,)
Is gach áras ina lóchrann geal
(And each house a guiding light)
Ag soilsiú an bhóthair do Chríost.
(Lighting the road for Christ.)

Anois ag triall ar bhóithre an doichill dom
(Now as I walk roads of unwelcome)
Is na cuimhní úd do mo chrá,
(And those memories tormenting me,)
B'fhearr liom go mór díchuimhne
(I'd much prefer to forget)
Ná méadú ar mo chás.
(Than have my concern increased.)

Examined together and in chronological order, these four Christmas poems give a general insight into the development of Ó Direáin's thought, which moves from celebrating the traditional and the idealistic to expressing the alienation of moral and cultural displacement. The central idea articulated in the earlier Christmas poems—that what is absent in the present (tradition, peace, justice, welcome, Christian faith, love) existed in the past and may be recaptured in the present or in the future—ultimately fails for Ó Direáin. In the final poem above, the poet's experience of alienation overshadows his present, rendering him unable to flourish or to take solace in recalling more joyful Christmases. What is most remarkable, though, is that this selection of Ó Direáin poetry articulates the intensifying nature of the experience of the modern 'displaced person' at Christmas with archetypal accuracy, making Ó Direáin, in the words of Tomás Mac Síomóin and Douglas Sealy, a 'representative figure of our time', and making these poems of particular relevance for all who are experiencing displacement and the emotional poignancy that Christmas brings to that experience.

SOURCES AND FURTHER READING

Síobhra Aiken (eag.), *An chuid eile díom féin: aistí le Máirtín Ó Direáin* (An Spidéal, 2018).

Louis de Paor, 'Contemporary poetry in Irish: 1940–2000', in Margaret Kelleher and Philip O'Leary (eds), *The Cambridge History of Irish Literature Vol. 2: 1890–2000* (Cambridge, 2006), 317–56.

Louis de Paor, '"Cnámh na seisce": crapadh na fearúlachta i ndánta Mháirtín Uí Dhireáin', in Meidhbhín Ní Úrdail agus Caoimhín Mac Giolla Léith (eag.), *Mo ghnósa leas an dáin: aistí in ómós do Mháirtín Ó Direáin* (An Daingean, 2014), 115–29.

Louis de Paor, 'Réamhrá / Introduction', in Louis de Paor (eag.), *Leabhar na hathghabhála / Poems of repossession* (Indreabhán, 2016), 13–28.

Peter MacKay, 'Scottish and Irish Second World War poetry', in UCDscholarcast Series 4, *Reconceiving the British Isles: the literature of the archipelago*, Episode 6.

Tomás Mac Síomóin and Douglas Sealy (eds), *Máirtín Ó Direáin: selected poems / tacar dánta* (Kildare 1984, 1992).

Máirín Nic Eoin, *Trén bhfearann breac: an díláithriú cultúir agus nualitríocht na Gaeilge* (Baile Átha Cliath, 2005).

Máirtín Ó Direáin, *Máirtín Ó Direáin: na dánta* (eag. Eoghan Ó hAnluain) (Indreabhán, 2010).

Marie Whelton, 'Ceannairí Éirí Amach 1916 agus gnéithe d'eitic agus d'aeistéitic na codarsnachta i ndánta le Máirtín Ó Direáin', COMHAR *Taighde* **6** (30 Samhain 2020), 1–16 (DOI: https://doi.org/10.18669/ct.2020.12; faighte 24 Lúnasa 2022).

'Bright be your Christmas'. Christmas greeting card with Celtic design by Brian O'Higgins (1882–1963). © National Museum of Ireland.

THE IMPACT OF CHRISTMAS ON IRISH FOLK TRADITION

Pádraig Ó Héalaí

The extensive range of customs associated with the celebration of Christmas is clear evidence of its importance in the lives of generations of Irish people. The focus of this contribution is on aspects of Irish folklore that reflect the Christian teaching on the pivotal significance of Christ's birth, the event traditionally commemorated by the feast of Christmas. The preparations for the feast involved mundane activities with a social dimension such as cleaning and decorating the interior of the house, whitewashing its exterior, laying in supplies of festive food and drink, and attending to items of seasonal cuisine. In addition to these, however, spiritual preparations were generally undertaken, both on an individual and family level, the main features of these being special prayers at the family rosary and the reception of the sacrament of penance.

While the provision of Christmas fare was intended primarily for the enjoyment of family and friends, an additional religious dimension may have attached to enhancing the appearance of the house. Acceptance of the traditional belief that heavenly guests would pay a visit on the Holy Night may well have underpinned endeavours to make the house attractive. This widely attested tradition is invoked in Máire Mhac an tSaoi's well-known poem *Oíche Nollag*, in which the repetition of the line *luífidh Mac Dé ins an tigh seo anocht* ('the Son of God will rest in this house tonight') suggests the intense emotion aroused by the prospect of heavenly visitors.

As well as whatever family prayers were said on Christmas Night, attendance at midnight Mass was widespread. Christmas Night was also a recognised occasion for telling religious tales—the practice is exemplified, for instance, by Peig Sayers in her autobiography, where she tells how a traditional tale and poem concerning the Infant Jesus were recited on Christmas Night to the children of the household in which she was in service.

In addition to embellishing the house, candles were lit and placed in windows to guide and invite the Holy Family, and it was customary for households in parts of the country to cover the ground near the entrance door with rushes, straw or hay as a welcoming gesture. Unlike on all other nights of the year (save Hallowe'en, when the dead were said to visit the house), the fire was not damped down but was left burning, as a further sign of welcome for the visitors. Underlying these practices is a desire to engage with the events of the first Christmas Night, and they can be viewed as an attempt to participate, to some extent, in a re-enactment of them, as households sought to create their own welcoming resting place for the Holy Family. In this, they conform to a well-documented pattern manifested in commemorative celebrations of events of cosmogonic significance to a culture—such as the birth of the Saviour constitutes for Christianity—whereby, through the symbolic re-enactment of the primal event, access is afforded to the benefits and energy conferred by it.

The importance accorded the birth of Christ in the traditional worldview is given expression in oral narratives. Holly, a central feature of house decoration at Christmas, was linked in a number of legends with the birth of Christ. An origin-tale explains that the holly's red berries were formed from drops of blood shed by a rushing shepherd when scratched by holly and briars on his way to the manger. According to another legend, a poor woman brought holly as a gift to the Infant Jesus, and because of that it is used as decoration at Christmas. Other aetiological tales variously claim that the practice originated because holly and ivy grew in the stable where Jesus was born, or, alternatively, that holly sheltered the Holy Family on the Flight to Egypt.

Some traditional beliefs relating to certain animals owe their origin to the role they are said to have played on the occasion of the Infant Jesus's birth. The donkey, for example, was thought to be blessed because of its presence in the stable on the first Christmas Night—a notion sometimes forcefully asserted in protesting its ill-treatment—and the cross on the donkey's shoulders is commonly said to be a reward for his helpful role on that occasion (or else in transporting the Holy Family on the Flight into Egypt, or carrying Christ on His triumphant entry into Jerusalem). The cow in medieval Irish literature is associated with the Otherworld, but in later folk tradition a spiritual dimension is attributed to her because of the belief that a cow was present at Christ's birth and helped with her breath to warm the Holy Infant. Unsurprisingly, this belief features in a charm to cure a sick cow which appeals specifically to the cow's presence in the stable at Bethlehem as grounds for divine intervention to save the stricken animal.

There was a tradition that at midnight on Christmas Eve both donkey and cow would kneel in homage, thus acknowledging the significance of the event being commemorated. The manner in which a cow kneels on her front legs before lying down was viewed as a sign of its blessedness. In this way, the phenomenon of the cow's kneeling, together with the cross on the donkey, might serve as everyday reminders of the significance of Christ's birth.

According to a widespread European tradition which was also prevalent in Ireland, animals become capable of speech on Christmas Night. Since it is asserted in oral tradition that animals originally had the power of speech, the belief that this faculty returns to them on Christmas Night might be viewed as an instance of the world reverting to its pristine state at this special point in time. The best-known legend based on this tradition, however, discourages any attempt to eavesdrop on the animals' conversation, as it tells how an inquisitive listener hears them foretell his own imminent death. While in Ireland, unlike in some other European countries, the cock's crowing was not generally interpreted as a version of *Christus natus est* ('Christ is born') but rather as *Mac na hÓighe slán* ('the Virgin's Son lives') in reference to the Resurrection, nonetheless, the cock's crowing in the lead-up to Christmas was nonetheless associated with the joyful foretelling of Christ's birth and was referred to as *rámhaillí na Nollag* ('the Christmas rantings').

According to a folk belief, the gates of heaven are wide open during the Christmas festival, signifying that during this period of time the normal dispensation of admittance is set aside. The belief in open access to heaven is reflected in folk prayers for a happy death, and the expression *fuair sé/sí cuireadh na Nollag* ('he/she received the Christmas invitation') is still commonly used of a death during the festive period.

A more worldly demonstration of the normal order being relinquished during the Christmas festival is afforded by the belief that water turns to wine for a brief moment at the exact hour of midnight either on Christmas Night or on the Twelfth, also known as Little Christmas and *Nollaig na mBan* ('Women's Christmas'). The liturgy undoubtedly played a role in propagating this belief, as the Marriage Feast of Cana featured as the Gospel reading for Mass on the feast of the Epiphany. Although water is most frequently mentioned in this context, it is not the only substance said to undergo transformation at this moment of time. A traditional formula in highlighting this Christmas midnight marvel proclaims that grass and rushes turn to silk, gravel turns to gold, stones on the seashore turn to silver and the eagle's heart turns to bread. The transformation was said to be momentary, and narratives based on the belief invariably serve the didactic function of discouraging people from attempting to observe the phenomenon. A typical example tells how individuals who went to the well to procure some of the wine were either turned into rocks or else were never heard of again.

Given the wondrous nature of Christmas, it is not surprising that music and dance were traditionally felt to be appropriate responses to the event being celebrated. This sentiment is voiced in the poem *Oíche*

Nollag by Eoghan Ó Tuairisc, discussed by Mícheál Mac Craith elsewhere in this volume, when the poet says *Dá mbeadh mileoidean agamsa / Ní bheadh Críost gan cheol anocht* ('if I had a melodeon, Christ would not lack music tonight'), and it underlies the lines 'My father played the melodion / outside at our gate' in Patrick Kavanagh's 'Christmas Childhood'. The notion that in celebrating this feast an elevated artistic response was called for is encapsulated in a proverb which declares it inappropriate to go to bed on Christmas Night without engaging in a bout of dancing—*Oíche Nollag, ní hobair dúinn insint, dul a chodladh gan greas beag a rince.*

SOURCES AND FURTHER READING

Mircea Eliade, *The myth of the eternal return, or cosmos and history* (Princeton, 1971).
Seán Ó Súilleabháin, *A handbook of Irish folklore* (Dublin, 1942).
www.duchas.ie

CHRISTMAS FOODWAYS IN RURAL IRELAND

Regina Sexton

C hristmas food customs in rural Ireland developed a distinctive character based on the intertwining of religious practice, the patterns and rhythms of agricultural work, and folk custom and belief. Throughout the nineteenth century the interplay between farm-produced and shop-bought goods had a further impact on Christmas food traditions as rural communities became both producers of festal foods and consumers of seasonal commodity goods. This movement between farm and shop was shadowed by dietary movements between fast and feast as the faithful followed the liturgical seasons of Advent and Christmastide. The mix of elements from traditional and modern food systems gave rural Christmas foodways a certain characteristic dualism. And, when infused with shared folk beliefs that held meaning and value for communities, rural Christmas foodways had a defined and dynamic identity.

The importance of farmyard fowl to the economic health of rural households, especially in the second half of the nineteenth century, influenced the value assigned to different fowl, which in turn determined the character of the rural Christmas dinner. Turkey-rearing was a lucrative farm enterprise that supported domestic economic well-being. The important commodity status of turkeys and their greater sale returns above geese meant for many fowl-keepers that the birds were destined for the market rather than for the table. In a nostalgia and memory piece about early twentieth-century Christmases in the *Ballina Herald* in December 1955, one Donegal account is typical of practice and sentiment: 'Turkeys were not eaten in the homes where they were reared. Their's was a cash value not cuisine, they were a too costly and an uncalled-for luxury.'

Where the economic returns of the turkey were valued above their culinary merits, the goose was the choice table bird for the Christmas Day meal. The home killing of a goose brought additional benefits beyond meat for the table: the fat had multiple household, cookery and medicinal uses; feathers and down were used in bedding; and the wing feathers served as hearth and griddle dusters. In areas where open-hearth cooking was practised in the absence of stoves and cooking ranges, large birds like geese and turkeys were boiled rather than roasted, as boiling best suited the range of hearth utensils. This method gave a strong broth that was often flavoured further with carrots, turnips and cabbage, and thickened with oatmeal. In coastal and upland areas, and for island communities, mutton—and sometimes goat—was the popular Christmas meat. The slaughter of an animal, often a fattened wether, gave fresh meat for the festival, together with additional and welcome items like blood puddings and fresh meat offcuts. In these community contexts, fresh meat was extended to those without stock. Often it was also shared between family and friends in a reciprocal arrangement that saw the favour returned when it was their time to slaughter a farm animal.

The varied and fluid approach to what constituted Christmas food is illustrated in the popular description of the Christmas meal as simply 'a big dinner'. This summation carried an inherent understanding that, in accordance with means, people would strive to create a special food environment where 'special' was relative to everyday consumption patterns. In an 1828 entry, the Kilkenny diarist Humphrey O'Sullivan remarked that Christmas and Easter were the two best days for the stomach as a break from the everyday diet of potatoes, milk and the occasional piece of bacon. He described his 1827 Christmas dinner as one with roast goose and potato stuffing, and on 27 December 1829 his 'excellent dinner' with Father Walsh in Waterford was meat- and fowl-rich and not bound to any sense of set convention. He enjoyed a 'chine of beef, new-salted, and white cabbage, roast goose with bread stuffing in it, a leg of mutton with turnips, bacon and chickens and roast snipe', with port and whiskey punch. He is also conscious, however, of the plight of the poor in their attempts to build a sense of distance from the everyday in their purchases at the 1828 Christmas Eve market of pigs' heads, joints of lean tough beef, remnants of an old ram and fatty bits of a sow's groin.

For the less affluent in rural Ireland, the luxury status of meat as an item that entered the diet only at Christmas and Easter persisted into the early decades of the twentieth century. In poorer households, the meat element of the Christmas meal was purchased, hunted or home-produced. Rabbit, as the poor man's chicken, was cheap at local markets and widely available to those who hunted; chicken was a substitute for market-valuable turkeys or geese, and salted bacon took the place of fresh meat. Foods that were everyday items in mainstream food practice but luxuries for those in strained economic circumstances assumed special status as vital ingredients to mark Christmas celebrations. *Caoineadh Fir Siúil* ('the Wandering Man's Lament') positions butter as essential for Christmas, and a season without it was seen as a disruption of the ordered norms attending the main religious celebrations: *Oíche Nollag Mór gan im, Máirt Inide gan feoil, Domhnach Cásca gan nibhe, Nach mise an diol deor?* ('Christmas night without butter, Shrove Tuesday without meat, Easter Sunday without eggs, isn't mine a tearful state?').

The fast–feast relationship directed by religious observance linked strongly to the agricultural patterns of winter and early spring. The relationship structured Christmas food culture around opposing periods of abstinence and indulgence. The beginning of Advent coincided with the period of winter stock culls and the preserving of meat for the leaner months of winter and spring. At Martinmas on 11 November, the slaughter of a pig or farmyard fowl and the sprinkling of the blood on the house and farm boundary points ritualised the secular culling period and set a contrast with the season's fast days in Advent and on the vigils of holy days. In accordance with a church ruling that was often locally directed, the appointed days in Advent, Christmas Eve, St Stephen's Day, New Year's Eve and the Eve of the Epiphany were kept as fast days. Christmas Eve was a day of fasting and abstinence that was not broken until into the evening of the vigil. Salt fish with potatoes and a white sauce (flour, milk, onions and pepper) was the traditional Christmas Eve dish. Popular fish for the meal were salted cod, ling, pollack, wrasse and herring. When fish was unavailable, *brúitín*, a simple dish of mashed potatoes with butter, was prepared, and its popularity highlights the importance of butter to a poor food economy outside the milking season.

The breaking of the Christmas Eve fast marked the beginning of the Christmas feast. Alongside the traditional fish and potatoes dinner, a sweet element ushered in the celebrations: the Christmas cake was cut and sampled, sweet fruit soda breads or soda bread and jam were taken with tea, fruit cordials, mineral waters, lemonade or alcohol, and an orange or apple or rice pudding might make an appearance. For those who could afford the expense, the break from routine food habits carried through to breakfasts of fried steak and cake taken after early morning Mass.

Food-related folk belief and superstitions shared many features with Hallowe'en popular custom and these brought a further distinctive character to rural Christmas foodways. Ritualised and symbolic action centred around meal provision and table place-setting for the Holy Family and family revenants on Christmas Eve. Marriage and death portents were encoded in the activities and engagements with sweet baked goods—in hiding rings in plum puddings, in attempts to guard against the crumbling of freshly boiled plum puddings to prevent a family death or, as described by a County Meath schoolchild to the National Folklore Collection Schools' Manuscript Collection (NFCS), in collecting nine pieces of pudding at Christmas with the intention that 'when the ninth piece has been tasted, the collector will marrie [*sic*] the first person he or she shakes hands with, before Christmas comes again'.

There are many local variations and expressions of these customs, but more universal and popularly executed were those performed on New Year's Eve and designed to bring food security for the year that followed. Rituals to banish hunger were common in rural and urban areas, and bread was used as a dietary staple to symbolically drive or beat hunger from the door. The execution of the ritual varied; bread was beaten against the door or was thrown out of the door, or one cake was thrown out one door and another cake was thrown in another to mimic endings and beginnings. Rings, charms and tokens baked into Twelfth Night cakes and barmbracks gave those who found them the opportunity to act out fantastic roles with an atmosphere of disorder that marked the end of Christmas indulgence. This theme of disorder and disruption also extended to the nature of celebrations on Little or Women's Christmas, when women withdrew for the eve of the Epiphany from household work and food preparation. The interconnections of symbol, religion and popular belief were also worked into the custom of saving sprigs of Christmas decorative holly as kindling for hearth fires used to bake Shrove Tuesday pancakes, thus anticipating one feast to follow another.

For rural populations, accessing commercial goods for Christmas became a defining feature of preparations for the festival and these were sanctioned in the ritual of 'bringing home the Christmas' on 8 December. The *Irish Farmers Journal* of December 1979 provides accounts of early twentieth-century Christmas shopping trips to the nearest towns. One Mayo account describes the *cúlog*, where the woman rode on a pillion attached to the back of the man's saddle on the trip to buy five-pound crocks of jams and a barrel of salted herrings for Advent and Christmas week. For trips where larger volumes of goods were purchased, neighbours came together to rent carts to travel to the nearest town on days other than the busy 8 December. And to reward loyal custom, grocers gave presents of Christmas boxes of wine, whiskey, tea, sugar, dried fruit and Christmas cakes.

In the first half of the twentieth century rural Christmas food customs conformed to standardised practice. Movement to align with a more universal way with Christmas food was encouraged by commercial, communication, infrastructural and economic improvements, and by government-promoted development drives in the post-Famine period. Essentially, rural Ireland embraced a more modern food system that would in time homogenise food practices. An improvement of living standards for certain groups and the circulation of commercial goods made mainstream what were luxuries in the mid-nineteenth century. These transitions towards conformity are often seen in the children's narratives returned to the NFCS. By the 1930s, turkey was the accepted and excepted celebratory meat for Christmas. A County Donegal account notes that 'At the present time every family, practically, has turkey and plum pudding—the latter is only quite recently introduced, and this is due to attendance of Domestic Classes in Technical Schools', while in County Leitrim a downward social movement of food practices may have been promoted by the plum pudding's perceived sophisticated status linked to its modern identity: 'The plum-pudding has not yet been introduced into the country districts except by the more modern families'.

The post-World War II period brought changes in farming methods owing to the application of scientific innovation, technological developments and economic policy to intensify food production and scale up supply. This had a wide impact on the choice, availability and accessibility of goods, although it can be argued that choice was a marketing construct that distracted from and shielded the increasing uniformity imposed by the spread of processed foods and their weak sense of connection to people and place. Turkey-farming was subject to considerable changes incentivised by the export market value of the birds, the import of American strains in the 1950s and the demand for white broad-breasted varieties especially amongst the American military forces stationed in the UK. The extension of the rural electrification scheme facilitated this development, making the white broad-breasted turkey the ubiquitous bird for the Christmas table. Bronze turkeys fell out of favour, while the goose was pronounced old-fashioned and oily. In more recent years, the demand for bronze turkeys and a reconsideration of the culinary merits of the goose represent the ethos of the informed consumer in connecting with the ethics and values of traditional and local food production.

SOURCES AND FURTHER READING

L.A. Clarkson and Margaret E. Crawford, *Feast and famine: food and nutrition in Ireland 1500–1920* (Oxford, 2001).

Kevin Danaher, *The year in Ireland: Irish calendar customs* (Cork and Dublin, 1972).

Revd Michael McGrath SJ (ed. and trans.), *The diary of Humphrey O'Sullivan*, parts I–IV (London, 1928–31; Dublin, 1936–7).

Regina Sexton, 'Food for humans, fairies and the dead at Hallowe'en', *History Ireland* **28** (6) (2020), 46–8.

FAST AND ABSTINENCE AT CHRISTMAS

Ultan McGoohan

Christmas is a season of feasting and to many people today the notion of fast and abstinence at Christmas is incongruous. Yet up until the mid-twentieth century fast and abstinence were an integral part of the Christmas season, regulated by Church law and also by local custom. The fast and abstinence on Christmas Eve was binding in Church law, but the custom of abstinence from meat on St Stephen's Day was rooted in popular Irish spirituality.

The *Catholic Encyclopedia* (1909) lists the fast days as follows:

> In the United States of America, all the days of Lent; the Fridays of Advent (generally); the Ember Days; the vigils of Christmas and Pentecost, as well as those (14 Aug.) of the Assumption and (31 Oct.) of All Saints, are now fasting days. In Great Britain, Ireland, Australia, and Canada, the days just indicated, together with the Wednesdays of Advent and (28 June) the vigil of Saints Peter and Paul, are fasting days.

The days of obligatory fasting, as listed in the 1917 *Code of Canon Law*, were the 40 days of Lent (including Ash Wednesday, Good Friday and Holy Saturday until noon); the Ember Days; and the vigils of Pentecost, the Assumption of the Blessed Virgin Mary, All Saints and Christmas.

Partial abstinence, the eating of meat only at the principal meal, was obligatory during all weeks of Lent (Monday–Thursday).

There is a distinction between fasting and abstinence. Under the 1917 *Code of Canon Law*, fasting meant one meal a day, but a little food might be taken in the morning and the evening. Abstinence prohibited meat, and soups made of meat, but it did not forbid eggs, milk and other condiments, even if taken from animals.

Christmas Eve was a day of both fast and abstinence that permitted only one main meal and prohibited the eating of meat. In Irish homes it was usual to delay the main meal of the day until late afternoon on Christmas Eve. The Schools' Collection, gathered by the National Folklore Commission, describes a typical Christmas Eve meal from the early twentieth century in Derryclogh Lower, Co. Cork:

> On Christmas Eve they did not eat their dinner until about six o'clock. For the dinner they only had potatoes, flour sauce, and fish which they caught in the local rivers. After this they boiled water in a pot. When it was boiled they put tea and milk into it. They then divided the tea in tin cans called mugs.

Another contribution from the Schools' Collection from Burren, Co. Cork, states:

> Christmas night is really kept on Xmas Eve here. About 30 years ago and before that Xmas Eve was a real day of fasting up to night-fall. Then at night-fall people had their dinner—potatoes and fish—ling with milk and melted butter poured over it. This seemed to end the fasting because they used have two suppers.

There is evidence that the keeping of the fast and abstinence on Christmas Eve in Ireland was respected even in the pre-Famine period. Amhlaoibh Ó Súilleabháin, a hedge-schoolmaster who lived in Callan, Co. Kilkenny, kept a diary that covered the period 1827–35. On Christmas Eve 1828 he made the following entry:

> Wednesday. Christmas Eve, a fast day … The poor people are buying pork chops, pigs' heads, soggy beef, big joints of old sows' loins, and small bits of old rams, as all the good meat had been already bought up by the well-off, well-fed people. He who comes last will be the loser as usual …

A further example of the keeping of the Christmas Eve fast can be taken from a popular Irish early twentieth-century novel written by Canon Patrick Sheehan (1852–1913), who was parish priest of Doneraile, Co. Cork. Canon Sheehan's novel *The Blindness of Dr Gray* (1909) contains an evocative scene set on Christmas Eve. The priest, Dr Gray, following an afternoon hearing confessions in preparation for Christmas, returned to the parochial house as dusk was falling, and he 'dined meagrely enough on a couple of fried eggs and a cup of coffee' because it was a fast day.

The Schools' Collection was compiled in the 1930s and, reading between the lines of the contributions, it is evident that by then a strict observance of the Christmas Eve fast was in decline. Yet Church law on the Christmas fast had not changed. The *Connacht Tribune* in 1935 published the local bishop's Lenten regulations, which included a reference to Christmas Eve as a day of fast and abstinence.

In 1941, with the outbreak of the Second World War, Pope Pius XII eased the regulation on fast and abstinence owing to the shortage of food at that time, except on Ash Wednesday and Good Friday, provided that there was abstinence from meat every Friday, and fast and abstinence on these two days and on the vigils of the Assumption and Christmas. As the war continued, a further easing of the regulations included Christmas Eve. The Irish bishops announced the easing in their respective dioceses. In December 1942 the *Drogheda Independent* reported that the archbishop of Dublin had dispensed with the Christmas Eve fast in his diocese.

In 1949 the pope restored the rules of fast and abstinence, including on Christmas Eve. In 1959 Pope John XXIII permitted the Christmas

Eve fast to be permanently moved from 24 December to 23 December, but the Irish bishops decided to keep the fast on Christmas Eve. By that stage it seems that the fast was no longer generally kept in Ireland, and the centrality of fast and abstinence in the spiritual lives of the people declined further with the changes that followed the Second Vatican Council, when fast and abstinence was reduced to two days only—Ash Wednesday and Good Friday. The traditional Friday abstinence from meat was no longer regulated by Church law; rather, the faithful were encouraged to embrace it as a spiritual exercise for its own sake rather than out of obligation.

The custom of abstinence from meat on St Stephen's Day was not a Church law, but it was a popular devotion among the Irish. Judging by the geographical spread of references to it in the Schools' Collection it was customary throughout the country, and even in the 1930s there is a sense that it was not only a historic custom but also a contemporary one. One informant from Ballinamuck, Co. Longford, recorded:

> Many of the old people and some people still keep St Stephens day as a day of abstinence. By doing so they believe that the family will be saved from all sickness and contagious diseases during the coming year.

Similar accounts come from other parts of the country and make particular reference to the belief that abstinence from meat on St Stephen's Day offered protection from fever.

An article on Irish folklore published in 1893 in the *Journal of American Folklore* included the following reference to St Stephen's Day:

> It is considered lucky to have been born on St Stephen's Day, the 26th of December, though why I do not know. Any one abstaining from eating meat on this day, in honor of our first martyr, will not catch any contagious disease during the year. We never ate any meat on this day, and consequently never were afflicted with infectious diseases.

In a time before antibiotics, even what began as a trivial illness had the possibility of becoming fatal. It is understandable that the custom of abstinence from meat on St Stephen's Day as a protection against illness proved popular, as people sought to achieve some power over the great enemy of sickness.

In my childhood a relative came to our house for dinner each St Stephen's Day because his wife abstained from meat on that day in their home. To this day a diminishing group of people keep the custom of abstinence from meat on St Stephen's Day, just as small pockets of the country retain the old custom of mummers and wren boys.

SOURCES AND FURTHER READING

National Folklore Commission, Schools' Collection (www.dúchas.ie).

Amhlaoibh Ó Súilleabháin, *Diary of an Irish countryman* (trans. Tomás De Bhaldraithe) (Cork, 1979).

Ellen Powell Thompson, 'Folklore from Ireland', *Journal of American Folklore* **6** (23) (1893), 259–68.

CHRISTMAS EVE IN THE SCHOOLS' FOLKLORE COLLECTION IN COUNTY MAYO

Yvonne McDermott

I GCUIMHNE CAITRÍONA HASTINGS

The blessed Virgin Mary had a son of a Christmas day in the morning.
She washed his face out of a silver cup of a Christmas day in the morning.
She combed his hair with an ivory comb of a Christmas day in the morning.

She dried his face with a linen towel of a Christmas day in the morning.
And sent him up to Heaven to school of a Christmas day in the morning.

(Collected by Annie Marie Dunleavy
from Mrs J.M. Dunleavy, Tavraun, Co. Mayo)

The Irish Folklore Commission was established in 1935 with the aim of collecting, cataloguing and publishing Irish oral tradition. It adopted a variety of methods of collection, from employing full-time collectors to distributing questionnaires. One of its very innovative approaches was the development of the Schools' Folklore Collection, which took place between 1937 and 1939 and involved 5,000 senior pupils in primary schools around the 26 counties of the Irish Free State becoming folklore-collectors in their localities, collecting from family members and neighbours. Roughly 740,000 pages of folklore were collected by these children over the course of the scheme. This chapter considers the material relating to Christmas that was gathered in County Mayo during this time. These contributions can be accessed on the www.dúchas.ie website, where the pupils' original handwritten contributions can be seen. A wealth of Christmas folklore was gathered, covering advance preparations, Christmas Eve and Christmas Day, in addition to the various traditions spanning the twelve days of Christmas up to *Nollaig na mBan* or 'Little Christmas'. This chapter will focus primarily on the material relating to Christmas Eve (often called Christmas Night in the manuscripts, from the Irish *Oíche Nollaig*).

Christmas was a popular topic among the informants who shared their stories with the children as part of the scheme. Much of the material concerns Christmas customs and traditions, but there are also some folk-tales, rhymes and various religious tales. The stories gathered varied from short snippets included in larger sections on themes such as calendar customs to longer, more detailed discussions of Christmas. Some

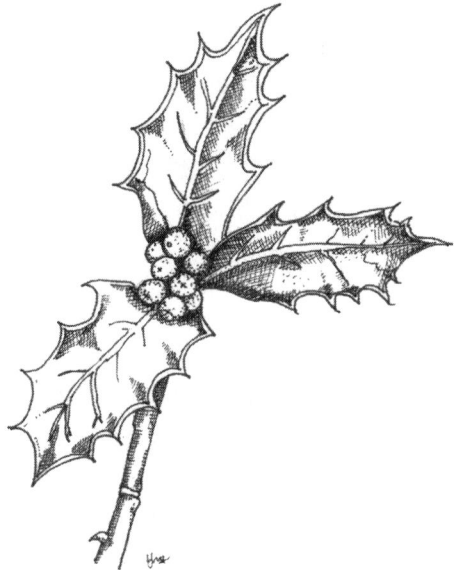

Holly was used to decorate the home at Christmas time. Image by author.

of the informants were discussing Christmas traditions and practices of their own time, while others harked back to earlier times with no specific sense of when that may have been.

The theme of welcome comes across strongly in the accounts, with clear emphasis on the idea that no one should be left out in the cold on Christmas Night. There are frequent references to candles being placed in each window of the house as a sign of welcome to passers-by; these might include homeless people who happened to be in the area or, more specifically, members of the Holy Family. The Blessed Virgin Mary is very frequently mentioned in these accounts, an indication of the extent of Marian devotion in 1930s Ireland, while the Child Jesus is also mentioned, with St Joseph appearing to a lesser extent. An account from Tooreen suggested that angels also pass by. The belief was that the Holy Family should find shelter if they came and not be turned away, as was the case in Bethlehem, according to an informant from Westport. Although the theme of welcome comes across very strongly, it was generally felt that Christmas Night was a time to be spent in one's own house and not a time to be visiting others. In the Neale, it was suggested that the Virgin Mary passes every house on that night. An informant called Ted Hastings in Derrymore stated that the door should be left half-open for the Holy Family, who come into every house seeking shelter and leave a blessing after them. Another account from Creganbane stated that no blinds should be put on the windows that evening and continued that the candle in each window should be lit by the youngest person in the house. If a stray dog came into the house that night, it would bring luck for years.

A religious story told by Mrs Thomas Munnelly of Muinrevagh tells of the Virgin Mary and St Joseph calling to a house looking for lodgings. The woman of the house agreed, although her husband thought that it was 'a queer thing to keep beggars on Christmas night'. The woman brought them to a stable, where there was an ox, an ass and some flax. After supper, the servant girl visited the stable to find it bathed in light and to see that Jesus Christ had been born. The man of the house then became ill, and the Virgin Mary gave the woman some flax to give to him and said, 'He will be alright'. The story exemplifies the importance for families of offering a welcome to those who may be in need on Christmas Night and the potential benefits for those who offer their kindness.

Household preparations are emphasised in many accounts, with cleanliness of the home being prioritised. The chimney would be cleaned so that Santa could easily pass through. The house might also be whitewashed, inside and out. Sprigs of holly and ivy would be used to decorate the kitchen and other rooms. Various goods would be bought for Christmas. An account from Tonroe suggested that 'the Christmas dainties' would include 'currants, raisins, lemon peel, jam, tea, sugar, meat, sweet cakes, fruit' and toys for the children, in addition to alcohol. An informant from Mount Pleasant recalled when tea was regarded as a great luxury, drunk on Christmas Eve and Christmas Day, with the rest being kept for any sick family members during the year. The men might make a 'round' of *poitín* (poteen) for Christmas.

At midnight, when the gates of heaven are opened, the cows and donkeys would fall to their knees and pray, as it was believed that they had the power of speech on Christmas Night, as discussed by Pádraig Ó Héalaí elsewhere in this volume. Special care would be given to the animals that night; they might be given bread or an extra heap of oats or sheaf of straw. No one should attempt to listen to the animals speak on Christmas Night. Mrs Derivan of Ballindine told of a boy who sneaked into the stable at midnight and heard a horse foretell the boy's death, which came to pass a week later.

For those whose Christmas preparation was not ideal, or who found themselves unable to provide the essentials, there was some hope in the following story. A tale of miraculous provision was recounted by Anthony Gavin of Fahburren. He told of a friar and his clerk at Kilgeever Abbey who were lacking supplies for Christmas dinner. The clerk enquired as to what they would eat, given that both were poor. The friar urged patience and was rewarded when his rich brother's Christmas table 'rose up and floated helter skelter across the fields' until it landed at the friar's house.

His brother arrived in its wake and accused the friar of orchestrating the journey, an allegation he did not deny. The friar urged his brother to sit down and be merry, and all feasted royally. The story suggests that everyone's experience of Christmas was improved by the act of sharing.

These various stories present some of the key aspects of Christmas Eve for people in County Mayo in the late 1930s and show how rich the observance of tradition was for families. It was a time of welcome and hospitality, as people learned lessons from the story of the first Christmas and the lack of accommodation for the Holy Family. It was also a time of preparation of house and food, and readiness for Santa's visit. Magic was possible at Christmas, and this influenced many aspects of the feast, as people sought to ensure good luck.

Candles would be placed in the window at Christmas time and the half-door left open as a sign of welcome to passers-by. This drawing is based on a house at Doolough in Co. Mayo. Image by author.

SOURCES AND FURTHER READING

Micheál Briody, *The Irish Folklore Commission, 1935–1970: history, ideology, methodology* (Helsinki, 2007).

Kevin Danaher, *The year in Ireland: Irish calendar customs* (Cork, 1972).

Caitríona Hastings, *Ag Bun na Cruaiche: folklore and folklife from the foot of Croagh Patrick* (Dublin, 2009).

National Folklore Collection (NFC), University College Dublin, (www.dúchas.ie).

IRISH CARMELITES'
CHRISTMAS IN THE
'MISSION FIELDS' OF
ZIMBABWE

Conor Brockbank

The Irish province of the Calced Carmelites, based in Dublin, expanded their missionary activities in November 1946 to the eastern territory of Southern Rhodesia, modern-day Zimbabwe, taking on the missionary area of what became the Diocese of Umtali in 1957, which changed to its current name of the Diocese of Mutare in 1982. This missionary area, previously run mostly by the Jesuits, covered 12,433 square miles from the most northerly mission of Avila in the Nyanga District to the most southerly mission of St Peter's near Chisumbanje, with a vast amount of this area being sparsely populated. Many Irish Carmelites have recalled their Christmases spent as missionaries in this area (around 8,100 miles away from Dublin) from the 1940s until the 1970s. They tell a story of the demands and toll of a missionary's Christmas and how the festive period was marked during periods of peace as well as conflict.

Christmas 1946 brought sharply home to the Carmelites the reality of a missionary posting. Fr Anselm Corbett wrote in his diary that this first Christmas was very lonely. Born in 1915 in Clonmel, Co. Tipperary, he was one of the first three Irish priests who were sent to establish the Carmelites' mission in Zimbabwe. These missionaries mostly spent Christmas apart, not only from their families and fellow Carmelites back in Ireland but also from each other. Fr Corbett and Westport-born Fr Luke Thomas Flynn celebrated Christmas at St Michael's Catholic Mission in Mhondoro, whereas their County Antrim confrère Fr Donal Raymond Lamont spent Christmas in Salisbury (present-day Harare) at the disposal of the bishop there. This distance alone would have reminded them of Christmases past, surrounded by their fellow Carmelites, but by 4 January 1947 Frs Corbett and Flynn had received Christmas letters from their fellow Carmelites in Dublin, which were forwarded on by Fr Lamont.

Owing to taking over the Triashill Mission in the Mutasa District from the Jesuits in mid-December 1947, their first Christmas as a community of Carmelites was one that 'crept up on us', according to Fr Corbett. By this time all the Carmelite priests, excepting Fr Eugene Andrew Wright from County Kildare, could speak the local Shona language, and their first Christmas Eve saw many crowds of people coming for Confession through the medium of this language. Fr Corbett notes in his diary entry for the day that Fr Wright and Dublin-born Brothers Bernard Joseph Clinch and Angelus James Kinsella were very lonely and quiet that day. Not being able to speak the language clearly made it harder for them to assimilate and take an active role in this first Christmas Eve and the Masses that included hymns in the local language, such as *Aimbirgwe Yawe* ('Blessed be God'). Furthermore, Christmas dinner that year 'bore little resemblance' to what they were used to, but Fr Corbett adds that they all accepted it as part of being a missionary.

The quality and size of Christmas meals enjoyed by Irish Carmelites working in Zimbabwe over the years varied enormously. A County Carlow Carmelite, Fr Michael Patrick Hipwell, reminisced in the Irish Carmelite magazine *The Scapular* in 1965 about one Christmas Eve in the mid-1960s at the St Charles Lwanga Mission in Chimanimani. He recalled spending it with Frs Corbett and Lamont around a log fire whilst sharing in a local family's supper before their two youngest daughters made their First Holy Communion. This meal consisted of *sadza*, a traditional Zimbabwean cooked maize meal, which was served with a goat meat stew. Meanwhile, Fr Mel Patrick Hill never forgot his first Christmas on supply at the Mount Melleray Mission in Nyanga in the early 1950s, as his dinner was just two fried eggs.

For some Irish Carmelites, however, the demands of missionary life, or the unexpected eruption of conflict, left them with no Christmas dinner at all! This was the case, for different reasons, for Frs Anthony Desmond Clarke and Michael Hender. Having celebrated both midnight and morning Masses at the Avila Mission one Christmas in the mid-1950s, Fr Clarke jumped into his jeep to answer a sick call in a remote part of the Mission. Owing to the state of the tracks, a series of punctures to his jeep (which he fixed during a downpour) and the rivers swelling, he didn't make it back in time for Christmas dinner, and when he did arrive home he went straight to bed after a long day. Similarly, on Christmas Day in 1977 Fr Hender also got back late and went straight to bed, having missed Christmas dinner, after his truck was hijacked by freedom fighters who were trying to evade army soldiers during the Rhodesian Bush War, a civil conflict fought between 1964 and 1979 against the white minority rule of Ian Smith's government.

The accounts of Irish Carmelites on mission in the region routinely note how Christmases often did not go according to plan for all sorts of reasons, including lightning hitting a grass-roofed classroom in the St Therese Mission in Chiduku at midnight on Christmas Day in 1956, causing a fire that consumed church records, tools and many personal items belonging to the missionaries. Fr Clarke recalls how the Avila Mission became a place of refuge in the middle of the night for the victims of a knife attack which had occurred in a nearby village during Christmas 1958, with the Carmelites bringing one of the victims some 60 miles to the nearest doctor. Nearly twenty years later, on Christmas Day 1977, Fr Hender and his parishioners were unable to mark Christmas in their usual way at St Columba's Mission in the Honde Valley after a grenade attack on an army truck near Makunike. The stark reality of war resulted in the road being blocked and the army retaliating, thus making it impossible to celebrate Mass that Christmas.

While Christmas on mission in Southern Rhodesia may have begun as a comparatively quiet affair for Irish Carmelites in 1946, this would not be the case for many of their subsequent Christmases, the only predictable feature of which was their unpredictability.

SOURCES AND FURTHER READING

A. Corbett, *Notes from a diary. Selected prose and poetry* (Dublin, 2003).

M. Hender (ed.), *Celts among the Shona: early experiences of Carmelite missionaries to Zimbabwe* (Dublin, 2002).

M. Hender, *Our 1970s in Zimbabwe* (Dublin, 2011).

J. McGrath (ed.), *Mvambo (The Beginnings). Celebrating 70 Years of Carmelite presence in Zimbabwe* (Naas, 2016).

THE THREE CHRISTMASES
OF C.S. LEWIS

Catherine Barry

I n 1949 the Belfast-born C.S. Lewis wrote to a friend, Vera Matthews: 'I couldn't agree with you more about the commercial rush of "Xmas" as distinct both from the Christian festival of Christmas and the old Germanic feast of Yule'. His dislike of 'Xmas' was a recurring theme of Lewis's letters and had been all his life. Aged fifteen, he wrote to his father: 'I suppose the aggravation of the social nuisance, which always accompanies Xmas has now died down'.

Nevertheless, this does not mean that Lewis disliked Christmas itself. It's telling that, when the boy writing from an English boarding-school turns to talk of home, even in May he thinks of Christmas. Writing *The Lion, the Witch and the Wardrobe* as an adult, Lewis would have chosen spring as a light of hope rather than Christmas if he disliked the latter. Instead, Tumnus the Faun, emphasising how complete is the eternal winter in which Narnia is trapped, tells Lucy that it is 'always winter and never Christmas, think of that!' 'How awful!', Lucy replies, without sarcasm.

In the 1950s, Lewis's decades of complaint about Xmas were distilled into two articles. The first is a satire about the strange winter customs in Niatirb ('Britain' backwards). These include the exchanging of pieces of cardboard or of gifts. Sending one obliges the receiver to send one in return, and gifts must be of a similar value to that received. This leads to the exchange of ridiculous objects made solely to be gifts, sold in market-places presided over by old, poor men dressed in red and wearing false beards. Over the weeks, 'the sellers of gifts no less than the purchasers become pale and weary, because of the crowds and the fogs'. When the main day of celebration comes, all are too exhausted to celebrate, retreating into excessive consumption of food and drink.

The second was a systematic outline of Lewis's objections to Xmas. He identifies three things called Christmas: the religious feast (of interest to Christians but not to anyone else); the popular secular holiday, 'an occasion for merry-making and hospitality' (Lewis adds, 'I much approve of merry-making'); and Xmas (the commercial racket).

Xmas is an adaptation of the customs of secular Christmas for commercial gain. The problem, says Lewis, is not that it is new but rather its effects. The first is that widespread gift-giving and card-sending is exhausting. It is mentally exhausting in that one must think of to whom to send gifts and cards (and what specifically to send) and physically exhausting in that one must go to crowded shops to buy what is required.

Worse, this is often done not for the sake of friends and family but out of obligation. 'The modern rule,' says Lewis, 'is that anyone can force you to give him a present by sending you a quite unprovoked present of his own.' Perversely, the receiving of a gift then causes not pleasure but pain and despair, as 'back to the dreadful shops one of us has to go'. This leads to the third effect: the creation of items whose only function is to be a gift. 'Have we really no better use for materials and for human skill and time?', asks Lewis.

The final effect is that these additional tasks and associated crowds complicate routine living, shopping and work (Lewis wrote often on how Christmas disrupted his work; his brief note to Fr Peter Milward on Christmas Eve 1960 is a good example). Lewis concludes that it is 'merely one annual symptom of that lunatic condition of our country … in which everyone lives by persuading everyone else to buy things. I don't know the way out.' Xmas means that the annual holiday brings more pain than pleasure.

What *should* Christmas be like? To find out, we return to Narnia. *The Chronicles of Narnia* is not an allegory. It is a work of speculative theological fantasy. In the overall story, Narnia is connected to 'our' world not only by the wardrobe but also through its first rulers, who presumably brought the secular Christmas holiday with them.

Lewis also tells us that things that don't exist in 'our' world but that we depict or talk about are real in Narnia. 'Our' world is further from ultimate reality than Narnia, I would argue, just as in Plato's *Allegory of the Cave* those who can see only the shadows of models cast by a fire against the cave wall are further from knowing what the outside world is like than those who see the models themselves. The Father Christmas whom Lucy and her siblings meet is so much more than the greeting-card figure, 'so big, and so glad, and so real' that they become solemn as well as joyful. Where better to find an ideal Christmas?

Christmas arrives in Narnia as suddenly as the sound of sleigh-bells on the wind. Gifts are given, but only to the children and to those who have left everything behind to help them. The gifts are not useless (Father Christmas calls them tools); they are described as beautiful, and there is no obligation to give a gift in return. Two meals are associated with the visit of Father Christmas. One is ham sandwiches with hot tea, the other a classic Christmas feast with plum pudding, but both are alike in bringing together family and friends.

Lewis's core problem with Xmas is clear. Xmas is parasitic on Christmas as mistletoe is on a tree, and it has become so large that it is killing its host. The essence of Christmas, merriment and hospitality, is undermined by the exhaustion and irritation at other people caused by Xmas.

The rush is mitigated today, but in ways of which Lewis would not have approved: by lengthening shopping hours and by how long the Christmas shopping season lasts. We have added further pressures: must-attend events and must-have items for the 'perfect Christmas'. As Plato would point out, perfection is not available in our world and, as Lewis might have added, it is exhausting to try to achieve it.

Now, as in the 1950s, there seems no obvious way out. Perhaps the best we can do is to try to protect our Christmas with a two-pronged test based on Lewis's insight (Lewis's Christmas Fork). Of what we do at Christmas, we ask: does it spark joy in ourselves or others? Does it support the exercise of hospitality? If not, why should we do it?

SOURCES AND FURTHER READING

H.D. Fisher, 'C.S. Lewis, Platonism, and Aslan's Country: symbols of heaven in the Chronicles of Narnia', in *Inklings Forever: Published Colloquium Proceedings 1997–2016*, vol. 7 (2010).

C.S. Lewis, *The Lion, the Witch and the Wardrobe* (various editions).

C.S. Lewis, 'Christmas and Xmas: a lost chapter from Herodotus' [1954], in C.S. Lewis and W. Hooper, *God in the dock: essays on theology* (Grand Rapids, 1970).

C.S. Lewis, 'What Christmas means to me' [1957], in C.S. Lewis and W. Hooper, *God in the dock: essays on theology* (Grand Rapids, 1970).

C.S. Lewis and W. Hooper, *Collected letters. Vol. 1: Family letters, 1905–1931* (London, 2000).

C.S. Lewis and W. Hooper, *Collected letters. Vol. 2: Books, broadcasts and war, 1931–1949* (London, 2004).

C.S. Lewis and W. Hooper, *Collected letters. Vol. 3: Narnia, Cambridge and Joy 1950–1963* (London, 2006).

'I'M FROM BELFAST': CHRISTMAS MEMORIES TOLD BY MAGGI KERR PEIRCE IN THE USA

E. Moore Quinn

I t's many an Irish woman or man who can recall cherished memories of childhood, like being hoisted to bed on the shoulders of a father singing

> I am the Wee Falorie Man,
> A rattlin', rovin' Irish man,
> I can do whatever you can
> For I am the Wee Falorie man

or listening to dandling rhymes like

> Round and round the garden
> Like a teddy bear,
> One step, two step
> And tickle you under there.

As well we know, though, once we become grown-ups such memories are shared only when occasions warrant—or, alas, sometimes not at all.

Fortunately, that is not the case for Maggi Kerr Peirce. Although she was raised in a 1930s Irish family who possessed few material comforts, she heard—and learned—an abundance of oral traditional lore, including many variants of 'The Wee Falorie Man' and 'Round and round the garden'. Rather than relegate them to the dustbin of amnesia, Maggi reveals:

> … they are as clear to me today as if, just this morning, I was running down the broad sweep of Irwin Avenue, scab-encrusted knees, short, bobbed hair from which a tartan ribbon is slipping, skipping madly towards school and mouthing 'wee rhymes' as I went.

Over time, and after having improved her mastery of the spoken word, Maggi married and moved to the USA. There she began to capture audiences with a powerful opening confession:

> I'm from Belfast.

Told with the sheer weight of pride of place, that one-liner took her far from what she calls 'the singing streets of Northern Ireland's capital city'. Eventually she was telling stories at the Newport (Rhode Island) Folk Festival, the Philadelphia (Pennsylvania) Folk Festival and even the national Smithsonian Festival in Washington, DC.

Childhood memories formed a large core of her repertoire, as she regaled audiences with reminiscences about secret places, culprits and 'frenemies'. Arguably, however, it is her collection of Christmas holiday material that wins the day. In *Christmas mince* she hits her stride, serving up a hodgepodge of festive stories, songs, games, plays and recitations. She even offers prickly advice for preserving maids-of-honour, current squares and German biscuits at Christmastime: 'Ye must keep the air out [of the tins] so as to keep the freshness in'. And when making 'Thin Scottish Shortbread', Maggi demands: 'One stick of butter (not margarine please!)'.

Despite such bossiness, *Christmas mince*'s pages contain 'the sweetness of raisins and sultanas … the bite and tang of lemon peel, and the spiciness of ginger and nutmeg'. These are all on full display in Maggi's tale 'The Good Midwife of East Belfast':

> The two shawlies stood in the glow of the fire, their timeworn faces crinkled with love as they bent over the wee one. 'Is it a wee girl or a wee fella?' they asked. 'A girl,' said the midwife, 'and now you must be going so that the Mother here can get her rest.' The two neighbors departed, murmuring promises of future help. 'Remember, dearie, weans can get thrawn at times, and we're right next door till ye.'
>
> The midwife bundled up her belongings, and just as she was ready to leave, Jo slipped a crown into her hand. 'I've been saving it for these last months,' he whispered. 'I felt it in my bones I'd get a woman who would do a good job by my Marie, thank ye kindly.'

The distinctive flavour of East Belfast can also be witnessed in 'Christmas, 1939 (a reminiscence of an Ulster childhood)'. Maggi writes:

> As far back as I can remember when I was a child in Northern Ireland, come Hell or high water, my mother, short of money the rest of the year, always managed to collect enough to take my sister Dorothy and me to visit Father Christmas (as we call Santa Claus in Ireland) to Robb's, one of the best Family Stores in the centre of Belfast City.

Readers accompany Maggi and her siblings as they enter 'the Good Ship Faeryland', which, owing to the public's preoccupation with war that year, had been transformed into a submarine. They eavesdrop on doled-out admonitions like 'Childer dear, you'll cowp over and break your necks, stop leppin' like spring lambs'. And they travel vicariously 'on the swaying tram' on the way home:

… with our noses pressed against the windows, watching all the shops flashing by, hung with turkeys, hens and holly wreaths for Christmas, the latter not for our doors, but for the graves of parents long since departed. People would swing onto the tram and chuck us under the chin and ask with beer-laden breaths, 'An' who's the lucky wee lassie who's been to see Father Christmas the day?'

Dorothy and I would smile shyly and clutch our parcels all the closer to our undeveloped buttoned bosoms. When finally Aunt Aileen's tram-stop hove in sight how happy we were, and off we children tumbled like bumbling puppies, hurtling ourselves over the road—which in those days of horse and cart traffic and only an occasional bouncy car, was as safe as houses.

Stories like these are replicated in Maggi's audio recordings and subsequent publications. 'Christmas 1939', for instance, is reproduced in *A Belfast girl*; so too are 'A Child's Christmas in Ulster', 'Change of Seasons' and 'Two Gifts'.

Although bearing similarities to other stories, 'Lest We Forget' redounds with magic, affection, thoughtfulness and caring even as it reminds readers of the real-life realities of Belfast. As Maggie tells it, when in 1941 a good-looking cousin who happened to be 'a petty officer in his Majesty's Royal Navy' came home for the Christmas holidays, he increased the aura of anticipation by inviting Maggi and a friend on a shopping spree. Despite maternal warnings that he was but a poorly paid enlisted man, the girls dreamed that 'perhaps he'd buy us something'.

Upon reaching the toy department, the young sailor offered to do just that, and as the youngsters ogled dolls and doll's houses they half-believed that dreams could 'come true'. Mammy's words, though, continued to screech 'nothing expensive', causing Maggi to choose 'a box of terrible gimcrack furniture in brittle poor wood'. It was then that her sailor cousin insisted that she 'must take' a doll priced at 'nine shillings and sixpence'.

'No, no,' she cried. But then, 'when I looked up into Norman's eyes and then back at the box in his hand, my eyes filled with happy tears, and I nodded speechlessly'.

Clearly, 'Lest We Forget', like the intimate songs and rhymes uttered on the shoulders of fathers and in the laps of mothers, has the power to renew Christmas memories year after year. Yet when it comes to this most heartfelt of stories there's something more, for, within months of resuming his seafaring duties, Maggi's generous cousin had been 'reported "missing in action, presumed killed" in one of the great North Atlantic battles'.

Maggi admits that she 'never really knew' that 24-year-old who had enriched her holiday that year. Not willing to discount the potency of that experience, however, she expresses a profound understanding of what she believes it meant to him—and to her:

> … something told him that day that he wanted to buy the best for two little girls who had never received 'the best' before. We, who had been brought up making do with what was offered to us, had our first taste of walking into the finest toy department in the city and choosing exactly what we longed for. It was a heady, wonderful feeling, and I still remember it clearly, and with deep, lasting thanks.

Maggi Kerr Peirce's songs, stories, games and rhymes can be visited at any time of year, but they are sure to add warmth at Christmas, especially if enjoyed with German biscuits, current squares, maids-of-honour or thin Scottish shortbread (all properly tinned, of course!).

SOURCES AND FURTHER READING

Maggi Kerr Peirce, *Keep the kettle boiling* (Fairhaven, Massachusetts, 1979).

Maggi Peirce, *An Ulster Christmas* [cassette recording] (Cambridge, Massachusetts, 1986).

Maggi Kerr Peirce, *Christmas mince* (Fairhaven, Massachusetts, 1983).

Maggi Kerr Peirce, *A Belfast girl* (Marion, Michigan, 2013).

EPIPHANY CANDLES, CUSTOMS AND STORMS: *OÍCHE NOLLAIG NA MBAN* BY SEÁN Ó RÍORDÁIN (1916–77)

Ríona Ní Churtáin

OÍCHE NOLLAIG NA MBAN

Bhí fuinneamh sa stoirm a éalaigh aréir,
Aréir oíche Nollaig na mBan,
As gealt-teach iargúlta tá laistiar den ré
Is do scréach tríd an spéir chugainn 'na gealt,
Gur ghíosc geataí comharsan mar ghogallach gé,
Gur bhúir abhainn shlaghdánach mar tharbh,
Gur múchadh mo choinneal mar bhuille ar mo bhéal
A las 'na splanc obann an fhearg.

Ba mhaith liom go dtiocfadh an stoirm sin féin
An oíche go mbeadsa go lag
Ag filleadh abhaile ó rince an tsaoil
Is solas an pheaca ag dul as,

Go líonfaí gach neomat le liúrigh ón spéir,
    Go ndéanfaí den domhan scuaine scread,
Is ná cloisfinn an ciúnas ag gluaiseacht fám dhéin,
    Ná inneall an ghluaisteáin ag stad.

Women's Christmas Night
(translation by Seán Ó Coileáin)

The storm that blew with such fury last night,
    Women's Christmas Night,
Escaped from some remote madhouse behind the moon
    And came screaming as a lunatic through the sky.
Neighbours' gates grated like the gaggling of geese,
    The throaty river roared like a bull;
My candle was quenched like a blow on the mouth
    That ignited a sudden spark of anger.

I would wish that same storm to return
    On the night when I am feeble,
Returning home from the dance of life
    As the light of sin is fading,
So that every moment be filled by shouting from on high,
    That the whole world become one uproarious din,
And that I would not hear the silence approach
    Or the engine of the car cutting out.

Since its composition in 1947, Seán Ó Ríordáin's poem *Oíche Nollaig na mBan* has been a source of fascination to scholars and artists alike. The poem vividly captures the ferocity of a storm on the eve of the Epiphany, as experienced from the isolation of the poet's sick-room. Afflicted with tuberculosis, Ó Ríordáin expressed a desire that a similar storm should rage during his final moments and assuage his fears as death approached.

The powerful imagery in the poem has inspired artistic works such as the short film *Oíche Nollaig na mBan* (2016), directed and produced by Oonagh Kearney, and *Fuinneamh* (2011), a choral work composed by Marian Ingoldsby. The poem has also been analysed in several academic texts, in particular for its potential insights into Seán Ó Ríordáin's views on death and the afterlife. Readers exploring Ireland's Christmas traditions, however, may find the imagery used in the first verse to be of particular interest, as several of the verse's images are reminiscent of aspects of Ireland's Epiphany traditions and history.

A series of similes in the poem's first verse effectively convey the fierce intensity of the storm. Although it's not unusual to experience stormy weather in early January in Ireland, history reveals that at least two exceptional storms have occurred on the night of the Epiphany. The Annals of the Four Masters describe how in 1478 'a great tempest arose on the night of Epiphany, which was a night of general destruction to all, by reason of the number of persons and cattle destroyed, and trees and houses, both on water and land, prostrated throughout Ireland'.

Another famous storm occurred on the same night over 360 years later in 1839, a night subsequently referred to as *Oíche na Gaoithe Móire*, or the 'Night of the Big Wind'. Winds that night developed to hurricane force, wreaking mass structural damage throughout the country and causing many injuries and fatalities. A week after the storm, the *Dublin Evening Post* of 12 January 1839 reported:

> Ireland has been the chief victim of the hurricane—*every part of Ireland—every* field, *every* town, *every* village in Ireland have felt its dire effects, from Galway to Dublin—from the Giant's Causeway to Valencia. It has been, we repeat, the most awful calamity with which a people were afflicted.

Such was the storm's intensity that some people felt that the end of the world was nigh. When the Old Age Pensions Act was implemented on 1 January 1909, many elderly people without appropriate documentation were able to prove their age to local committees by recounting their memories of the night. A poem by Michael Burke of Esker, Co. Galway, reputedly composed on the day after the storm, was published in *An Gaodhal* in 1884 and again in 1895. It survived in folk tradition, and the following version was collected from Peadar Ó Riallaigh in Elly, Co. Mayo, in the 1930s as part of the Schools' Collection. Some of its lines evoke similar sights and sounds to those of Ó Ríordáin's poem, describing the world as 'bellowing', the moon as 'destructive' and the sea as being comparable to a lunatic:

An domhan uilig ag géimneach
'Gus an mhuir le gealt ag léimneach
Ainmhidhthe dúil is éanlaith
Faoi eagla agus faoi uathbhás.

[…] Chaill an ghrian a soillse
An ghealach fuilteach millteach
An spéar ag caitheamh réalta ina
mílte céadta anuas

The entire world bellowing,
And the sea leaping like a lunatic,
Animals, creatures and birds
Fearful and terror-stricken.

[…] The sun lost its light,
The bloody, destructive moon,
The sky throwing down
hundreds of thousands of stars

Ó Ríordáin's candle imagery captures yet another aspect of the Irish Epiphany, as quenched candles were frequently associated with death divination in Irish tradition. In the Schools' Collection of the Irish Folklore Commission, a collection of folklore and local tradition compiled by pupils from 5,000 primary schools in the Irish Free State between 1937 and 1939, there are numerous accounts of candle-burning customs for Twelfth Night. According to these traditions, twelve candles were lit on this night. In some accounts this practice was accompanied by a rosary in honour of the twelve Apostles. These candles were traditionally made from dried rushes and dipped in tallow or oil. They were then placed in a cake made from clay or from cow manure mixed with ashes. Each member of the family chose a candle, and the person whose candle quenched first would be the first to die.

The poem's very title reminds us of another Epiphany custom in some areas of Ireland, that of Women's Christmas. This tradition, whereby men made a special effort to be kind to their wives on the Epiphany in gratitude for their work on Christmas Day, seems to have been particularly strong in County Cork. In the Schools' Collection, one account provides another possible reason for the feast's name:

> It is thought if a person remained up till midnight on that night he would see water turned into wine. It is believed it occurs in memory of the time Our Lord changed water into wine at the wedding feast of Cana at the request of His Blessed Mother. Probably that is why it is known here as the Women's Christmas.
>
> (Collected by Jeremiah Mahony, Crookhaven, Co. Cork)

The belief that water would change into wine on the night appears to have been a popular one, with numerous accounts thereof included in the Schools' Collection. Observing such a spectacle was considered to be bad luck, with some stories recounting the deaths or disappearances of those who attempted to do so.

Seán Ó Ríordáin's poem captures the unsettling experience not only of witnessing a ferocious storm but also of realising one's own vulnerabilities and mortality. Its evocation of Irish epiphanic history and customs situates these experiences amongst those of our ancestors, thereby emphasising the universality of such emotions. It is little wonder that its powerful imagery has inspired both academics and artists, and will likely continue to do so.

SOURCES AND FURTHER READING

S. Ó Coileáin (2017), 'A Poem on Women's Christmas' (https://www.ucc.ie/en/news/archive/2017/a-poem-on-womens-christmas.html).

L. Shields and D. Fitzgerald, 'The "Night of the Big Wind" in Ireland, 6–7 January 1839', *Irish Geography* **22** (1) (1989) (https://www.met.ie/cms/assets/uploads/2017/08/Jan1839_Storm.pdf)

The Schools' Collection of the Irish Folklore Commission (1937–1939) (https://www.dúchas.ie/en/cbes).

CHRISTMAS IN FAUGHARY, CO. LEITRIM, 1944–60

Francis Kelly

My mother (Mae Kelly, née Fox) is the eldest of five sib-lings raised in Faughary, Co. Leitrim. Faughary is a large townland that spans a mountainside a few miles north of Manorhamilton, between Saddle Hill and Dough Mountain. Its two extremities are differentiated as upper and lower Faughary. During the period described here, the Fox clan lived in a two-roomed thatched cot-tage, one of eight families in upper Faughary. Today the townland has no residents. This essay has been compiled from conversations I recorded with my mother and two of her siblings (Anne and Patsy) about their Christmas experiences.

CHRISTMAS PREPARATIONS

One custom on the mountain that had died away by 1960 was the Christmas raffle. As Mae and Anne explain:

> **Mae:** 'Raffles were a big thing in the locality in the run-up to Christmas. I remember a few being held in our house. People came in to play cards (Twenty-five), with a turkey as the prize for the winner (supplied by

the host family). There wouldn't be a big crowd, maybe seven or so at most (only men), and Daddy would make it up to eight players. Every year a number of houses in the townland held raffles as well as ours: the Connollys, the "Jimmy Cormacks" and the Monaghans. They were a big thing for the woman of the house because there was a fair bit of preparation with bread and jam and cakes to be baked for it.'

Anne: 'Raffles were held during December until about the twentieth. Each person who came to the raffle would pay some money at the start and that money would usually go to the woman of the house. The raffles provided some nice entertainment. A person got a turkey very cheap, while the host got a bit of extra cash in the run-up to Christmas.'

Another source of cash for the household at this time of year was through the sale of home-reared turkeys. Mae's mother usually reared ten to twelve turkeys each year for sale in the run-up to Christmas. There was a fair day in Manorhamilton on 12 December, followed by two turkey markets held on the last two Thursdays before Christmas. Anne describes how the turkeys were sold: 'Daddy brought the turkeys into town on the ass and cart but it was Mammy who did the selling. They were put in a wee pen on Main Street, opposite the market house (in the centre of Manorhamilton). It was a big thing to get in early and get them sold early because the poor turkeys became stressed.' Money received for the turkeys was spent on the Christmas shopping. Whatever presents were got for the children came out of the 'turkey money'. Extra flour (for the Christmas baking) and meal (for livestock) was also bought, which had to last until mid-January, the next shopping trip into town.

CHRISTMAS PRESENTS

Mae: 'I can remember the Christmas of 1950 in upper Faughary. I know that Patsy and I got little toys. He got these wee lead soldiers and I think we also got some pencils. I remember the Christmas stockings being hung up—our own knee-high stockings. All I remember being in them on Christmas morning was a few raisins and currants and a few small things like that. And there were also these little rolls of sweets. Later on we used to call them "a penny-ha'penny roll of sweets"—little pale brown sweets; sure we thought they were great. These were the Santa presents. As a child I don't ever remember getting any other presents.'

CHRISTMAS FARE

A special Christmas Eve tea was customary in Faughary but not necessarily the norm elsewhere. Anne explains that 'the Christmas Eve tea was a big thing in the countryside outside of Manorhamilton, but within in the town Christmas Eve was just an ordinary day'.

Christmas cake and mince pies were not part of the Christmas fare in Faughary: 'Mammy made cakes at Christmas, but we wouldn't have had the Christmas cake we know of now until later years (after a range was installed) because it was very difficult for her to bake that kind of heavy fruit cake on the open hearth. What Mammy made was a slightly richer version of a treacle cake with a small quantity of mixed fruit added.' According to Anne, it was Mae who first brought an iced Christmas cake into the house: 'The first real Christmas cake that came into the house was made by Mae in the Technical School [Manorhamilton, *c.* 1959]. I didn't know anything about a richer fruit cake until she brought this iced cake home.'

Marble cake, however, was a big novelty. Anne remembers the first time her mother made it: 'Mammy had found a recipe in a magazine to make a cake with three different colours. I remember her making it at about one or two o'clock in the morning (the night before Christmas Eve). I was in the settle bed (in the kitchen) watching her as she added treacle to make the brown part of it, stirring this mix in a mug. Cochineal was got for the red colouring and we were absolutely fascinated by this. We thought it was a miraculous cake.'

Similarly, the first box of chocolates to come into the house was a source of great delight. To Mae it was a marvel: 'For us to receive a present like that from a neighbour at that time was unprecedented. Maybe my memory has exaggerated it, but it seemed such a big box. It was given to us by one of the Connolly girls who had gone to England and was working in the Cadburys factory in Slough. It was a long single tray of chocolates, and the box was beautifully decorated with flowers. We'd only get one chocolate at a time, and they might not be taken down again for another five days or so. Mammy used to keep the box on the top of the delph cabinet, and sometimes when she and Daddy were out we'd take the box down and just look at all these lovely chocolates. We never took any of them out; we'd just look at them because it was only Mammy who could give them to us.'

BELIEFS

Most of the old beliefs have since been forgotten, but Mae and Anne recall some that prevailed in Faughary. According to Anne, 'there was a tradition of leaving the house door unlocked on Christmas Eve, and a belief that at midnight the cows in the byre would go down on one knee'. Mae recalled how 'a red Christmas candle was got each year that was lit for the Christmas Eve supper and the dinner on Christmas Day. It was left in the window on Christmas Eve night into Christmas morning in case the Lord would still be looking for a place to put his head.'

THE MUMMERS

The mummers were a feature of the Christmas festivities in the area until the late '50s (see Linda May Ballard's article in this volume). Mae and her brother Patsy remember them calling in to the house on a couple of occasions. Patsy recalls: 'They'd be dressed up in bits of costume and wore straw hats or some sort of a disguise. But sure we'd know them from their voice or the way they walked. There'd be a couple of musicians and a bit of a dance before they'd head off again.' There were different groups in the locality. A couple of neighbours from Faughary went out with the Brackary mummers, and there was another troop further down the road in Ballaghameehan with whom there was a keen rivalry. Patsy recalled, however, that if the mummers visited before St Stephen's Day they wouldn't be let in: 'Our father wouldn't let them in because he believed it was bad luck'.

Mae remembers going to the mummers' dance in 1959: 'In those days a girl couldn't go unless she was invited. We must have given them money when they called to us and that's how I came to be invited. It was our neighbour, "big" Joe Connolly, who invited me.' Mae was fifteen at the time: 'Dad wasn't happy about me going, so Patsy was sent along with me'.

Patsy, however, explains that there was another reason for their father's reluctance: 'My father was concerned about us going because of the shenanigans that had happened the year before'. The dance was to be held in Bradley's of Brackary, a few fields away from the house. This was where it had been held the previous year: 'Whatever went on during the dance that night, by the end of it the gable at one end of the house had collapsed'.

Nothing so dramatic occurred the year that Mae and Patsy went. Instead, it was the number of people in attendance that stands out in Mae's memory: 'The year we went there was a load of people at the house. However many were inside, there were far more people outside. It was the biggest gathering I'd ever seen at a house. There was music in one room and food in the other: tea and cuts of bread and jam and the like. Mind you, we didn't stay too late because Daddy had warned us to be back home at a reasonable hour.'

SOURCES

Interviews with participants.

LIGHT IN THE DEPTH OF WINTER: FOLKLORE AND MEMORIES FROM COUNTY CLARE

Michelle Dunne

A local saying in north-west County Clare, recorded by part-time folklore collector for the Irish Folklore Commission (1935–70) Seán Mac Mathúna (1876–1949), described the period between Christmas and St Bridget's Day as the worst part of winter. It is unsurprising, then, that the inhabitants of Luogh North, located near the Cliffs of Moher, eagerly awaited Christmas. This article explores the Christmas customs in this area from the late nineteenth to the mid-twentieth century and Mac Mathúna's memories as described in his diaries and the folklore he collected. His writings in his native Irish-language dialect depict the camaraderie and excitement of the season while highlighting the role that women played in the preparations and festivities. This is unusual, perhaps, because Mac Mathúna never married.

Preparations for Christmas began in earnest around 12 November, when the pig kept by the family was slaughtered and its meat preserved by salting. Women's share of the work involved making puddings using the pig's blood, which they then shared with their neighbours. It was a communal activity, as neighbouring women helped the farmer's wife even if she had a daughter of her own to help her. The other ingredients included flax meal, rice or white bread, salt, pepper, lard, spices and milk or water.

From 1 December families began 'bringing home the Christmas', i.e. buying the necessary Christmas goods like tea, sugar, the Christmas candle(s) and the raisins that women would add to the Christmas cake mixture along with treacle and porter. Mac Mathúna stole some of the raisins set aside for Christmas in his youth and believed that they tasted sweeter because he ate them unobserved.

The house, farmyard and chimney were cleaned in preparation for Christmas each year. Mac Mathúna described the local women bustling around cleaning the houses and tidying everything inside them. While the women he knew in the 1930s and 1940s used shop-bought brushes, the previous generations used home-made brushes made from local heather to wash and sweep the floors.

Mac Mathúna highly praised women's generosity, as they provided food, such as a spare goose, to families who had very little. As milk and butter were scarce at that time of year, a day or two before Christmas women would churn and give the buttermilk, butter, milk and cream to their neighbours who had none.

After Hallowe'en, everyone counted the days until Christmas. When December arrived, the children's constant refrain was, 'Where is Christmas now?', as they believed that Christmas came to Luogh day by day from abroad. Their parents would gently tell them, 'Oh, it's at Ballyvaughan', and then, as Christmas Day grew closer, 'It's now at the Spa' (i.e. Lisdoonvarna), and finally 'It's at the crossroads' (i.e. a mile away). In the only reference to Santa Claus in this collection, Mac Mathúna suggests that children were wary of trusting in Santa's existence when adults tried to instil the idea in their heads.

Christmas Eve truly was a light in the darkness of midwinter. On that day Mac Mathúna's nieces decorated the windows with candles, coloured paper and plants like ivy. Three candles were lit by the head of the household in the kitchen window in honour of the Holy Family, and one in each of the other windows in memory of deceased relatives or those who had emigrated. Doors were left unbolted to show the Holy Family that they were welcome, as they had been unable to find accommodation on the first Christmas. Mac Mathúna referred to the red Christmas candle as the Red Star, which may illustrate an association with the star that appeared in the sky on the first Christmas. A large turf fire was lit in the kitchen of each home in Luogh, illuminating and warming the people gathered around it. The family prayed the Rosary before (or after) the evening meal, which consisted of tea, cake, butter, jam, jelly and rice. Midnight Mass was not a custom in the area at that time.

Mac Mathúna's writings do not provide much detail regarding Christmas Day or St Stephen's Day. He mentioned that he attended the first Mass at 8.30am and again at 11am. Letters from relatives who had emigrated would be read on Christmas Day. St Stephen's Day was also spent with family and friends. Mac Mathúna looked forward to the visit from the mummers, a group of boys and men dressed in disguise who played music, sang songs and danced in each house they visited in exchange for money and beverages. Women did not cook meat on this day and used the Christmas Day leftovers for the main meal. Older generations did not eat meat on St Stephen's Day, hoping that the saint would protect them from illness during the year.

The 28th or 29th of December was known as the cross (i.e. unlucky) day of the year. It was believed that any new work or other endeavour should not be started on this day; for instance, people should not get married or buy land. If it fell on a Monday, for example, people believed that these activities should be avoided on every Monday during the year. It was also unlucky for a woman to visit any house on that day.

Young children visited their neighbours and were given a buttered slice of bread to eat in each house on 1 January or *Lá na gCeapairí* (Sandwiches' Day), as it was locally known. Mac Mathúna observed this custom in his own childhood and described how at the age of ten or twelve he left his neighbour's house tipsy because the woman of the house also gave him and his friends a drink of whiskey. No woman should be the first to enter a house on this day for fear of ill luck befalling the household during the year. Each household would ask a certain man to visit their house in the hope that he would bring them luck for the year. If the family had a good year, they would ask the same man who visited them on 1 January to do so again in subsequent years.

The 5th of January was known as Little Christmas Eve or the Night of the Three Kings, referring to the Three Wise Men who visited the infant Jesus. A fireside game with similarities to the cake baked on Hallowe'en and its fortune-telling contents, such as a ring, thimble and coin, was the cake baked by the farmer's wife on Little Christmas Eve. She would add a ring (her own wedding ring, an iron ring or one made from straw or rushes) to the dough. She divided the cake between her family members in the evening and whoever found the ring in their portion would marry by that time next year.

Older people said that 6 January was the first day of Shrovetide, and parents began arranging marriages for their eligible sons and daughters at the fair in Liscannor which was held on that day. This practice had died out by the 1930s. The day was known as Women's Christmas in other areas in Ireland, as women did not do any housework and met each other socially on this day. Perhaps it was not a custom in Luogh North, as it is not described in the collection.

Mac Mathúna's collection illustrates how Christmas was celebrated very humbly in north-west County Clare in the nineteenth and twentieth centuries. The value of such collections, which capture a snapshot in time of Christmas during this period, can be appreciated. They highlight a wide variety of customs, some of which no longer exist, and women's role during the festive season. This may not have been documented elsewhere owing to women's work in the home being the norm and the smaller body of folklore which was collected from women by the Irish Folklore Commission's collectors.

SOURCES AND FURTHER READING

M. Dunne, *Saintréithe de thraidisiún béil na mban agus léiriú na mban i gCnuasach Sheáin Mhic Mhathúna* (Ph.D thesis, Dublin City University, 2023) and at https://doras.dcu.ie/27975.

Seán Mac Mathúna's Collection, Main Manuscript Collection, National Folklore Collection, University College Dublin, and at www.dúchas.ie./en/people/315676825.

P. Ó Héalaí, 'Seán Mac Mathúna: diarist and dedicated recorder of Clare tradition', *The Other Clare* **40** (2016), 26–36.

R. Uí Ógáin, 'Part of the family: correspondence between the folklore collector Seán Mac Mathúna (1876–1949) and the Irish Folklore Commission', *The Other Clare* **27** (2003), 63–70.

CHRISTMAS OBSERVANCES IN SOUTH-WEST CLARE: MEMORIES RECORDED IN THE 1950S

Patricia Lysaght

While working as a collector for the Irish Folklore Commission in south-west Clare in the 1950s, Seán Mac Craith, a Kilrush resident, sent material that he had recorded about Christmas observances in Kilrush town and environs to the Commission in January 1955. This consisted of reminiscences by a number of elderly local tradition-bearers about the celebration of Christmas in the area from the closing decades of the nineteenth century. A sense of change, particularly concerning community aspects of the Christmas season, is discernible in the accounts, while the collector, Mac Craith, occasionally noted elements of continuity.

In the Kilrush area, as elsewhere, the Christmas festival cycle, consisting of both religious and secular elements, commenced on Christmas Eve (*Oíche Nollag*, 24 December) and concluded at midnight on 6 January, referred to traditionally as Small or Little Christmas (*Nollaig Bheag*), or Women's Christmas (*Nollaig na mBan*). Throughout this period—and mirroring what Alessandro Falassi has characterised as 'time out of time', 'a special temporal dimension devoted to special activities'—only essential work was done so that people could participate in festival activities. Thus, in the Kilrush area, tradesmen such as painters, coopers, journeymen shoemakers and blacksmiths ceased work from Christmas Eve until after 6 January. Mac Craith, writing in 1955, noted that 'even to this day, this old custom is rigidly observed'. No tradesman would put 'a hand to a tool until after Little Christmas'. Even St Peter, according to local tradition, left the gates of heaven unguarded during the Christmas period, so that the souls of those who died 'went straight in'.

The commencement of the Christmas festival cycle was preceded by an intense preparatory period, both spiritual and secular. While Christmas Eve was 'confession day' in the Kilrush area, the previous days involved thorough house-cleaning, the setting up of seasonal decorations and the Christmas candle, and the procurement and preparation of foods traditionally linked to the Christmas period.

Sprigs of red-berried holly, especially prized as a household Christmas decoration, were placed over pictures, on the mantelpiece and around the container holding the tall Christmas candle. This candle, 'always white and about twenty inches tall', was set up in the principal window of the house and was lit on Christmas Eve to commemorate the birth of Christ, 'the Light of the World'. A fresh candle was lit on New Year's Eve, and the third and final one on the eve of Small Christmas. Each candle was lit on successive nights until it had burned out. In Kilrush itself, 'candles were always placed on the sill of the window, and what a sight it was to see so many lights in all the small houses', while candles burning 'in all the little windows of the houses in Scattery Island were something grand to see from Cappagh Pier'.

As elsewhere in the country and in the wider European context also, festive food and drink were central elements of the celebration of the Christmas festival in the Kilrush area. Meat of different kinds, especially that of fowl, was a prominent feature. Three geese (often supplied to townspeople by country relatives) were normally consumed—on Christmas Day, New Year's Day and Small Christmas Day respectively. Shopkeepers gave grocery presents ('Christmas boxes') to their regular customers and public houses presented a bottle of whiskey or wine to regular patrons, while householders themselves had purchased bottles of porter 'for callers over the holidays'. Fruit cakes and Christmas puddings were made by the woman of the house for family and callers, including, it was said, the Holy Family: 'Women long ago used to leave a glass of wine and a slice of cake on the kitchen table for St Joseph, in case he would be hungry or tired on his travels, looking for a place to stay'. Little toys were placed in stockings for the smaller children, but ''twas nearly always fruit like apples or oranges we used to get long ago'.

Christmas Day was the most significant religious day of the Christmas cycle, with the Irish-language proverb *Aifreann na Geine, Aifreann is fiche* ('the Mass of the Birth of Christ is worth twenty-one Masses') express-ing people's perception of the importance of Christmas Day Mass. In Kilrush, walking to seven o'clock Mass in the dark and wishing one another 'A Happy Christmas' were typical features of Christmas morn-ing. Two half-crowns were given to the priest as Christmas dues. 'And then after Mass when you came out, you'd meet all your pals, and if you had anything new on you, like new breeches or a new jumper, they would be codding you as to was it Santa Claus that brought it to you!'

Christmas Day was also devoted to family. On returning from Christmas morning Mass, breakfast was eaten; for one Kilrush resident this included meat from a boiled pig's head, while his dinner, served around two o'clock in the afternoon, featured 'a goose stuffed with bread-crumbs and onions' together with 'a bit of home-cured salty bacon'. His evening meal consisted of leftovers from the dinner 'and the pig's head again', and then his 'mother used to cut slices off the [plum] pudding, and she used to fry them in dripping … and that used to be the nicest of it all'. Tea, an expensive beverage, was also drunk on Christmas Day.

While young male members of the household might go out 'croost-ing' (*ag crústáil*, 'throwing stones')—'trying to kill a wren so as to hang him off the bush on the wren day [St Stephen's Day]'—or to play pitch-and-toss or quoits with their friends after breakfast, attendance for the Christmas dinner was required. The Kilrush resident added: 'We would have our tea at seven o'clock but the devil damn the one of us would be let out afterwards …'. Mac Craith added: 'This persists in many homes in this district'.

St Stephen's Day (*Lá Fhéile Stiofáin*, 26 December), on the other hand, brimmed with out-of-doors community activity. Involving performance, entertainment and the setting aside or reversal of social codes and norms, emblematic of community renewal and continuity, large groups of wren-boys in disguise and playing lively music traversed Kilrush town and environs, visiting each house, rich and poor, Catholic priest and Protestant clergyman alike, to collect money 'to bury the wren'. Then, in the evening, the different wren groups joined the parade of the Kilrush Temperance Hall Brass Band, and they used to 'sing, dance and shout as they went [on] their way'. In the 1950s, however, Seán McGrath noted that the large 'wrens' were a thing of the past in Kilrush.

Welcoming the New Year was formerly a prominent social activity in Kilrush, according to a local narrator. The church bell would ring out, and Glynn's factory hooter would sound, at midnight on New Year's Eve (*Oíche Chinn Bliana*); boats on the River Shannon 'would join in the ringing of sirens', and people would gather outdoors to celebrate New Year's Day (*Lá Coille*) with 'singing and well-wishing'. His father and older brothers would leave the house just before midnight and, on hearing the sirens signalling the New Year, would rush back in to wish the household 'A Happy New Year'. Neighbours, too, visited each other to offer New Year greetings. The narrator also remarked that this kind of customary behaviour was 'sadly fading away …'.

Small Christmas, or Women's Christmas, the last day of the Christmas cycle, was celebrated with festive fare and house-visiting. Family members and neighbours visited each other and partook of refreshments and entertainment. As the last candle of Christmastide burned out by midnight on 6 January, the season of goodwill drew to a close.

SOURCES AND FURTHER READING

Kevin Danaher, *The year in Ireland* (Cork and Dublin, 1972).

Alessandro Falassi (ed.), *Time out of time: essays on the festival* (Albuquerque, 1987).

Alessandro Falassi, 'Festival', in Charlie T. McCormick and Kim Kennedy White (eds), *Folklore: an encyclopedia of beliefs, customs, tales, music, and art*, Vol. 2 (2nd edn, Santa Barbara, 2011), 497.

Sylvie Muller, 'The Irish wren tales and ritual', *Béaloideas* **64–5** (1996–7), 131–69.

National Folklore Collection (NFC), University College Dublin (www.dúchas.ie); NFC 1391: 121–44.

'MY HEART GOES BACK TO MY CHRISTMAS IN THE ISLAND': AN ANONYMOUS WOMAN'S GREAT BLASKET MEMORIES

E. Moore Quinn

I am out in this country fifty years and have seen some beautiful decorations but nothing like my Christmas in Ireland.

So begins a two-page, typewritten narrative—all in caps—with no author. It arrived in the post some 30-odd years ago in an envelope with no return address. Discerning the place from which the post originated is impossible, but the contents' importance is established in handwritten words, written in red ink, across the top of the first page:

I think that my mother's words are a beautiful recollection of a very happy time in her life, a time so dear that it was cherished all her life.

The next typewritten sentence reveals the author's subject:

I was born and brought up in the Blasket Island and my heart goes back to my Christmas in the island.

For many Irish people—and a good many Irish Americans as well—Ireland's Blasket Islands call to mind the autobiographers Peig Sayers, renowned for her remarkable storytelling, Tomás Ó Criomhthain, clever at vividly describing the personal features of island life, and Muiris (Maurice) Ó Súilleabháin, whose grandfather is said to have uttered the now-famous lines:

Twenty years a-growing, twenty years in bloom, twenty years a-stooping, twenty years declining.

When it came to the Great Blasket's abundance, that same grandfather reminisced that he had at his disposal 'the gathering of the strand, the hunt of the hill, the fish of the sea and the wool of the sheep'. Christmas held unparalleled riches, overflowing with song, poetry, hurling matches, food, drink and brightness.

Tomás Ó Criomhthain describes the Great Blasket's exquisite 'lighting up' on Christmas Eve:

On 'God's Blessed Eve', if you were coming towards the village from the south-east—for that's the direction in which every door and window faces—and every kind of light is ablaze that night, you would imagine it a wing of some heavenly mansion, though it is set in the middle of the great sea.

The mainland, essential to the Great Blasket Island's survival, featured prominently at all times of the year, but especially at Christmas. The unknown woman who spent her girlhood there writes:

Lots of times [I think of] how good the people in Dunquin were when they [people from the island] were coming with their Christmas food. All the young boys in Dunquin were there to help with their packages. How can one forget such people? The people in Dunquin always ready to help.

Peig Sayers expressed similar sentiments. Before she married into the island, she found her joy in collecting songs and rhymes and witnessing the *craic* and merriment in Dunquin's streets and pubs at Christmastime:

> Your health, my friend, and drain your glass
> Our common welfare will come to pass!

When she wasn't eavesdropping on singers, Peig was staring with awe at the labours that had gone into the designs of holly, ivy, paper flowers and candles:

> When all the lights were lighted and the kitchen was decorated, I thought that I was in the Kingdom of Heaven because I had never before seen such a lovely sight.

If those activities were taking place in Dunquin—and all over Ireland at Christmastime, for that matter—so, too, were they under way on Great Blasket Island. Intense energies were directed towards preparation and readiness in anticipation of the special visitors who were about to arrive. Looking back, the anonymous writer recalls:

> For a week before Christmas, all we did was get ready for Our Lord's birthday. Christmas was Our Lord's coming into our home and hearts. The house was decorated with ivy over the windows with little posies stuck here and there and a big candle lit on every table. To us, Christmas was the little Baby Jesus's birthday. We could feel his presence all over in our hearts and home.

Once the candles and flowers were perfectly placed, dictums were laid down as to what would be expected and what would ensue:

> We had to be in Christmas Eve. Then my mother would get a shieve of straw, open it and place it outside the door. Our Blessed Mother gave birth to her Baby Jesus in the stable laying on the straw. We knew she would walk on the straw to come in the house. The next day my mother would put that shieve in the cradle to take care of the baby.

In this manner, preparations made for the sacred child extended to the baby of the family as well.

There were Mass rituals to attend to, with alternate plans put in place if there could be none:

> On [Christmas], if no boat could cross over to Dunquin to Mass, every family in the island would go on our knees and beg God to give us the grace of the Mass. We knew the time the priest was coming on the altar and we went on our knees. The oldest in the family would be the one to start.

Memories of prayers said might have even overshadowed those of the actual Mass:

> I remember how they prayed for their family in America and all over. Everyone's name was mentioned.

It was then that thoughts turned to the all-important matter of preparing the Christmas feast. What were the items on the menu and how were some of them made?

> Christmas day we would have creamed cod fish. My mother took care of that. There was nothing to eat all day waiting for our big supper around

six that evening. The supper was creamed cod fish, potatoes, creamed onions. Then we had tea, raisin bread [and all] kinds of jam, butter. The bread was made by my mother. She also had a big baker's cake she brought from Dingle. It was delicious. I was told it was wet with porter, not milk.

And the practices following the meal?

After supper, we young girls would go from house [to house] to see the decorations. We spent part of the night looking out at the lights in Dunquin. They used to look beautiful.

    Christmas Day, our friends would drop in. My father would have a bottle of whiskey. They all [would] have a shot of whiskey or two and codgers of porter. After a while, my father would go out to his friends and come home feeling good and merry and singing.

As the two pages proceed, the goodness, the merriment and the singing are summed. The different foods served on the island are compared to those served on the mainland, accompanied by a poignant explanation (again, handwritten in red ink) as to why such information is relevant:

Baker's Bread from Dingle

Christmas Eve:
Kill [the] best sheep on the island
Creamed cod fish: Dunquin and Island

Christmas Meal
Dunquin:
Goose or Hens
Potatoes
Tea

Baker's Bread and Jam

Island:
Lamb Chops
Black Sausage
Bread, Jam, Tea

My mother was from the island. My father was from Dunquin (main-land).

As if to bring the two pages to a close, at the bottom of the second page the following words are handwritten in red:

Life was simpler then, but the impact of the love expressed and exchanged spawned more than half a century.
Kathleen

In these brief pages, a fourth voice is added to the chorus of words that emerged from famous Blasket Island autobiographers Tomás Ó Criomhthain, Peig Sayers and Muiris Ó Suilleabháin. Like theirs, it is a voice overflowing with the sights, sounds, tastes and scents of Christmas life on Great Blasket Island. Exceeding them, however, it is a voice with *a sense of touch*.

Ensuring that the Great Blasket's cultural heritage will not be forgotten or dismissed, this anonymous woman gives readers a chance to *feel* what Christmas meant to her when she was a child, and what it continued to mean to her many years later.

Who wouldn't want a set of Christmas memories as powerful as hers?

SOURCES AND FURTHER READING

Tomás Ó Criomhthain, *An tOileánach. The Islandman* (trans. Robin Flower) (Oxford, 1951 [1929]).

Muiris Ó Súilleabháin, *Fiche bliain ag fás. Twenty years a-growing* (New York, 1933).

Peig Sayers, *Peig* (trans. Bryan MacMahon) (Dublin, 1983 [1936]).

Great Blasket Island village, 1932. Reproduced with permission of the National Folklore Collection, University College Dublin.

THE IRISH
MUMMING TRADITION

Linda-May Ballard

In Ireland the tradition of mumming, or Christmas rhyming, was usually observed either during Advent or between Christmas and Epiphany. It is related to a more widespread tradition known in England and Scotland, where it was sometimes observed during the Christmas season, at Hallowe'en or at Easter. R.A. Gailey comments that 'The earliest known mummers' play text anywhere is of the Revesby Plough Play in England. It is known in a manuscript of 1770.' Gailey also refers to eighteenth-century chap-book publications of the texts of mummers' plays, and elsewhere remarks on a version of this kind published in Belfast by the firm of Smyth and Lyons during the first decade of the nineteenth century. These printed versions of the texts no doubt helped to facilitate the spread of the custom, but only when social and cultural circumstances made this appropriate. A map published by Gailey in 1971 shows that in Ireland the mumming tradition was well known in a broad horseshoe-shaped band around the northern coast of Ulster from Donegal to Down, and in pockets around Dublin and Wexford. He remarks on the challenges of interpreting the reasons underlying this distribution pattern, while Kevin Danaher comments on the distribution of another seasonal custom, the wren-boys' rhyme, that 'Except in the northern part of Ulster, from Donegal to Antrim, the wren men and procession was known all over Ireland'. It seems that the

Christmas rhymers and the wren-boys may have complemented each other, and it should be noted that some Ulster versions of the mummers' play incorporate a form of the wren-boy rhyme.

The rhyme recited by the wren-boys refers to the fact that this tradition is characteristic of St Stephen's Day (Boxing Day) when the wren, the 'king of all birds', was described as being 'caught in the furze'. Groups of young men would parade with a branch holding either a dead wren or an effigy of a wren, and the association with St Stephen's Day is traditionally explained by the suggestion that it was a wren that betrayed St Stephen to the Romans. Describing the custom as they observed it in Limerick in 1840, Mr and Mrs Hall explain that the tiny wren became the 'king of all birds' through trickery. When an assembly of birds determined that their king should be the one who could fly the highest, it was assumed that the eagle would win. Unbeknownst to the soaring eagle, a wren had concealed herself in his feathers, and when he had flown as high as he could she fluttered her wings and rose above him to become the acknowledged leader of the birds. The wren-boys often dressed in colourful costumes and sometimes wore masks, and they expected to receive a reward in return for their performances.

The Christmas rhyme or mumming play can be expanded or contracted by the addition or omission of some rhymes, no doubt to accommodate differing numbers of young men prepared to participate. The essential characters are a 'captain' to introduce the action, two warring champions who engage in a fight in which one is killed, a nonsense-talking doctor who resuscitates the 'slain' knight, and a character, often a demon, who collects money, usually reciting a rhyme along the lines of:

Here comes I, Beelzebub,
And over my shoulder I carry my club
And in my hand a dripping [frying] pan
I count myself a jolly wee man.
[The pan is here extended to the audience]

All silver, no brass
Bad pennies won't pass.

The money was sometimes distributed among poorer members of local communities, but more usually it was used to provide refreshments for a 'mummers' dance' to entertain everyone on a dark January night.

The mummers' play is usually interpreted as a time of fun and enjoyment but, like many folk customs and traditions, it could also be used as a way of settling scores or perhaps giving vent to jealousies. An important element of the tradition was that all participants were carefully disguised in a variety of ways, so if there was an antisocial element to the event the culprits could usually expect to escape unscathed. During 1976, one observer from the north Antrim coast explained:

> Every Christmas the Christmas Rhymers came … They were nearly all boys in their teens. All were dressed up, all were masked. The favourite mask was a bit of cardboard, just with eye holes cut out in it, and pieces of flax tow to imitate hair and beard … The masks were called 'facicks' … There was a lot of vandalism went on too … The scones of soda bread was stolen and a basket or two of apples … And very often people chased the Christmas Rhymers when they came in. I knew many a family that took great delight in sitting with their loins girded and their boots on, ready and waiting for the Christmas Rhymers, and immediately they came in they went out again. Because the boy would be sitting with his family cudgel and his family dog and maybe the family shotgun and the whole lot just ready … for the pleasure of chasing the Christmas Rhymers. [Ulster Folk and Transport Museum Cassette Recording C76.68]

Doors were seldom locked, and the mummers used to burst into kitchens unannounced, so it is perhaps understandable that on occasion they caused consternation, especially if intent on mischief, but in general they were welcomed and provided an unusual evening of entertainment.

Nevertheless, the same speaker remarked on a deeper meaning underlying the entertainment and nonsense of the Christmas rhymes.

> I think the idea was that it was a scary thing. They were supposed to come in and scare the devil out of you … prepared your soul for Christmas … You had Oul' Nick scared out of you, with these boys coming in clattering and fighting in the kitchen … it was quite an event. It was a play you remembered more than any of your horror things on TV yet. [Ulster Folk and Transport Museum Cassette Recording C76.68]

Clearly, the mummers made an impression that was difficult to forget.

The costumes worn by the Christmas rhymers differed from place to place and perhaps also changed over time. In many areas they wore brightly coloured ribbon streamers hung from caps to disguise their faces. In other places they wore masks and even entire outfits plaited from straw. Costumes of this sort point to a link with the Scottish guizers, who performed either at Hallowe'en, Martinmas or Christmas and are described by McNeill as wearing suits of straw, 'the helmet usually ornamented with long streamers of ribbons of different colours'.

The Irish mumming tradition clearly relates to a much more widespread set of customs, but it could also be developed in distinctive, localised ways. For example, Danaher refers to the complex sword dance associated with the Wexford mumming tradition. He also refers to revivals of the mumming tradition and to competitions organised for rival groups of mummers, as the tradition continues to intrigue participants and audiences alike.

ACKNOWLEDGEMENT

I am indebted to Donal MacAnallen, Library and Archives Manager at the National Museums Northern Ireland, and to his colleagues for facilitating my research so graciously.

SOURCES AND FURTHER READING

K. Danaher, *The year in Ireland* (Cork and Dublin, 1972).

R.A. Gailey, *Irish folk drama* (Cork, 1961).

R.A. Gailey, 'The Christmas Rhime', *Ulster Folklife* **21** (1975), 73–84.

R.A. Gailey, 'Mummers' and Christmas rhymers' plays in Ireland, the problem of distribution', *Ulster Folklife* **24** (1978), 59–68.

Mr and Mrs S.C. Hall, *Ireland, its scenery, character, etc*, vol. 1 (London, 1841).

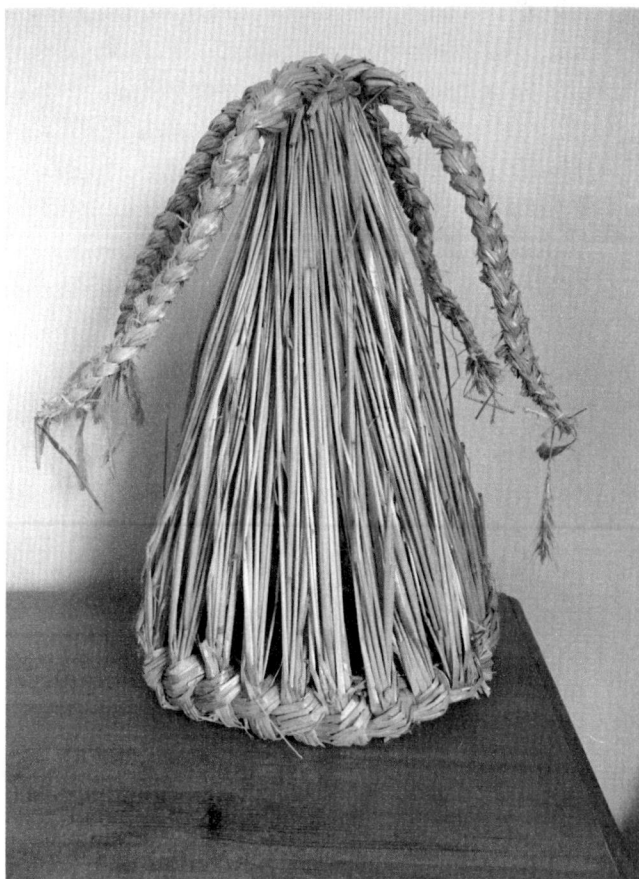

Mummer's mask made of straw. Leggings, skirts and capes could be constructed using the same technique and the heights of the masks could even be varied to make all participants appear to be equally tall. Image courtesy of R. D. Ballard.

THE RATHLIN 'COALIN'

Linda-May Ballard

Rathlin, the only populated island off the coast of Northern Ireland, sits like a punctuation mark off the north-east of County Antrim, adjacent to Ballycastle. During the medieval period it belonged for a time not to Ireland but to Scotland, and the 'Coalin' or 'Coullin' has close parallels in the tradition of the Scottish Highlands and Islands. John Braidwood suggests that it may have been known at one time in the Glens of Antrim. He also suggests a relationship with the Welsh Mari Lwyd tradition, in which a horse's skull is draped with ribbons and paraded to the accompaniment of recited rhymes. A similar tradition was known in parts of Cork and Kerry, where it was observed on St Stephen's Day (Boxing Day). The Coalin was performed by a group of young men who visited houses and recited a rhyme in return for a small reward. According to Braidwood, the name is likely to derive from the word 'calends', or first day of the month, and it was observed at New Year or Hogmanay, appropriate to its role in Scottish tradition.

Braidwood points out that the tradition is described in a manuscript history of Rathlin written in 1851 by Mrs Gage, a member of the land-owning family on the island. She describes how the leader of the Coalin band would dress up in a sheepskin, which would be beaten with a stick by the person immediately following him. The rhymers would enter homes and walk round a chair placed in the centre of the kitchen as they gave their recitation. According to Mrs Gage, after the rhymers were rewarded they gave a small piece of the sheepskin as a 'blessing' to the family. An alternative version is that the sheepskin was held over the fire, singed and passed from person to person to sniff. Apparently, as they did so they inhaled benefits that would protect them during the coming year.

In Scotland the tradition was sometimes known as 'the Procession of the Bull', as a bull's hide was usually kept from year to year to be worn for the event. The Scottish version might alternatively feature the hide of a goat, a deer or another animal. According to McNeill, on the Island of Mull 'the principal singer of the party carried a singed sheep's tail', which was sniffed by observers as 'a talisman for fertility and protection from disease in the coming year'.

Commentators on this custom both in Scotland and on Rathlin are agreed on its pagan origins. As Braidwood points out, 'Dressing up in animal skins is certainly a legacy of paganism'. He highlights that the seventh-century Penitential of St Theodore specifically prohibits the practice of dressing up in animal skins 'in Kalendas Januarii', and as early as AD 578 the Council of Auxerre stated that 'During the Kalends of January, it is prohibited to disguise oneself as an old man or calf or indulge in diabolical gifts'. It is therefore evident that the custom of wearing animal skins on the first day of January was known and possibly widespread in Europe in the early medieval period. It is also clear that for centuries these prohibitions had little impact, at least in the remoter regions and islands.

The Coalin was still being performed on Rathlin, at least in the remote Upper (west) End of the island, until the early decades of the twentieth century. In March 1981 one islander explained: 'They used to have rhymes—at New Year's Eve they would lift the Coalin—that was somebody would dress up in a sheepskin and two or three of them would go with him and take a bag and go round and collect for the poor … and they gave them meal or money' (Ulster Folk and Transport Reel Recording R81.62). He was one of the last speakers of Rathlin Gaeilge and, although he did not say so, it is likely that he himself had been a

Coalin rhymer as a teenager or young man, as he clearly remembered the rhyme:

Coalin, coalin, fu na bhfoitín
Eadar cloch is cnámh.
Beannaigh Dia taighe tán
Mná, fir is páiste.

He also gave this translation:

Coalin, coalin, below the bottle of straw
Between the stone and the bone.
Blessing of God, the house is still standing
Men, women and children.

This is perhaps the last personal recollection of an ancient tradition that persisted in island life almost into living memory. Even in the early twentieth century the sheepskin was still singed and sniffed, presumably to impart benefits to those who observed the custom, and in turn they provided benefits for poorer neighbours by donating food or money to be distributed as needed throughout the community.

ACKNOWLEDGEMENT

I am most grateful to Donal MacAnallen, Library and Archives Manager at the National Museums Northern Ireland, for his perceptive comments about the Coalin rhyme, and to him and to his colleagues for facilitating my research so graciously.

FURTHER READING

J. Braidwood, 'The Rathlin rite of the "Coullin"', *Ulster Folklife* **14** (1968), 44–50.

F.M. McNeill, *A calendar of Scottish national festivals* (Glasgow, 1961).

Alessandro Testa, *Rituality and social (dis)order: the historical anthropology of popular carnival in Europe* (Abingdon on Thames, 2020).

SANTA'S GRAVE

Helen Doyle

Ireland is often called the 'land of saints and scholars', sometimes imagined as a nation steeped in legend, folklore, myth and magic. As discussed elsewhere in this volume, there are many rituals and traditions that take place in Ireland over the Christmas period, such as the lighting of the Christmas candle, *Nollaig na mBan* and the visit of the wren-boys, each of which have their own distinctive histories. More recent in origin are traditions that emerged elsewhere but have become an integral part of the fabric of Irish life, such as Santa Claus and his visit to all good children on Christmas Eve.

The name Santa Claus only dates from the late eighteenth century, and it was not until the mid-twentieth century that he emerged as a jolly old man in a red suit. Santa Claus evolved from St Nicholas, from the Dutch nickname *Sinter Klaas*, which was a shortened version of *Sint Nikolaas*, the Dutch for 'Saint Nicholas'. The story goes that in 1804 John Pintard, the founder of the New York Historical Society, gave out woodcuts of St Nicholas at the society's annual meeting. The background of this woodcut portrayed the now-familiar image of Santa Claus with stockings filled with fruit and toys. It was from that time onward that Santa's popularity spread, and he became almost universally known for his gift-giving at Christmas time. What many do not realise, however, is that the original 'Santa Claus' was St Nicholas of Myra, a saintly bishop who performed deeds of great kindness and many miracles during his lifetime. Less commonly known still is the link that Santa Claus has with

Ireland, and more specifically with the county of Kilkenny. It is said that in this county, amid the ruins of St Nicholas's Church in the lost medieval town of Newtown Jerpoint, is the location of Santa Claus's grave.

While this may be regarded by some as Santa Claus's final resting-place, it is not where he began—or, indeed, ended—his life. Santa Claus began his life as St Nicholas, who is believed to have been born around AD 280 in a place called Patara, near Myra in modern-day Turkey. He was born into a very wealthy family, but his parents died when he was very young, leaving him to be raised by his uncle, a bishop. From early on St Nicholas showed signs of his saintliness; for instance, when he inherited his parents' wealth, he travelled the countryside giving alms to the sick, the poor and the suffering. Even during his own lifetime he was venerated for his extraordinary kindness and generosity. In time, he was ordained a priest and eventually consecrated bishop of Lycia, in what is now Turkey. One of the most enduring stories of St Nicholas's generosity concerns how he saved the three daughters of a merchant who had fallen on hard times from lives of destitution by throwing bags of gold into the house to provide them with dowries. One version of the story tells of how St Nicholas threw the bags of gold down the chimney and that they landed in the girls' stockings, which were hanging at the fireside to dry. Perhaps this is the origin of the tradition of hanging a Christmas stocking on the fireplace.

On account of St Nicholas's great generosity in life, and the miracles he performed for the poor, he came to be revered as a saint following his death, reportedly at the age of 73, on 6 December 343. Henceforth this date was celebrated as his feast-day. In the intervening centuries, St Nicholas has come to be revered as the protector of children, sailors, merchants, archers, repentant thieves, brewers, pawnbrokers and students in various cities around the world.

Following his death in 343 it is believed that St Nicholas was buried in the local church at Myra, and there he lay until 1087, when Italian sailors seized half of his skeleton and brought it to Bari, where his remains are said to be today, resting in two churches, one Catholic and one Orthodox

Christian. Venetian sailors later claimed the remaining fragments of his skeleton and brought them to Venice, where the church of St Nicholas was built. This story, however, does not consider a set of circumstances that may have led to St Nicholas or Santa Claus ending up at his final resting-place at Newtown Jerpoint in County Kilkenny.

The origin of the claim will become clear when the history of Newtown Jerpoint is explained. This was one of two towns, the other being Thomastown, that were established in the early thirteenth century near Jerpoint Abbey. The abbey was founded in 1160 by the Cistercian Order on 20,000 acres of land donated by Domnall Mac Gilla Pátraic, who was the king of Ossory at that time. The abbey was a working monastery from its foundation until 1540, when, like many others, it was dissolved under the rule of King Henry VIII. It would be reasonable to assume that the two towns, Newtown Jerpoint and Thomastown, sprang up close to the abbey, where there would have been the opportunity of employment on the

Grave of St Nicholas,
Newtown Jerpoint.
Wikimedia Commons.

extensive farmlands and industrial units set up by the monks. Newtown Jerpoint survived as a bustling village with over a dozen taverns until sometime in the seventeenth century. With the loss of its toll bridge and the re-routing of the local road, it appears that its residents simply abandoned the town and moved elsewhere. There is, however, another legend that relates to the demise of the town, and that account claims that it was burned by Silken Thomas, the 10th earl of Kildare, in 1534.

So how did St Nicholas, or Santa Claus, arrive in Kilkenny? Although there is no definite answer to this question, it is thought that his remains were brought to Kilkenny by a Norman French family who were living in the locality at that time. The de Frainets held lands near Thomastown and also in France. The story goes that when in 1087 these Norman overlords went on Crusade to the Holy Land to fight the Saracens, they were overcome and were forced to retreat. Determined not to allow any of the sacred Christian religious relics to fall into the hands of their enemies, they brought everything they could with them. One of these relics was the body of St Nicholas, which they exhumed as they were passing through Myra in Turkey. The remains were brought by the Norman crusaders to southern Italy, and there they remained in a church in Bari until the Normans were forced out of Italy by the Genoese. St Nicholas's remains were later taken to Fraxinet, a Moorish town near Nice, where they were entrusted to the French branch of the de Frainet family. Nicholas de Frainet, who lived in Ireland, was fearful that the Normans' days in southern France were numbered and he decided to bring St Nicholas's remains to Kilkenny, where the church of St Nicholas was built at Newtown Jerpoint. The ruins of this church remain to this day, with a memorial stone slab on the ground marking the spot of St Nicholas's grave. This memorial slab depicts the effigy of a cleric overlooked by two stone heads. This effigy is believed locally to be St Nicholas, bishop of Myra, and the two heads on either side of the saint are thought to be those of the two crusaders who brought his remains back to County Kilkenny.

We all realise that on Christmas Eve, as the crackling fire turns to ashes and embers and the house settles to stillness, the plate of cookies, the carrot and the glass of milk will be waiting for one very special visitor. As little children dream of what Christmas morning will bring, they may half-wake to the sound of jingling bells on the snow-covered rooftop. As they drift back into their dream-filled sleep, there will be no doubt in their minds that the individual they have just heard was jolly old Santa Claus and his reindeers. Santa Claus is alive and well, and he will live on as long as there are those who believe in the magic of Christmas—and, for those who do, the story of Santa Claus's grave is, of course, nothing more than just another winter's tale.

SOURCES AND FURTHER READING

Gerry Bowler, *Santa Claus: a biography* (Toronto, 2007).
'In Search of Santa', *Irish Times*, 19 December 2019.
'St Nicholas: a life', Talking History, *Newstalk*, 24 December 2020.

EOGHAN Ó TUAIRISC'S
OÍCHE NOLLAG /
'CHRISTMAS EVE'

Mícheál Mac Craith

Eoghan Ó Tuairisc (1919–82) belonged to that small but select band of writers who write in both Irish and English. On 4 December 1964 he published an anthology of verse in Irish, entitled *Lux Aeterna*. The very same day, under the English form of his name, Eugene Watters, he published a long poem in English, *The Week-end of Dermot and Grace*. By March 1970, 2,135 copies of *Lux Aeterna* had been sold, while sales for the *Week-end* in the same period were but a mere 217 copies. This discrepancy in sales is largely explained by the fact that the Irish volume was selected by *An Club Leabhar*, the Irish-language book club, though it is debatable just how many of the subscribers actually read the volume. During his lifetime Ó Tuairisc attained much more recognition for his writings in Irish than in English, but since his death in 1982 his work in both languages has attracted renewed interest.

The first poem in *Lux Aeterna* is simply called *Oíche Nollag*, 'Christmas Eve', and in the opening lines the narrator says that if he had a melodeon he would welcome the infant child with music that would set the very stars dancing in the night skies. A more literal translation states that if he had a melodeon, Christ would not be without music tonight, the negative second conditional clause implying that he actually has no melodeon. The situation, however, is somewhat more complex than that. Building on the theme of music, the narrator muses on Christmas Mass the following morning, his grandchildren singing *Adeste Fidelis* with great gusto in the church choir despite not having a word of Latin. He contrasts their zealous but patchy efforts with the rich music that he himself would play if only he had a melodeon. All this is wishful thinking, however. In fact he has a melodeon, but it is discarded and damaged beyond repair, broken by his beloved grandchildren. Their mother, his daughter, totally unresponsive to her father's gift and passion for music, is deaf to his pleas and sides with the children. Her decent but useless husband is dismissed with a shrug of the old man's shoulders.

And so it's late on Christmas Eve, the family have gone to bed, and the old man is sitting alone in front of the hearth, feeling as if the fire is rebuking him for not welcoming the babe of Bethlehem with his music. All is silence save for the drumming of the rain on the roof that lulls him to sleep. The raindrops, however, gradually morph into the old man's fingers as he releases the richness of his musical talent from the buttons of his melodeon, the wealth of his repertoire deftly captured through ingenious use of alliteration, assonance and onomatopoeia. For a short time player, instrument and music become one, as the artist celebrates the birth of Jesus from the depths of his being. Then the old man awakes, the spell is broken and he returns to reality, back to where he started. Alone, unappreciated and unwanted in his own home, his memories are his sole solace: 'if only I had a melodeon Christ would not be without music tonight' (*Dá mbeadh mileoidean agamsa / ní bheadh Críost ga cheol anocht*).

While focusing on the grandfather's isolation, Ó Tuairisc simultaneously exposes the superficiality of his daughter's piety. Convinced of her Christian righteousness in taking care of her father's material needs, she is totally neglectful of him as a human being. He has become a victim of 'the throw-away culture' so frequently criticised by Pope Francis, jettisoned in his own home just like his melodeon.

In many ways *Oíche Nollag* can be seen as a total subversion of the Old French legend *Le Tumbeor Nostre Dame* ('Our Lady's Tumbler' or *Le Jongleur de Notre Dame/*The Juggler or Jongleur of Notre Dame'). This tells of a successful minstrel/acrobat who abandons his craft and becomes a monk. Not knowing Latin, he is unable to chant the psalms and pray with his confrères. As his frustration grows, he goes into a crypt one day and chances on a statue of the Blessed Virgin Mary. Taking off his habit, he goes through his gymnastic routine in honour of Our Lady. This turns into a regular routine until his absence from choir is noted. One of his fellow monks stealthily follows him and discovers him performing before the statue. Horrified, the snooper summons the abbot, who is equally dismayed. Their distress is further amplified at the end of the performance, however, when the statue of Mary comes to life, descends from her pedestal and fans the acrobat with a cloth.

A Latin *exemplum* of this tale dating from *c.* 1277 has the tumbler explain the rationale behind his actions: 'I see everyone serving God according to his faculty, and for that reason I wish to celebrate God according to mine, as I know how'.

The original Old French tale was not formally edited until 1873, but an adaptation into modern French by Anatole France in 1892, entitled *Le Jongleur de Notre Dame*, proved immediately popular and inspired Jules Massenet to compose a three-act opera under the same title. Giving the first draft of his work as a Christmas present to the wife of his publisher, Massenet forged a link between Christmas and the original story that has remained fixed in the translations and adaptations into many languages that flourished up to the second half of the twentieth century. It is hard to believe that Ó Tuairisc was not familiar with one of these. It would have appealed to him on a number of levels, as a storyteller, as a primary teacher and as a creative writer, but the sentimentality and happy ending of the original are completely subverted in *Oíche Nollag*.

'Fairytale of New York' is another Christmas composition in which lived reality is far removed from the religious significance of the feast. The contrast, however, between the grandfather's solitary melancholy musings in *Oíche Nollag* and the raucous, vulgar and alcohol-fuelled invective of the protagonists in 'Fairytale of New York' could hardly be greater. Nevertheless, this anti-Christmas song, first released by the Pogues in 1987, has been regularly voted the best-loved Christmas song in the United Kingdom. Despite all the bitter recriminations between the Irish emigrant couple who have fallen on hard times, the conclusion still holds out the possibility of reconciliation. According to Shane McGowan, 'You really don't know what's going to happen them. The ending is completely open.'

Whereas the bells ringing out for Christmas Day suggest a glimmer of hope, even that minimum is denied by the negative second conditional of Ó Tuairisc's *Oíche Nollag*.

SOURCES AND FURTHER READING

Colbert Kearney, 'Between birth and birth, Lux Aeterna', *The Poetry Ireland Review* **13** (Spring, 1985), Special Eugene Watters Issue: 'The Week-End of Dermot & Grace', 90–105.

Dorian Lynskey, 'Fairytale of New York: the story behind the Pogues' Christmas anthem', *The Guardian*, 6 December 2012.

Eoin Ó Tuairisc, *Lux Aeterna* (Baile Átha Cliath, 1964).

Jan M. Ziolkowski, 'Juggling in the Middle Ages: the reception of *Our Lady's Tumbler* and *Le Jongleur de Notre-Dame*', *Studies in Medievalism* **15** (2006), 157–97.

A WEST OFFALY CHRISTMAS

Seamus Dooley

Christmas in west Offaly began with the annual Sale of Work at St Mary's Parochial Hall by the banks of the Brosna River at Gallen, Ferbane. Long before the ubiquitous *Late Late Toy Show*, discussed by Béibhinn Breathnach elsewhere in this volume, on the first Friday of December we had our own harbinger of Christmas, deeply rooted in a parish tradition of fund-raising for the missions.

Built by public subscriptions and local voluntary labour in the 1930s, St Mary's Hall was for long the centre of social life in the town. Now disused and neglected, it still evokes childhood memories of school concerts, variety shows, youth club discos, parish draws and the annual grand bazaar run by the Sisters of St Joseph of Cluny to support their missionary work.

The Sisters of St Joseph of Cluny are a French missionary order founded in 1807 by Anne Marie Javouhey. In 1896 Canon Patrick Sheridan welcomed four members of the order to Ferbane for the purpose of providing education for young girls. The Cluny nuns, in their simple blue and black uniform, were for many years a dominant—and, at times, domineering—force in the parish, in the field of primary and secondary education, parish work, social services and pastoral care. They were enormously proud of their foundress, and the annual Christmas Sale of Work was the primary fund-raising effort for their missionary labours.

It was many years after I left St Joseph's and St Saran's Secondary School that I learned of Anne Marie Jahouvey's disdain for the French

Revolution. According to the Heritage Statement of the Sisters of St Joseph of Cluny, Anne Marie was nine years old 'when the Paris mob stormed the Bastille, and barely fourteen when the French royal family were beheaded'. Her response, even at that early age, was to help hide fugitive priests, and in a dream St Teresa of Avila inspired her to set up a religious order dedicated to education. Little did I know then that the raffles, the wheel of fortune, the jams and the lucky dip were all part of a counter-revolutionary movement.

The souks of Morocco or Dubai had nothing on Sr Mary's stalls. For a few pence you might win wine, cider, lemonade, sherry or cans of ale. Sr Mary was farm manager, and effectively in financial control, of Gallen Priory, a boarding-school and novitiate, and she was a force to be reckoned with. She would beg, borrow or blackmail parishioners into donating gifts and buying raffle tickets.

On the wheel of fortune, Joe Claffey boomed out numbers and we excitedly checked our tickets to see whether we had won some exotic prize—Yardley soap, tins of USA biscuits, boxes of Lemon's sweets and assorted items of hardware, jewellery, make-up, arts, crafts, religious icons, candles and general bric-à-brac (or, perhaps less generously, tat).

My big moment came when I won a pair of ducks in a raffle, which I delightedly chose instead of a hand-crocheted suit. My sister Lily would have liked the suit and instead had the task of cooking the ducks. I was devastated, having assumed that I'd won two pet ducks rather than a culinary treat.

The clattering, rat-a-tat-tat of the noisy wheel of fortune, spun with all the enthusiasm of Marty Whelan in full flight, is an abiding memory of the Sale of Work. Joe was forced to compete with the delighted squeals of excited children queuing to meet Santa. There was nothing flashy about Santa or his carefully wrapped presents—best described as cheap and cheerful—but to a child the climb up the steps to what seemed an enormous stage was a wonderful adventure.

The annual St Mary's Boys NS Christmas concert was another high-light of the season and an occasion of communal excitement. Row upon row of parents would gather to see the Nativity play, in which I was once called on to play the part of one of the Magi; dressed in a pink brides-maid's dress and a turban carefully made from a tweed scarf, I solemnly proclaimed 'I bring gold'.

There was no toy shop in Ferbane, but Mrs Gunning would trans-form her sitting room into a virtual wonderland every December. Her sweetshop-cum-chipper assumed an air of magic, and she had a special arrangement with Santa Claus whereby she would take your order on his behalf. Among the Santa gifts I recall are guns and holsters, a cowboy and Indian outfit, Batman and Robin outfits, and kaleidoscopes for myself and my twin sister. From my sister in England we sometimes got more exotic presents; I still regret throwing out my Monkees car which played the band's signature tune, 'Hey, hey, we're the Monkees'.

My childhood memories of Christmas are shaped by family back-ground. My mother died in November 1961, leaving my father, a Bord na Móna worker and Fianna Fáil councillor, to raise seven daughters and two sons. My sister Barbara and I were thirteen months old and, as the baby twins, were adored by our siblings.

My mother's death, so close to Christmas Day, undoubtedly cast a shadow over the festive season, but every effort was made to make the event special. I recall the eagerly anticipated trips to Kenny's bar and gro-cery store for the special Christmas shop. Mrs Bridget Kenny observed the rural tradition of a Christmas box—usually a tin of biscuits, a cake and perhaps whiskey. Christmas was one of the few occasions when I remember my father buying drink—Guinness, Smithwick's or Phoenix Ale, and always Winter's Tale sherry.

Daddy would spend hours writing his Christmas cards. He had worked in Turraun with the Turf Development Board in the early days of mechanical peat production in Ireland, and his list included former Turraun colleagues from across the country. In return, we would receive a wonderful selection of cards, and I especially looked forward to let-ters from abroad, including from Sr Pauline Egan, his first cousin, who worked in the papal household in Rome. As a councillor he was the recipient of hundreds of cards from ministers, TDs and senators, and as a child I'd count and recount the cards to see whether we'd beaten the previous year's tally.

As I grew older, Midnight Mass in the Church of the Immaculate Conception was a joyous event, made memorable by a wonderful parish choir. Garda Eddie Mitchell singing 'And He Shall Reign' was an annual highlight, and to this day when I hear Handel's *Messiah* I'm transported not to Bethlehem but to a small rural town in the Irish midlands where Christmas was marked by simple pleasures.

After Midnight Mass I'd sometimes call next door to Lally's, where Liam and May would serve brown bread, rashers and sausages. Liam would take down the accordion and play 'The Castle of Dromore', while trying not to wake the young children before Santa arrived.

Over Christmas I'd often visit Paddy Devery, who lived by the edge of the bog with his brother Christy. He had an amazing collection of records, ranging from Dame Nellie Melba, the Australian coloratura soprano, to Canon Sydney MacEwan, and from Delia Murphy to the Donegal singer whom he simply adored, Bridie Gallagher.

The RTÉ broadcaster Gay Byrne was for long associated with Christmas, and Gay's request slot was enormously popular. On one occasion Gay answered Paddy's appeal and announced that he had indeed tracked down a Bridie Gallagher record, which was now in the post. Alas, when it arrived there had been an accident, and Paddy proclaimed to the embarrassed shock of the postman, Jim Spollen, 'Jesus, Mary and Joseph, Bridie Gallagher is in shite!'

CHRISTMAS CARDS IN THE 1960S: ANNUAL RITUAL BEHAVIOUR REVISITED

Thomas O'Loughlin

One of my regrets at the rise of the connectivity brought about by the communications revolution is the gradual disappearance of the Christmas card. Each year we send fewer of them and have fewer to display around our houses as part of 'the Christmas decorations'. The constant contact engendered by an array of systems—all linked to our computers—means that the card with its merry picture and 'a few words' seems to belong to a time when the post was the normal means for keeping in touch. The Christmas card was more than a missive: it was somehow an event. It was often the only link—kept up as an annual ritual—with people on our periphery. Distant cousins and friends from 'way back' still got a card, despite the fact that we had not been in contact in the previous year, nor were we likely to be in touch in the coming year, for which, however, we wished them every happiness.

DOMESTIC RITUALS

The actions related to writing and receiving the cards were also very much part of the necessary preparations for Christmas. For many, the thought of sending a whole batch of items in the mail at one time made 'doing the Christmas cards' a significant task, not to be undertaken lightly. Indeed, it was an annual literary event, somehow on a par with James Joyce setting out to write *Ulysses*. Along with making the puddings and the Christmas cake (and, closer to the time, procuring the tree), sending off the cards was a serious moment in the domestic liturgical cycle, and it was understood that such a task was to be respected and considered worthy of comment: 'I must get down to the cards this coming weekend, please God!' Moreover, the ritual had its own timescale that had to be respected. In the late 1960s, I saw a handwritten sign in the local post office giving the latest dates for mail for Australia, New Zealand, the USA and Canada—an interesting indication of the main locations for cards for abroad—and then a rider: 'except airmail'. Airmail was still a luxury that was only for the few, or for those too disorganised to get their cards written in time!

When cards arrived—delivered at unusual times by an army of special auxiliaries, such as university students, who had a silver badge with a number pinned to their coats and a bulging bag of envelopes but no other uniform to indicate their authority to deliver the mail—each sparked another series of rituals. First of all, the handwriting on the envelope was scrutinised, and more often than not this indicated who had sent it: everyone took it for granted that one could identify the whole suite of scripts found among one's family and circle of acquaintances. Thus identified, further reading of the enclosed card was often rendered unnecessary. Second (at a time when most children collected stamps to some extent) was the matter of the stamp. Those from Ireland or Britain merited no comment, but there was a definite hierarchy for those from further afield. In my family, US stamps were the most common of those worthy of interest, followed by those from Canada and Australasia, and so Canadian and Australian stamps were somehow more valuable. Any other stamp was an item truly exotic that would stand virtually alone on the designated page in the stamp album. Third, there was the matter of reading some of the cards—the duplicated Christmas letter with its listing of children's academic, artistic and sporting prowess had not yet appeared—which was akin to semaphore: 'Hoping this finds you as it leaves us. All well here' or 'All the family are well' or 'Will write soon' (with a strong hint that they should have already done so). At this point there was an optional extra ritual: panic. Did we send them a card? Have we got their new address? Is it too late to get a card in the post to them now? Whatever the answers, the issue was a flurry of anxious activity! The last ritual of the reception of a Christmas card was that of display. Smaller cards had to be placed at the front. Less colourful cards were relegated to the background. Cards with a top fold—like a tent—had a tendency to splay and so had to be held upright by cards to front and rear. And with each new arrival the display was altered: a really nice card could cause the whole mantlepiece to be rearranged! Finally, there was analysis: why did we not get one from … and did we have more cards, or fewer, than last year? The display of cards was a veritable index of the range and wonder of our social network: a fictive, but very real, community.

With each expansion of the display, the coming of Christmas became just that little bit more real.

THE MEDIUM IS THE MESSAGE

Looking back on that time when the physical, posted card was the means of sending 'season's greetings', we have a perfect example of McLuhan's dictum that 'the medium is the message'. Unlike all the other items that came through the letterbox—whether letters or bills—one did not see the card as a vehicle from which one extracted information. One valued the actual card—the medium—for itself. One might comment that one 'got a card from …' and this was enough; there was no need to refer to anything it might convey. One did not say 'Aunt Nan was in contact to wish us a happy Christmas and a prosperous new year', for such was to miss the point of the whole operation. We had sent a card to her, and we had received a card from her. It was a perfect semaphoric event, *res* and *sacramentum* coinciding, complete in itself!

Sometimes there was a message in addition to the medium, but this was always accidental. It usually was just a new address. And those who used the card as a form of note often had their missive only read *after* Christmas, when it was noticed at the time of taking the cards down. In those jolly December moments when several cards might arrive on a single 'post', the thought of opening and arranging the new arrivals was much more exciting than pausing to read any added details. For someone studying rituals, the Christmas card was a case of semiotic singularity: once you had engaged with the card, you had engaged with its meaning.

BEYOND THE CARD ITSELF

But the card did, of course, carry a message, and in fact there were several distinct messages on it: meaningful marks that were open to decipherment. There were the handwritten words of the sender; there were the formal printed greetings on the inside, which said more or less the same thing as most of the written comments; and there was the image on the outward face of the card which made it worth displaying. Curiously, I only recall one form of charity card—which are now almost *de rigueur* as a justification for sending cards—in those seemingly distant days: cards in support of disabled artists. These meaningful marks were, however, very secondary. I do not recall ever reading the printed 'glad tidings' on the inside of a card, and barely ever recall paying much attention to the written greetings either: one knew one's own name, was interested in the sender's name, and could safely assume that the wishes were consistent with those of the season.

But that left the picture. I cannot recall anyone making comments in the 1960s about the covers of cards except in terms of that subjective absolute: prettiness. The pretty cards were given prominence. And, by the way, if you received 'two of the same', one had to be relegated to obscurity behind larger cards. At a later time people might comment on how many, or few, 'religious cards' they had received, as a subtle consciousness emerged that there was a difference between the festival and the liturgical season, just as there is a difference between the carol and the Christmas song. Nevertheless, in Dublin at least, the issue of whether some could be designated 'overtly religious' while others were 'seasonal greetings' was, as yet, a distinction known to few.

The themes—thinking back on them—fell into three categories. First, there were the still-familiar Christmas memes: holly, robins in the snow, trees with presents, and Santa in various poses. Second, there were those invoking a nostalgia for a mythic Victorian Christmas: men in top hats and women in crinolines and bonnets greeting neighbours on their way to a country church when the snow lay deep and crisp and even. Lastly, there were the religious cards. The variants went from figures on camels heading towards a distant town, through the familiar crib scenes to Madonna-and-Child images: the iconography fitted with the compounding of the accounts of Matthew and Luke that is at the core of the liturgical calendar for Christmas. Significantly, an occasional cave-like crib scene aside, it was an iconography that was strictly confined to the canonical accounts—possibly a result of the emergence of Christmas cards in nineteenth-century Britain—and ignored other traditions about the birth of Jesus that still formed a fuzzy hinterland to Catholic discussions and are still prominent in Orthodox iconography. I wonder how many, if any, opening a card in the 1960s in Ireland were willing to engage with the subtle consumerism of the first category of card; the implicit social snobbery and colonialism of the images of a happy 'Home Counties' squirarchy; or the demythologising called for by the crib scenes. The joy of another card, another word of contact and a fuller array of cards banished such fears.

Significantly, I cannot recall any instance of those two staple themes in contemporary cards: the Christmas joke or the campaigning card advocating a cause. Perhaps they did exist—I can certainly recall them from the 1970s, when the arrival in 1971 of a 'Long Kesh' Christmas card was a matter for comment in my home—but they were certainly not plentiful. Just as all recurring festivals create expectations that what was done last year is both a guide to next year and a witness to what 'always happens', so Christmas cards seemed to be the same every year. This notion of cyclic continuity is, of course, one of the great human illusions: change is always occurring to some extent, and the Ireland of 1970 was very different socially, culturally and in terms of religion from that of 1960, but I doubt whether the Christmas cards of the period would be a good index of the dramatic evolution that was occurring.

Looking back from our climate-change-conscious world also alerts me to another silence. All the images of holly, robins, Santa, 'the quality' wending their way to church and even those of Bethlehem assumed that a genuine Christmas—that deeply embedded Platonic form recalled annually in the Christmas cards—required a deep blanket of snow worthy of an Alpine village. Yet no one seems to have remarked that on an island on the eastern edge of the Atlantic, blessed by the mild weather of the Gulf Stream, where cattle and sheep could be left out all winter, such a Christmas would be a once-in-a-lifetime event. And, on the occasions when it did occur, it would not be a dreamy 'white Christmas' (no matter what Bing Crosby was singing on the radio) but a very 'bad winter' indeed. But that comment is unfair: Christmas cards belong to our shared mythic life. Within our myths, in which we live so much of our lives, we find that rationally derived empirical laws, such as those of climatology, do not apply. That is both the glory and the horror of our human condition.

THE FINAL ACT OF CHRISTMAS

Every successful ritual needs a distinct ending, a marker that the significant activity has run its course. The arrival of the last post on

Opposite page: Christmas cards from the 1960s. From the family papers of Paddy Waldron. With thanks to Paddy Waldron for permission to reproduce these images and to Dr Paul O'Brien for sourcing them.

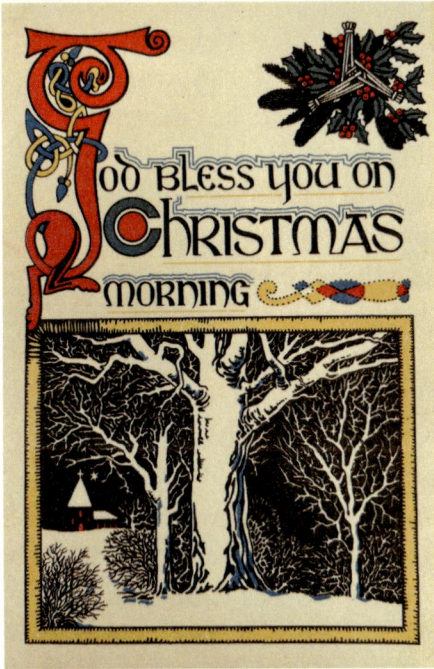

Christmas Eve—it might be as late as the early afternoon—marked a crucial moment in the whole ritual. Now the last cards had arrived, the final moments of excitement at opening the envelopes had passed, and the final arrangement of the cards around the house was made. They would now cease to be part of the activity of Christmas and become an exposition: interesting, perhaps worthy of a comment to guests such as 'D'y'know we got a card from Betty, so she must be OK', or a more meditative 'We did not get one from Jack this year, I hope he is OK', but, effectively, static for the twelve days.

And, yes, as with all rituals there were exceptions: an odd card that had 'missed the post' arrived between Christmas and New Year; it was squeezed into the display but without the pleasure that it would have given had it arrived on 24 December. And in my family there was always the card from 'Uncle Myles' which arrived around New Year. I place his name in inverted commas because no one recalled having seen him or being in contact with him except through this annual ritual, for he had emigrated before the Great War. But, funnily enough, half a century in Australia had not yet alerted him to the need to get his cards posted in time for Christmas.

The final days of the festival heading towards Epiphany had a melancholy character for myself and my friends. Weeks earlier we had counted down—echoing the tones of NASA at a launch—towards the holidays with mounting joy; now we counted down grimly towards 'going back' (to school) and the cards, still enthroned, seemed to alert us to time passing as they seemed less interesting with each passing day. Then came the night of 6 January and their formal deposition along with everything else relating to Christmas, which all of a sudden seemed long ago. One or two were kept so that new addresses could be extracted; the rest went into the basket to become part of the paper for setting the fire next morning. The mantelpiece seemed awfully naked, and larger and emptier than ever before. Christmas was truly ended. The schoolbag had to be retrieved from its hiding-place; the drudgery of 'back to school' was but hours away.

A CHRISTMAS MEMORY
FROM THE STREETS
OF SLIGO

Padraic Rooney

I don't like Christmas. Not for me the time of fellowship of man and good cheer. I stopped liking it a long time ago. Don't get me wrong, that's just me. For an awful lot of people it can be the highlight of their year, and I'm not just talking about kids. For me, it's like a big bubble of expectation that on too many occasions bursts when you least expect it, leaving you with a puff of air and wondering what all that fuss was about. No, I like to get the winter out of the way and spring with all its growth, budding flowers, and the evenings stretching out like a swan's neck when it's angry. St Patrick's Day can come and go without my participation. Easter, if it comes near the start of May (if you have any religion in you), is the best religious festival, regardless of your creed.

But this morning, as I answered a phone call, for some reason a long-forgotten Christmas memory came sailing into my head. It was a memory from, I'm guessing, 1964 or 1965, an event that happened in the dark days running up to Christmas. I'm sure many older and not so much older people can remember knocking on doors and singing a carol or two for whatever the people inside might give you—money hopefully, but nothing was refused. I remember one time going into Feehily's old pub at the bottom of the Mall in Sligo with a friend of mine who has spent a lifetime since then living in Australia. We had two guitars and three or four chords, and a repertoire of two or three songs, though we found it hard to match the lyrics with the chords. We struggled through the first song and, before we could even start the second, pennies and a few threepenny bits and a rare tanner were given to us—I'd say more to stop us starting again with the next song than for the enjoyment of the first one. On the way out, a town character called Johnny Rainsfort, who drank there regularly, came up to us as we approached the door and handed us a guitar string. 'Here,' he said, 'you might get a better tune out of that.' I think that was the end of that night's gig.

But the memory that stood out when I was on the phone was from a few years earlier. Times were tough in the Rooney household, as they were for most of the families in the street at that time. At best it was tuppence looking at a penny. That evening I said to my four sisters, 'Why don't we go round the houses for "da wran"; sing Silent Night and see what we might make'. They all said 'No, don't be daft! Who would want to hear us?' But I convinced my older sister Mary, and she reluctantly agreed to come with me. So we donned old coats, two of my mother's scarves and blackened our faces up with shoe-polish.

The only song we had was 'Silent Night', so away we headed. We started knocking at doors, and when the doors opened we hit them straight away with two versions of the carol. My sister Mary had all the words, while my words were rimming it, to say the least. She would sing 'Silent Night, Holy Night, round yon Virgin, mother and child'; I was singing 'Silent Night, Holy Night, round John Verdon's mother and child'. It didn't matter; if they didn't close the door in our faces on the opening note, they threw a penny or two into our hands, maybe after half the first verse. Seldom did I get to 'John Verdon's mother and child'. We soldiered on, and it was getting close to freezing; the clothes and shoes we had on weren't exactly providing thermal heating. I had a pair of shoes on me, and the sole was so thin that if I stood on a coin I'd have been able to tell you if heads or harps was turned up. We had most of the street done and were totting up our rewards, which were only a few coins and a slab of Cleeves toffee. Even for those days they were like John Wayne's sidekick in the western movies—Slim Pickins! We were about to head home when we saw a light in Mrs Farrell's house at the bottom of the road, a lovely quiet lady who I think lived alone at that time. As we approached the door, we could hear voices and laughter inside. Obviously, some of her family were home from England for the Christmas holidays.

We knocked on the door and it was answered by a man I don't ever remember seeing before, and away we went: 'Silent Night, Holy Night …'. We even got by John Verdon's mother and child, and on to verses that I was ad-libbing as fast as I could: 'Holy Infidel, so mental and wild … Sleep in heavenly fields, Sleep in heavenly fields', while my sister Mary seemed to be singing well, with no slip-ups of any kind. We finished the carol and the man clapped but wasn't moving towards his pockets for his money. 'Miserable so-and-so', I was thinking. But then he said, 'Come on into the house—I'm sure my mother would love to hear you'. So in we went. Mrs Farrell was sitting in the corner, close to the range, keeping herself warm and sipping on some type of dark drink; I reckon it was port or a glass of sherry. That's what most women of her age might drink at that time. There were four or five other people there drinking glasses of Guinness and ale whom we didn't know either, and one of them had a strong English accent.

We were asked by Mrs Farrell who we were and did we live in the street and, when we answered, she said she knew our family well. The Englishman said 'Hold on', and he went mooching in behind the sofa and came out with a yoke that I had only ever seen in a film at the cinema or on TV. It was a two-reel tape recorder. He fiddled about with it and shortly after said that it was ready. '*FFS!*', I thought, 'he's going to record us'. He held it close to us and away we belted. By this stage we were actually sounding like we were singing. The carol was sung and I'd like to think we loosened a few slates on the roof of No. 31 St Anne's Terrace, Sligo, with the cheers and clapping we were receiving. As the clapping and the cheers died down, we were handed glasses of lemonade, Christmas cake, biscuits that you'd only see on the telly—USA Assorted—and a pocketful of Cadbury's chocolate sweets. We were stars for those few minutes.

But I've learnt one or two things in life—the Yin and the Yang of living. Like a stone thrown in the air, as far as it rises and as long as it rises, it always comes down again. And as sure as a politician filling out his expenses sheet, our Yang arrived. The Englishman called for silence. The tape recorder was rewound and, out of the silence, the song we had sung began to play. But what was coming out was not what I had been hearing in my head as we sang. No, this was a mixture of Mongolian throat singing, Aran Island female wake-house keening and the last song of the night in the Shoot the Crows pub. But as the last wails were ending, the applause and cheers rose again. Now that I think of it, maybe that was my first realisation of the parallel world of drunkenness. It set me back musically, I have to admit. The sound of my voice from then on at school in Brother Einard's (Sharkey's) choir was never heard again.

And yet, as hands were shaken and our hair was tousled and we were heading for the door, I heard some shuffling. Hands in pockets, coins rattling and whispers. At the front door, Mrs Farrell's son held out his hand and placed two half-crowns in both of our hands … five bob each—a fortune for kids from the streets of Sligo.

That's the memory that came flooding back to me this morning as I was on my phone. Maybe it was the Ghost of Christmas Past telling me to cheer up and enter into the spirit of the season.

Incidentally, I heard many years later that the Englishman's wife kept the tape recording and threatened to play it for him if he ever got drunk again.

FESTIVE JOY: CHRISTMAS AND NEW YEAR'S BABIES

Clodagh Tait

My brother David was born on a New Year's Day, the first boy born in St Munchin's Maternity Hospital, Limerick, in that particular year ('Beaten by the girls', my father still remarks). David's wife, Julie, was a Christmas Day baby, an accident of timing that brings with it endless questions about 'What is it like having a birthday on Christmas?' and necessitates bearing with good grace the task of eating birthday cake on top of all the rest of the day's fare. Adding to the 'specialness' of the days themselves, nowadays Christmas Day is the rarest birthday, and New Year's Day the second-rarest, as Caesarean sections and other interventions like induction are unlikely to be scheduled to interfere with the holidays.

Under titles like 'The perfect present', 'Bouncing into the new year', 'Nappy Xmas' and 'Festive joy', pictures of bemused Christmas Day and New Year's Day infants and their exhausted but proud parents are a staple of national and local newspapers. The earliest 'New Year's babies' articles in the Irish newspapers appear in the 1950s, but the papers' attention to the first babies of the year increased during the 1960s. Interest was doubtless fed by photos of the new arrivals and by stories like that of 31-year-old Alice Nelson of Sion Mills, Co. Tyrone, who gave birth to her fourth set of twins on New Year's Day 1964, bringing her complement of children to ten. In earlier publications, the New Year's babies are to the fore, but Christmas Day babies have begun appearing more recently as the 24-hour news cycle grinds on through even that holiday. The maternity hospitals seem pleased to be associated with Christmas 'good news' stories: a special mention has to go to the Coombe in Dublin for supplying the 2018 arrivals with Santa-style 'Coombe special delivery' baby sacks, as pictured in the *Irish Mirror*.

The Republic of Ireland's accession to the EEC in 1973 focused particular attention on that January's crop of New Year's babies, who became European citizens from the moment of their birth. The *Munster Express* celebrated the County Waterford New Year's 'Eurobabies' with a group photo of seven of them. New Ireland Assurance presented £1,000 educational grants to the first ten babies born in 1973 to mark the occasion (the headaches of fairly administering the scheme are noted in an *Irish Press* article). The Irish Council of the European Movement also distributed specially designed and personalised 'Europa' medallions to all babies born on the day: 160 were distributed in total.

Many Christmastime babies carried a key sign of the timing of their births throughout their lives: their name. Nineteenth-century Catholic parish baptism registers from December regularly show modest peaks in the use of the names of SS Nicholas (commemorated on 6 December) and Thomas (feast traditionally on 21 December). Mary and Joseph appear too. In the Catholic registers of Wexford and elsewhere, another saint's name especially associated with the days around Christmas was Anastasia or Anstace (Christmas Day also being the feast of St Anastasia), though there is little sign in the Civil Registration birth records that this connection was widespread or consistent by the end of the nineteenth century. However, the Christmastime emphasis in the parish registers on the name Stephen, the martyr whose feast on 26 December has long been enthusiastically celebrated in many parts of Ireland, is also obvious in the civil registers. In 1900, for example, 131 Stephens were registered from January to November, and 79 in December (39% of the total for the year); the first week of January 1901 also shows a disproportionate number of Stephens.

Other Christmas-related naming patterns are evident. The clergy of the busy Catholic parish of Kingstown (Dún Laoghaire, Co. Dublin) may have actively encouraged the flourishing of the names Christopher and Christina during Decembers in the 1870s. On 27 December 1874, the three children baptised were Christopher Kelly, Christina Darcy and Christina Kelly. In 1876, of the sixteen children baptised between 12 and 26 December, half were named Christopher or Christina (five Christophers, three Christinas). The tradition continued in the parish, facilitated by the growing adoption of middle names, which expanded naming potential: of the fifteen baptisms over 12–26 December 1897, eleven children were given Christopher or Christina as an element of their name. The pattern is still visible in 1911 (the last year of the online parish registers), especially for the five children born exactly on 25 December, all of whom received the name Christopher or Christina. A similar trend towards the Christmastime use of Christopher/Christina is evident, though usually to a lesser degree, in other Irish parishes at around the same time: examples include Wexford and Cork. It can also be seen in the civil registers: of the 364 Christinas whose births were registered in 1900, more than half (52%) were born in December; 173 of 397 Christophers (44%) in the same year were December babies.

From the end of the nineteenth century, Noel (given to both boys and girls) and Noelle (usually given to girls) came to be deployed as names for Christmastime babies. The civil birth registers show the use of Noel beginning to take off from the late 1890s and that most Noels had December birth dates. In the 1901 and 1911 censuses the vast majority of Noels were aged under twenty. In 1911 there were about 470 people with Noel as a first or middle name, nearly 90 of them female. This represented a doubling of Noels since 1901, when there had been fewer than 200 (32 female). At that point it seems that the use of the name, especially for women, was strongly concentrated among members of the Protestant churches.

There was a short burst of Noeleens in the 1910s, though the name disappeared for a while until a relatively short-lived revival (along with the occasional Noelene) in the mid-twentieth century. Ten Noelles were named in the period 1894–1927, all but one born in December. According to the Central Statistics Office name-tracking app, which allows users to follow the popularity of Irish first names (though not middle names) from the mid-1960s, Noelle enjoyed a minor revival in the 1970s and '80s, but nowadays there are three or fewer a year. Noel, already in decline from about 400 first names per annum in the mid-1960s, plunged precipitously thereafter to about twelve a year at present. The CSO graphs show some limited use of Nodlaig and Nollaig (Irish for 'Christmas') as a given name for girls in the 1970s and '80s, and some people also use Nollaig as a cognate or translation of Noel or Noeleen.

The 'festive joy' newspaper articles indicate that Christmas babies still sometimes get called Noel, if only as a middle name. Holly also appears as a Christmas name, though its recent relatively high rankings in the Irish naming charts (no. 31 in 2021) indicate that it's not used just at Christmas. These days, the internet conveniently offers a range of Christmas baby name suggestions that the nineteenth- and twentieth-century inhabitants of this island could not possibly have dreamed of. They range from the established (Noel, Holly, Nollaig) to the *faux*-traditional (one list has Cuilinn, meaning 'holly', and Aoire, meaning 'shepherd'—or cow or goatherd), the international (Emmanuel/le, Angel, Felix) and the exotically monosyllabic (Starr, Yule, North).

Such exoticisms were far from the minds of those at the baptism of Patrick Christopher O'Sullivan at St Finbarr's Catholic church (South Parish), Cork, on Christmas Eve 1878. The same day also saw the baptism of Stephen Winter, a foundling. Only one godparent was mustered for a ceremony that constructed a scanty identity for Stephen out of chilly fragments: the season of his finding and a Christmastime martyr. I can find no other mention of him in the civil or church registers. Unless he was reclaimed and renamed, I fear that he may not have experienced much by way of festive joy.

SOURCES AND FURTHER READING

Baby Names of Ireland, Central Statistics Office (visual.cso.ie/?body=entity/babynames).

Catholic Parish Registers database at the National Library of Ireland (registers.nli.ie).

Civil Registration Archive (www.irishgenealogy.ie).

Irish Newspaper Archives (www.irishnewsarchive.com).

Helen McGurk, 'Meet the Ulster folk who were born on Christmas Day', *[Belfast] News Letter*, 22 December 2019 (newsletter.co.uk/news/meet-ulster-folk-who-were-born-christmas-day-1346017).

Emer Twomey, '1972: Ireland votes for change' (blogs.ucc.ie/wordpress/theriverside/2017/11/07/1972-ireland-votes-change).

AIFREANN, ACHRANN AGUS TELLY AR CÍOS: NOLLAIG SNA 1970Í

Adrian Ó Ceallaigh

Is maith is cuimhin liom ceiliúradh agus contrárdhaí na Nollag siar sna 1970í. Bhí an tAifreann agus an t-achrann ann, an chastacht agus an chneastacht, an tsaoltacht agus an naofacht taobh le taobh, fite fuaite ina chéile i gcarachtair agus i gcoitiantacht na féile.

Is cuimhin liom bean, ball den lucht siúil, a tháinig chuile Nollaig chun croíúlacht agus cairdeas a bhronnadh ar mo thuistí agus orainn féin, bean a bhí taithí aici ar chor agus ar chasadh an tsaoil.

Is cuimhin liom an bhliain a tháinig Daidí na Nollag faoi dhó, nuair a d'fhág sé lear mór bronntanas dúinn i gCorcaigh agus i Sligeach. Bhí achrann sa bhaile an Nollaig sin ar chúiseanna nár thuig mé ach bhí faoiseamh agus fuascailt ar fáil dúinn i dtithe ár muintire. B'in an bhliain a thuig mé i gceart go mbíonn gach eolas ag Daidí na Nollag. Thuig mé freisin, den chéad uair b'fhéidir, go mbíonn an chruálacht agus an chneastacht in adharca a chéile amanna ar an saol seo. Agus go mbíonn an daonnacht agus an dínit níos treise ná an doicheall agus an dochma sa deireadh.

Is cuimhin liom an bhliain a chuala mé Daidí na Nollag ag baint triail as an traein a d'fhág sé dom faoin gcrann Nollag, an bhliain a thuig mé ní hamháin go bhfuil tuiscint faoi leith ag Santy, ach go bhfuil stuaim aige, agus é ag cinntiú go raibh gach rud ag obair i gceart sular fhág sé aon fhéirín. Is cuimhin liom an bhliain a chaill Santy céanna a bhróg sa seomra suite, bróg atá fós sa bhaile i mbosca mhaisiúcháin na Nollag agus rian na mblianta air.

Is cuimhin liom an mainséar a dhein mé féin agus mo Mham as sean-bhosca cairtchláir, crepe paper agus cochán, mainséar atá fós sa bhaile agus peannaireacht chruinn mo mháthair le feiceáil ar bhosca na ndeil-bhíní, 'Clery's 1977'. Is minic a chodail an cat sa mhainséar céanna, é ar a chompord sa tuí agus ag déanamh muintearais leis na hainmhithe trí chéile. Ar mhaithe leis féin, dar ndóigh.

Is cuimhin liom na cuairteanna laethúla a thugamar ar an leanbh Íosa sa mhainséar mór sa séipéal gach lá ó Lá Nollag go dtí Nollaig na mBan, an séipéal chomh ciúin leis an luch a dhein leaba dó féin i gceann tuí an mhainséir chéanna.

Is cuimhin liom cráifeacht agus creideamh na Nollag agus na paidrea-cha faoi leith a bhain leis an am sin den bhliain. Bhí an Choróin Mhuire á rá go laethúil sa teach an t-am sin, agus paidir na hAidbhinte curtha leis na trimmings, míorúilt agus draíocht i ngach focal: '*Hail and blessed be the hour and moment, in which the Son of God was born of the most pure Virgin Mary, at midnight, in Bethlehem, in piercing cold …*'. Comhartha a bhí sa phaidir sin go raibh an Nollaig ag teacht. Agus go mbeadh Santy sa teach go luath. Bhí liodán eile ann don Nollaig féin: '*Sweet Infant Jesus, Infant Divine, Make me, O make me, forever be Thine*'.

Is cuimhin liom dáileadh amach idir mé féin agus mo dhearthái, ceann ar cheann, gach íomhá de Santy a bhí sna páipéir chun iad a dhathú.

Is cuimhin liom buaicphointe na Nollag, is é sin an tiomáint chuig Cnoc an Línsigh go luath Oíche Nollag chun telly a fháil ar cíos. Ní raibh telly againn sa bhaile an tráth sin, dubh, bán ná riabhach. Ceann dubh agus bán a fuarthas. Bhí amhráin ag Johnny Cash tráth leis an líne, '*we were born and raised in black and white*'. Bhuel, bhí sé sin fíor dúinn i rith na Nollag pé scéal é. Is cuimhin liom a bheith lán den bhrón tar éis na Nollag agus an saol ag normalú arís agus an telly tugtha ar ais.

Is cuimhin liom Coinneal na Nollag ar lasadh san fhuinneog Oíche Nollag, nós a thug mo mháthair léi soir ó Shligeach chuig machairí na

Midhe, an lasair mhaorga ag cur fáilte roimh an Maighdean Mhuire agus ag soilsiú an bhóthair do strainséirí agus dóibh siúd a bhí ag filleadh ó Aifreann na Gine, nó a bhí ar an drabhlás ar an tslí abhaile ón teach tábhairne b'fhéidir. Bíonn an naofacht agus an tsaoltacht taobh le taobh i gcónaí. Cheannaigh mo mháthair coinneal chaol dhearg na Nollag i Murray's ar an gcearnóg. Las an duine ab óige sa teach é le clapsholas Oíche Nollag. Cuireadh Coinneal na Nollag sa chistin, agus bhí coinnle beaga bána ar lasadh sna fuinneoga eile, iad ag cruthú íomhá dhraíoch-tach i dtost séimh na hoíche.

Is cuimhin liom mo mháthair ag déanamh gach iarracht Nollaig mhór mhaith a chur ar fáil dúinn. Ise a dhein chuile rud chun muid a chothú chuile lá den bhliain. Ise a bhí mar chroílár na Nollag againn. Thosaigh sí amach go luath i mí na Samhna ag ullmhú féasta na Nollag, ag déanamh na gcístí agus na plum puddings, maróg na Nollag. Roimh an lá mór féin, bhí an obair déanta aici agus prog na Nollag bailithe aici.

Is cuimhin liom scéalta mo mháthar faoina hóige féin agus í ag fás aníos ar fheirm bheag cúig mhíle ó bhaile Shligigh. 'Bringing home the Christmas', a ghlaoigh sí ar shiopadóireacht na Nollag an t-am sin. Bhí áit faoi leith ag an am sin den bhliain i saol mo Mham. Ag tús na seachtóidí fuair a hathair, mo sheanathair, bás Lá Nollag, an t-aon lá den bhliain a bhíonn geataí na bhflaitheas ar oscailt do chách gan choinníoll. D'fhág an eachtra sin rian ar an lá do mo mháthair. Blianta ina dhiaidh sin fós d'fhág tubaist eile rian uirthi, an bhliain a fuair sí stróc tubaisteach í féin, maidin Nollaig na mBan, lá ar leith do mhná. An bhliain dár gcionn, bhí amhras orm nuair a d'fhiafraigh mé di conas mar a bhí a céad Lá Nollag sa teach tearmainn.

Is cuimhin liom freagra na ceiste. Gur dhúisigh sí an mhaidin sin agus faoiseamh uirthi nach raibh uirthi turcaí a chur san oigheann. Splanc inti agus meangadh gáire ar a gnúis. Rinne mo mháthair chuile rud chuile Nollaig chun muid a chothú agus a bheathú. An bhliain sin, ghlac sí leis an saol mar a bhí le stuaim.

Sea, is maith is cuimhin liom an tAifreann agus an t-achrann, an draíocht agus an doicheall, an dínit agus an daonnacht, an naofacht agus an tsaoltacht a mbaineann leis an am áirithe beannaithe seo. Agus tuigim anois go raibh na gnéithe sin den saol go smior ann an Chéad Oíche Nollag úd i mBeithil.

FOUR THOUSAND
HAIL MARYS

Miriam Moffitt

I first encountered the custom of 4,000 Hail Marys in December 1970 when our teacher, a nun recently arrived in our school, instructed the girls of fifth class to say 150 Hail Marys each day from the start of Advent until Christmas Eve. These Hail Marys, she said, would add up to 4,000, and would represent the 4,000 years that people waited for the birth of Jesus.

I had never come across this practice and certainly did not embrace it wholeheartedly. One hundred and fifty Hail Marys a day was an awful lot of Hail Marys. Even if we said three at the start of class, three before going out at break, three more when we came back in, and another three before going to lunch, three after lunch and three before going home, we had only managed eighteen in the course of a school day. Attendance at the evening rosary in the church added another 50. I could usually manage about ten during the walk to the school, and ten more on the way home, which, considering I came home for my dinner in the middle of the day, gave me 40 more—but only if I ignored my friends for four weeks. And even with all that, I went to bed every night terrified because I knew that I was still 40 or 50 short of my quota. What if I fell asleep before I got them all said? How could I raise my hand in class, where a full show of *lámha suas* was expected in response to the daily enquiry?

My older sister, with whom I shared a bedroom, defiantly opted out; this hadn't been imposed on her and she was having none of it. The incessant mumbling from my side of the room grated on her nerves and, in true sisterly fashion, she made it her business to mess up my counting whenever she could, and my rendition of Hail Marys was drowned out by the music played loudly on her crackly transistor radio. It was an unequal contest and the Hail Marys were losing out.

As was often the case, it fell to my mother to sort things out and, fed up with finding me awake half the night, she sat on my bed to get me over the line: she would 'give out' the first part and I would say the response and then we'd swop over. We rattled them off so fast that even the Blessed Virgin herself would have difficulty making out the words. I got the distinct impression that my mother wasn't hugely taken with the practice, but of course she wouldn't say so. After a week or two, she got a bolt of pure inspiration and told me she was certain that if I fell asleep saying my Hail Marys the angels would finish them off for me. But angels or no angels, the 4,000 Hail Marys said in the weeks before Christmas 1970 became deeply imprinted in my ten-year-old consciousness. The Advent Hail Marys was a one-off event for me and, with a new teacher the following year, I didn't repeat the experience. Interestingly, my mother didn't suggest it either.

Although I grew up in an extremely devout household in east Mayo, this tradition of 4,000 Hail Marys was not part of my religious upbringing—apart from this single episode. It was, however, found throughout Ireland and was even practised close to where I grew up. Folklore evidence gathered in the neighbouring parish of Carracastle confirms that people near Rooskey school recited 4,000 Hail Marys by Christmas Eve 'because of the four thousand years that the world waited in expectation of the Saviour'. Accounts of 4,000 Hail Marys turn up the length and breadth of the country in the folklore collection. In Knockcarron, Co. Limerick, it was described as 'a very old custom', with the belief that God would grant any request if the Hail Marys were said. In fact, there was a general belief that three requests would be granted to those who completed the task, with the first granted after 1,500 Hail Marys, the second after 3,000 and the third when all 4,000 Hail Marys were said. A folklore account from Moyvore, Co. Westmeath, described little tally books called 'Hail Mary Books' in which children marked an X for every ten. In County Cork a mark was made on a piece of paper for every Hail Mary, and it was believed that the requests would be granted when these papers were burned in the candle on Christmas Eve. It was customary to recite 150 Hail Marys each day from the beginning of Advent, as we had done, but an account from County Limerick described an all-night vigil of Hail Marys which started at 12 o'clock on Christmas Night and was completed before first Mass.

Although the tradition of reciting 4,000 Hail Marys appears to be most strongly embedded here, it can be found in places with no obvious influence from Ireland. When we read that in 1929 Fr Joseph Lavin, an American-born missionary to China, urged his sister to continue the practice, we may look to his mother, who was from County Armagh. Other memories of the practice are less easy to connect, such as the reminiscences of St Mildrid Lustig, a Franciscan nun born in Idaho in 1913 who remembered the practice from her childhood, or Hilda Noetzel's account in the *New Zealand Tablet* of 9 March 1922, in which the seventeen-year-old girl described how she felt under pressure to complete her 4,000 Hail Marys in time for Christmas.

The recitation of 4,000 Hail Marys does not seem to have left much trace in the written record, and studies of folk customs connected to Advent generally describe wreaths and the sequential lighting of four candles without referencing the Hail Mary tradition. Advent is covered in detail in Francis Weisner's *Handbook of Christian feasts and customs: the year of the Lord in liturgy and folklore* (1958) but without any mention of the 4,000 Hail Marys. I have been unable to locate an origin for the practice, or any reference to it in written studies, but its traditional use throughout Ireland is unquestionable.

CHRISTMAS IN MAYNOOTH COLLEGE

Penelope Woods

Seventy-eight years ago, the main road from Dublin to the West was winding and narrow, with only one lane each way. Fifteen miles out, in County Kildare, lay Maynooth, its main street hemmed in to the east by Carton, the demesne of the dukes of Leinster, and to the west by St Patrick's College, the national Catholic seminary for the training of diocesan priests.

The College, founded in 1795, had gained a Gothic character at the hands of A.W. Pugin in the 1840s, with towers, buttresses and mullioned windows in stone. Beyond its two large squares and ancillary buildings lay parkland with magnificent avenues of lime trees, and a farm, with further acreage at Killick, to supply and feed some 500 students.

Late in November 1945, the bursar, Daniel Hourihane, sat writing in his diary, lamenting the bitter cold and hugging his electric fire. Out on the bog with the lorry it had been wintry. He had had a difficult time as assistant bursar managing the College, with notable resourcefulness, through the shortages caused by the Second World War. An impromptu trip to the port when a ship came in had landed him four chests of tea, which had lasted the duration. He had commandeered classes to unearth potatoes with their bare hands and cross-saw great tree trunks for fuel. Now, finally, the war was over, but Europe lay desolate and shortages remained.

Meanwhile, the students had just launched a magazine, *The Silhouette*, and in an article, '*Adeste, Fideles*', the editors were catching the mood—the first hint of Christmas, the beginning of Advent. 'When does the "Adeste"* begin, lads?' A quick calculation and they have it worked out—four Sundays before Christmas, so 2 December. They were looking forward to that first singing of it and the weekly repetitions—each, they said, ever more joyful. Impishly, they describe *Adeste Fideles* as a spiritual 'Come all ye', adding that 'We Irish love Come all ye's'; sung by 500 young men in the frosty air and against a Gothic backdrop, resounding round St Joseph's Square and 'across the plain of Nuadha' far beyond, the Adeste became a potent memory for many. According to Neil Kevin, writing *I remember Maynooth* in 1937, it had been sung thus at midnight Mass on Christmas Eve long ago. It was special, too, in another way, though they may not have been aware of it.

Adeste Fideles is thought to have been written in the 1740s and is generally attributed to John Francis Wade, Dominican-educated and a fervent Jacobite, who fled to Douai after the failed attempt to restore the Stuarts to the throne in 1745–6. The hymn was said to have been heard for the first time, in Dublin in 1748, in the Dominican Convent of Channel Row, a known centre for church music. In Clongowes Wood, a Jesuit school founded in 1814 and just along the road from Maynooth, they once had a Wade manuscript (now lost) containing the *Adeste* and dated 1746. Though missing, it helps the dating. It would have been the earliest but one of ten known manuscripts of his containing the hymn. Wade was immensely influential in the revival of plainchant and wrote music with a beautiful scribal hand.

December in Maynooth brought plays and concerts. After the Junior House play, the students were permitted to lie in—a rare treat. The bursar was disappointed by the First Divines, for they performed a play but with no carols or songs. There were at least carols on Radio Éireann and he, as a professor, was entitled to a radio. There was a play put on at Clongowes Wood two days later and the bursar cycled the seven miles over to see it. It was a good one, with tea at half-time. The Maynooth professors held their Christmas 'banquet' in the parlour. A former colleague, Paddy Brown

(Pádraig de Brún), was fêted and Denis O'Flynn (Donnchadh Ó Floinn) was the 'tit-bit' of the night, parodying Churchill telling the House of Commons of the death of Mrs Hubbard.** In the past, students would go home after Christmas, but with shortages of food and fuel they left before Christmas, as became the custom, and the only person to remain on this occasion was the bursar. It was a lonely time. Someone had to stay to mind the premises, and as overseer of the College farm he needed to be on hand. His lot was tempered, though, for he said Mass daily at the Presentation Convent at the top of the village and was fed well there by the Sisters; he tuned in on his radio to carols from Tuam Cathedral and a Dublin performance of Handel's *Messiah*, an Irish Christmas favourite; there was a trip into the city to the Astor cinema and again the next day, the 21st, to post all his Christmas letters. On Christmas Day itself he headed into Dublin again and called on his Aunt Hannah, whom he found in 'restful mood', and they had a long chat and a meal together; afterwards he stopped at Mulligan's before catching the bus home.

The students continued their light-hearted banter in succeeding issues of *The Silhouette*. At Christmas in 1951 they cheerfully headed home by bus, car and cart, 'confident of sharing the fate of one of their number who was assured by the professor in the Latin oral examination that if ignorance were bliss, he would have a very happy Christmas!' And echoing down the Main Street, from the departing buses, a final 'Adeste'. Note the Latin oral: it was still a spoken language and the language of the Mass. Lectures were at one time given through Latin. Until 1970 the College calendar (*Kalendarium*) gave details of course topics in the Faculty of Theology entirely in Latin.

Twenty-five years later, when I joined the library staff in 1976 after an interview by the president, Tomás Ó Fiaich, the road from Dublin to the West was a lot busier but still narrow and winding, and if the No. 66 bus to Maynooth got stuck behind a lorry the journey could be slow indeed. The College had begun opening to lay students in 1966, so the population was growing and nearing 1,000, but still most professors were priests, dressed without exception in black with a white clerical collar—

for a newcomer it was hard to distinguish one from the other, but in fact there were many great characters among them. On occasion the Irish bishops, in black cassocks edged in purple, would hold their meetings there—at that time in St Mary's Library on the cloister—and one of the College staff members, the late Tom Corcoran, would stand patiently nearby with a special telephone line at the ready.

The much-loved carols had been drafted into a carol service for all, held in the magnificent main chapel with carved wooden pews and high vaulted roof, its painted stars and saints lost in shadow and mystery. In mid-November, in the serried seating of Callan Hall, the choral society would abandon their earnest practising of the choral work chosen for Easter and instead would practise the carols, their muffled voices carrying outside into St Joseph's Square. Instituted by Noel Watson in 1969, the service was to become such a favourite under Gerard Gillen and then John O'Keeffe that it was eventually performed three nights running, with tickets having to be allocated by lottery and the College president obliged to give his homily three times over. The 'Adeste' always came at the end, with choir and congregation singing their hearts out, the organ in full swell, and trumpets in the gallery sending a tingle down the spine. Apart from a single chorus, the choir never performed the *Messiah* at Christmas, but Gerard Gillen would always choose it regularly as the Easter performance to ensure that each student had an opportunity to sing in it. And so it was in his time that practising the *Messiah* was a regular part of anticipating Christmas.

In the mid-eighties, messages within the College still travelled by envelope and were delivered in and out of the post room daily—no emails then. In early December everyone on the wider staff received an envelope announcing a Christmas Dinner Dance, to be held in the evening and open to spouses and partners also. Tickets could be purchased at five pounds apiece. These came by return post—with pink fluted edges, and were printed by the local Cardinal Press. Holly was cut from trees in the grounds by gardener Maurice Dunne for Pugin's great refectory, and a 12ft Christmas tree was erected. The evening began with a sherry reception.

Tables had been laid with white cloths. The College president sat with most of his priest colleagues at a very long table to the side under portraits of former presidents. A few joined their lay colleagues and proved to be lively raconteurs. After a good Christmas dinner, the plates were cleared away. There was a sudden skirl of pipes and the late Micheál Mac Gréil, Jesuit and lecturer in Sociology, emerged from the kitchen with white chef's hat and apron, bearing a flaming Christmas pudding. He marched to the sound of the piper with great ceremony, carrying the pudding aloft and, amidst cheers and clapping, laying it before the president. After that, pudding and coffee were served to all, speeches followed, and then tables were moved back and a band appeared. Some danced, some watched, but further conversation was drowned out!

Term ended, the College emptied and the gates were locked. But it was not entirely empty. A priest was still deputed to 'mind the house' over Christmas. Turns were taken. It was a custom that continued into the 21st century. A vivid memory for one—Professor of French Breandán Ó Doibhlin, recalling for me—was the heavy snow blown in by the east wind a few days after Christmas in 1978. It drifted up to reach the high ground-floor windows. The corridors were intensely cold and silent with a strange brightness. The only heat was his own turf fire.

---

* *Adeste Fideles*, 'O come, all ye Faithful'. Find the full intriguing story of it on www.hymnologyarchive.com.

** A speech made by Churchill in 1919 had been described as based on Mother Hubbard's Cupboard evidence (the cupboard was bare, according to the nursery rhyme); the phrase must have followed him.

SOURCES AND FURTHER READING

Salvador Ryan and John Paul Sheridan (eds), *We remember Maynooth: a college across four centuries* (Dublin, 2020).
Daniel Hourihane's diary for 1945 is held in the Maynooth College Archives (https://sppu.ie/archives).

My gratitude to the late Monsignor Breandán Ó Doibhlin for sharing his memories with me, and for his unfailing kindness.

Maynooth College Carol Service. Image credit: Tony G. Murray, Photography, Naas. Maynooth College Collection.

'THE LATE LATE TOY SHOW NO MATTER YOUR AGE': A UNIQUELY IRISH CHRISTMAS TRADITION

Béibhinn Breathnach

During the 2022 *Rose of Tralee* competition, the Queensland Rose reduced some viewers to tears with her poem on the meaning of Irishness. Listed amongst Irish peculiarities like Tayto sandwiches and 'grand stretches in the evening', '*The Late Late Toy Show* no matter your age' is considered one of the many 'things that are Irish that we cannot describe'. Albeit a quaint depiction, the poem's reference acknowledges the extent to which this relatively young Christmas tradition has become embedded in our festive celebrations. While the *Toy Show* is indeed a difficult phenomenon to capture for the non-initiated, the beloved annual programme where children rule the screen epitomises the beginning of the Christmas season for many Irish families. The programme defies the restrictions of age, as nostalgia for the *Toy Show* of old and an eagerness to participate in tradition ensures strong engagement from even the grown-up audience.

The viewing figures consistently support the status of the special as a Christmas mainstay, with the *Toy Show* often topping the charts as the No. 1 programme on Irish television. According to RTÉ, the 2022 consolidated viewing figures indicate that 1.6 million people watched the programme over the weekend of its broadcast, with the streams on the RTÉ Player reaching 139 countries. The consolidated figures emphasise the place of *The Late Late Toy Show* as a major television event for the Irish at home and abroad, even in the world of on-demand streaming services. In addition to viewing figures, the popularity of the programme is evident through social media engagement on *Toy Show* night. The metric is particularly helpful in capturing the shared experience of the show, with #LateLateToyShow trending on both TikTok and Twitter over the *Toy Show* weekend in 2022. As people participate in the commentary in person and online, certain moments and children are initiated into the *Toy Show* hall of fame, thus immortalising aspiring horologists or grand elephant entrances. *The Late Late Toy Show* is a product of and a mirror into Irish society, ensuring its status as a feature in the landscape of Irish Christmas celebrations.

THE RIGHT-HAND WOMEN

Working with host Gay Byrne for 30 years, Maura Connolly was the presenter's right-hand woman on a variety of productions, including *The Late Late Show* and *The Rose of Tralee*. As Special Assistant on *The Late Late Show*, Connolly played an instrumental role in the humble origins of the special Christmas episode, and her experience offers a unique insight into the early years of the show.

In 1974, Senior Researcher Pan Collins pitched the idea for a Christmas toy segment during a planning meeting for *The Late Late Show*. The concept was received with little enthusiasm by the team and was dismissed. Following the meeting, the two aforementioned women discussed the idea over coffee. A plan was put in place, with Connolly agreeing to support her colleague when the segment was suggested again. In her own words, Connolly liked the idea because it allowed the show to 'go with the season'. *The Late Late Show* team at this time were no strangers to innovation, constantly seeking fresh content and actively engaging with the concerns of the public. The *Toy Show* simply operated as a seasonal extension to the programme's ethos to entertain, educate and inform the Irish people.

The topic of the toy segment was broached again. True to her word, Connolly reminded Gay Byrne that, in addition to the religious festivities, toys and children were the images conjured up when people thought of the season. The segment was given the green light and its success laid the foundation for the now-annual tradition. From the beginning, the festive episode was marked as different from the show's usual tempo. The *Irish Press* wryly commented afterwards on Pan Collins almost upstaging Gay Byrne on his own programme: 'He didn't actually tell her to sit down, but I feel he would have found her a chair if she had asked for it'. It was *The Late Late Show* that the Irish public knew, but with a difference.

ALL HANDS ON DECK

Speaking on *The Late Late Toy Show Unwrapped* (2015), comedian Mario Rosenstock observed that on *Toy Show* nights Gay Byrne 'gave you the feeling that there was nobody working. It didn't look like working, it looked like he was on a night off.' This playful performance was not as effortless as it may have appeared on screen, with the team industriously working both in front of and behind the cameras.

In the earliest days of the special programme, Pan Collins filled *The Late Late Show*'s workspace with toys for her research. The items collected would go 'bump' and 'ding-a-ling' as her colleagues carried out their usual tasks around her. To avoid disturbing her colleagues further, toys were instead brought to Collins's apartment, but later the overflow found its way into Maura Connolly's sitting room. On the day of the *Toy Show*, a van from RTÉ whisked the toys to the studio, where they were assembled into a set by the team, which was no mean feat in itself.

While working on the *Toy Show* was fun, it was also 'hard work', according to Connolly. Describing herself as Byrne's 'legs outside the studio', the Special Assistant was responsible for getting guests to the studio floor. Reflecting on her role, Connolly recalled: 'People used to say to me "How do you remain so calm?"' when working on the programme. The answer was 'Preparation, preparation, preparation'.

For *The Late Late Toy Show* team, their role did not always stay behind the scenes. While many viewers today associate the Christmas special with children as the stars, the programme initially aimed to assist the show's regular adult audience in navigating Christmas toy-shopping. The toy testers were also adults, led by Pan Collins, and later Colman Hutchinson and Mary O'Sullivan. They were assisted by their colleagues; for example, the series' music director, Frank McNamara, showcased musical toys and instruments. While Maura Connolly preferred to remain behind the camera, she too was enlisted to help, recollecting her own involvement with a makeshift *Toy Show* band and testing art supplies. Gay Byrne noted in a 1992 *Sunday Independent* obituary for Pan Collins that the *Toy Show* was the only episode of the series where the two would drink a whiskey before going on air, and 'then we'd drink during the show to get us through the night'. The festive fun of *The Late Late Toy Show* may look like child's play, but it owes its success to a team who worked tirelessly to bring the programme to the nation at its inception.

ENTER THE CHILDREN

As *The Late Late Toy Show* progressed, children became more active participants in the programme as both the esteemed toy testers and performers. Initially, the tester roles were filled by children the team already knew, and so, when the opportunities were opened to the public, children were already familiar with the important role they could play during the programme. This platform even provided many future Irish perform-

Gay Byrne with several young toy testers/demonstrators on the annual toy show edition of RTÉ Television's *The Late Late Show*, broadcast from Studio 1 on 13 December 1980. Gavin Sexton and John Kearns are to the left of Gay; the remaining testers are unidentified. Senior researcher Pan Collins is in the background. Gay Byrne presented and produced this edition of the programme. Photo: Des Gaffney. With thanks to the RTÉ Stills Department.

ers (such as Imelda May, Michael English and Samantha Mumba) with their first television appearances.

The types of toys promoted, and the attitude of Gay Byrne towards them, reflected the adult-focused sensibilities of the programme's early years. Irish-made products and traditional toys were lauded over the electronic options, with the presenter commenting in 1981 that the latter were often 'useless and a bit tedious at times'. The selection of more 'appropriate' toys was not always enticing for children, as the comedian Dara Ó Briain reminisced in *The Toy Show Unwrapped*: 'It was invariably craft, and no child wants craft'. In 1975 the *Toy Show* responded specifically to adults' concerns regarding children's toys. As outlined in one article in the *Sunday Times*, toy guns and armaments were a taboo present in Northern Ireland, where 'make-believe can turn to chilling reality in a flash'. This decrease in product popularity extended to the Republic of Ireland, and Pan Collins assured the paper and parents that the *Toy Show* would not promote such toys. As the chair of the Irish Toy Fair Committee observed to the *Sunday Times*, this reaction came from the parents and not the young boys, who 'will always be fascinated by weapons'. The *Toy Show* sided with the grown-ups.

The *Late Late Toy Show*'s ability to respond to the Ireland around it has allowed the programme to flourish as a Christmas tradition. Through advertising and the internet, children have become more aware of the toys available to them and the need for a televised toy fair has decreased. Nevertheless, the *Toy Show* has ensured its continued success, as its modern incarnation, until this year hosted by Ryan Tubridy, has removed toys from its centre and opted instead to place children, entertainment and sentimentality at its heart. This adaptation has been achieved without jeopardising the existing nostalgia for the original concept. The popularity of children such as Adam King and his 'virtual hug' during the Covid pandemic is evidence of the programme's ability to anticipate the emotional pulse of the Irish public. This goodwill of the viewers towards the programme has even given rise to an annual charity appeal which has raised millions of euros for Irish children in need.

CELEBRITY SELECTIONS

Like Christmas jumpers and musical numbers, celebrity cameos have become a staple of *The Late Late Toy Show*, with appearances ranging from Irish sporting heroes to international stars. The image of a starstruck child meeting his or her idol live on air is often a fan-favourite moment, particularly when the famous face comes from an unexpected field, such as the appearance of meteorologist Evelyn Cusack in 2015. Such segments are not a new feature of the *Toy Show*, although the definition of well-known figures has altered over time. One feature of the programme under Gay Byrne invited adults described as 'friends' or 'acquaintances' of the show to pick a toy to present. These special guests included figures such as the broadcaster Thelma Mansfield, politician Brian Lenihan Senior and historian Sister Benvenuta. For Maura Connolly, this segment gifted her a favourite memory from the programme in the form of Monsignor James Horan, the force behind the foundation of Knock Airport. As Connolly recalled, the guests usually discussed their selected toy in advance to ensure that Gay Byrne was familiar with the product. Prior to the 1983 broadcast, Monsignor Horan did not indicate which toy he would present until he appeared on the studio floor with a baby doll. The selection was initially met with some confusion, with Byrne jokingly enquiring as to why the toy was 'not a Boeing 707'. Monsignor Horan explained that he had selected 'an ordinary child' as it reminded him of his Saviour and the love of parents for their child. He continued that toys were simply a 'symbol of love' and 'the most expensive ones that you showed, they're no use unless there is love'.

It is obvious why the poignant moment became a treasured memory for Connolly, and the studio audience appeared to agree with her, reacting more favourably to Monsignor Horan than to any other celebrity that year. This particular famous cameo would be unusual in the modern *Toy Show*, which carries expectations of appearances from singers like Ed Sheeran or video messages from actors like Emma Watson. Even as the programme has turned from insular to global stars, reflecting a change in Irish expectations, *The Late Late Toy Show* continues to speak to the shifting values of our society. One small way in which celebrity appearances still reveal such changes is through the increased inclusion of sporting stars like the Republic of Ireland women's football team, and boxers Katie Taylor and Kellie Harrington. Their appearances are the culmination of increased support amongst Irish society for women in sport, making them significant idols for young Irish children. The celebrity appearances on *The Late Late Toy Show* therefore reveal just one small way in which the programme can chart a change in Irish society over the decades of its broadcast.

FINAL THOUGHTS

The Late Late Toy Show, as a televised toy fair elevated to a national tradition, is undeniably an unusual phenomenon. The programme's charity appeal, merchandise collection and musical theatre production are testaments to its unique legacy in Ireland. The stage was set for the nation's favourite festive television show in 1974, but it owes its success to the teams past and present who have ensured its continued appeal. *The Late Late Toy Show* remains, in the words of Gay Byrne, for 'all the children around the country from nine months to ninety years of age'.

ACKNOWLEDGEMENTS

With special thanks to Maura Connolly for sharing her memories of *The Late Late Show*.

SOURCES AND FURTHER READING

John Bowman, *Window and mirror: RTÉ television, 1961–2011* (Cork, 2011).
RTÉ, *The Late Late Toy Show Unwrapped* (2015).

A CHRISTMAS FEELING

Norrie Gibney

(with an introduction by Fiona Hurley)

*This piece was written by my aunt, Norrie Gibney (1936–2009), and origi-
nally appeared in the anthology* If you can talk, you can write, *published
by Kilbarrack Women's Writing Group in 1983. Norrie lived all her life in
Dublin: in Fairview as a child and in Kilbarrack after she married. She was
very involved in her community, and was one of the founders of the adult
education group KLEAR (Kilbarrack Local Education for Adult Renewal).*

*Obviously, this piece has personal meaning for my family. My grandpar-
ents appear at the beginning, working hard to create the Christmas feeling
for their children. My mother appears twice: first as the baby who gave
the family 'two Christmases' when she was born in January, and again as
the sister in Sheffield minding Norrie's middle children. It captures much
of my aunt's spirit: her positive attitude in tough times, her love for her
family, and even her fondness for picking out just the right ensemble to
wear! But it also captures the spirit of working-class Dublin people in the
twentieth century, and how even in hard times they managed to create that
Christmas magic.*

The most important thing about Christmas for me is the feeling.
I don't mean atmosphere; I mean the feeling I get deep inside
when Christmas arrives. I'm sure I developed it from my mother
and father. They managed to achieve it for all the family, no matter what

the circumstances were, and I know for them it was often pretty grim. It would often appear that Christmas was just going to be like any Sunday, with baths on Saturday night, but Christmas morning dawned like magic, with presents from Santa, a large ham boiling on the cooker; we always had a ham, but not always a turkey.

I remember very distinctly the year I was ten years old [1946]. My mother was expecting my sister. Mammy took bad three weeks before Christmas. She was taken to hospital. Christmas was entirely forgotten about, or so I thought. Mammy was allowed out of the hospital on Christmas Eve and she slipped on the way home. A kind person helped her up and wanted to take her back to the hospital, but with six children at home she couldn't delay another minute. She scrubbed and polished, bathed the children and put us to bed. In the meantime, Daddy was looking after the food and Santa. It was a wonderful Christmas. My youngest sister was born on 13 January. That year we had two Christmases.

I spent two Christmases in hospital. One as a child three years old. I don't remember it very well. The second time was ten years ago, and my children's ages were, at that time, eleven, ten, seven and four years old. I went into hospital in November and I didn't expect to be out for Christmas, so I made my plans accordingly. Michelle, ten, and Jim, seven, went to stay with my younger sister who lived in Sheffield at the time. Donna, my youngest child, went to stay with another sister who lived in Portmarnock. Robert, eleven, was staying at home with his daddy. He was told he could visit me on Sunday mornings, but being the stubborn child he was and also being lonely after school, he arrived up to visit me the next day after he finished school. The Sister on the ward gave him permission to visit me every day.

As Christmas drew near, he asked if I was coming home for Christmas. I asked my doctor who said no way could he allow me home. I expected to have the worst Christmas of my life. How could you possibly get the Christmas feeling with your children scattered everywhere? My sister in Portmarnock assured me that Donna was looking forward to Christmas and the bike Santa would bring her. My brother-in-law came over from Sheffield, and also assured me that Michelle and Jim were having a good time, with several parties to look forward to as well as a visit to see my brother in Wales. They had written their letters to Santa and he had to travel to Ireland to get the guitar Michelle wanted.

Christmas Eve fell on Sunday that year. I had lots of visitors with loads of presents during the day. My husband, Bobby, came up that night. Both he and Robert would spend Christmas with Bobby's mother. He told me Robert was quite happy when he left him, being fussed over by his Nana. I was miserable, and when Bobby left I cried. One of the nurses offered to do my hair and asked what I was wearing for Christmas Day. She went through my presents with me. One of my sisters had given me a white nightdress and a white bedjacket, so we decided on this ensemble. At about ten o'clock I heard carols being sung. A few minutes later the nurses' choir had arrived in our ward and it was beautiful. When they left, something else had arrived—the Christmas feeling. I began to feel very excited. I found it difficult to get to sleep.

Christmas dawned once again for me like magic. We had a beautiful service. At eight o'clock Robert arrived dressed in his new clothes. He was very upset. Christmas had not dawned for him like magic. He had caught the first bus out of Ringsend garage to take him where Christmas was for him. The nurses gave him breakfast and then took him to the kitchen where they had a Christmas tree with a present underneath for him. He came back to me, this time smiling.

Bobby arrived shortly after, in a state. Robert had left his Nana, Grandad and Daddy outside the church after Mass and had run to the garage. He hopped on the first bus he saw and told the conductor he wanted to go to his mammy in hospital and the driver drove him straight to the hospital. His daddy and I chatted with him for a while. We explained he would have to go back to Nana's for dinner and then they could both come back later and stay for the rest of the day, which they did. He brought cards and games and we played for a few hours. We had tea together and at eight o'clock they went home, promising to see me the next day.

I couldn't say it was the best Christmas I ever had. What is the best Christmas? Once I get the Christmas feeling, they are all the best. I did leave the hospital in February, on Robert's birthday, but that's another story.

IRISH POETS IMAGINE CHRISTMAS

Kevin Williams

Two characters in Umberto Eco's novel *Foucault's Pendulum* see the world through the lens of literary sources. They do not perceive what is in nature but rather what they have learned to find there through works of art. This mind-set reflects the well-known remark of Oscar Wilde that 'Life imitates Art far more than Art imitates Life'. Now there is a sense in which our perception of Christmas is shaped by art—by sacred music ('Silent Night', 'O Holy Night'), by paintings of Nativity scenes and perhaps, too, by Dickens's *A Christmas Carol*. In this piece I propose to explore how poetry can give expression to a perception of Christmas that may inform and enrich the lives of readers. I shall concentrate on two poems of Patrick Kavanagh that were widely studied in school in the past, but first I shall consider a powerful but less well-known short poem of eight lines, 'Magi' by W.B. Yeats, which has perhaps been overshadowed in the popular imagination by Eliot's 'Journey of the Magi'.

In 'Magi', the speaker explains that the Magi are ever-present in his 'mind's eye', as he envisages them dressed in 'stiff, painted clothes' and looking 'pale' and 'unsatisfied'. Their eyes are 'fixed' in the effort to make sense of the birth of Christ, which the poet calls the 'uncontrollable mystery on the bestial floor'. The Magi also foresee the Crucifixion, but they do not understand the 'turbulence' of this awful event and their quest for meaning remains unfulfilled or 'unsatisfied', the second time

Yeats uses this word. As we shall see, the Magi also make an appearance in Kavanagh's 'A Christmas Childhood', but their appearance there prompts a positive response in the speaker.

But first we shall examine Kavanagh's poem 'Advent', which concerns the search for childhood innocence through penitential exercises and religious renewal. The speaker rejects the world of indulgence and self-conscious questioning to find again the innocence of a child. Indulgence in pursuit of pleasure has brought satiation and a craving for childhood's sense of guiltlessness. The satiation is conveyed in words stating that the speaker and his lover, meaning his inner self, 'have tested and tasted too much'. His experience has opened a 'chink too wide' in his world and he is no longer capable of enjoying the 'wonder' of things. By doing penance, and through the severe self-restraint of limiting himself to 'dry black bread and the sugarless tea', he hopes to recover what he calls rather paradoxically 'the luxury / Of a child's soul'. Following this period of penance, he will come to find 'newness' in 'every stale thing', as it would be seen through the eyes of a child. The penitential purging will allow him to find delight in the 'ordinary plenty' of life. Rather than being a time of self-indulgence, Christmas will lead to the discarding of the 'clay-minted wages / Of pleasure, knowledge and the conscious hour' to appreciate the enduring presence of Christ, who 'comes with a January flower' in his new way of life.

The other poem by Kavanagh, 'A Christmas Childhood', is probably more embedded in the imaginative world of the Irish Christmas in the minds of many readers. The speaker is again reflecting on the transition from childhood to adult life. All of this makes the poem a marvellous symphony of images and insight into the delight of Christmas. It is a eulogy to childhood and a lament on the erosion of innocence by the experience of the adult world. It is also a hymn to the magic of Christmas. The transition from childhood's Garden of Eden to the realm of adult corruption is registered in the first verse. Eve was 'the world that tempted me'. This was the temptation to 'eat the knowledge that grew in clay', which contained within it the 'germ' of 'death'. This knowledge led to his ignoring 'the transfigured face' of the universe of the ordinary, everyday 'beauty that the world did not touch'.

The long second verse of the poem situates this beauty in the wonder-filled season of Christmas. This world was permeated by a religious spirit and by the speaker's response to the Nativity narrative. As his father 'played the melodeon', stars appeared 'in the morning east / And they danced to his music'. His mother made the 'music of milking', while the lamp that she used 'was a star' made to 'twinkle' by 'the frost of Bethlehem'. As the people headed for Mass, he could hear them crunch 'the wafer-ice on the pot-holes'. All of this creates 'the wonder of a Christmas townland'. Looking towards the horizon, he sees 'three whin bushes' transformed by his imagination into 'the Three Wise Kings'. In the final verse of the poem, the speaker returns to the images of the father playing the melodeon and the mother milking, to conclude with the lovely lines 'And I had a prayer like a white rose pinned / On the Virgin Mary's blouse'.

To be sure, not all poems about Christmas by Irish poets are as positive as was the speaker in Kavanagh's poems. One of the most famous poems that takes a jaundiced view is the book-length *Christmas Day* by Paul Durcan—a poem that, like 'Advent', was featured in *The Guardian*'s poetry section. For the speaker, a single man on his own, Christmas is the 'Feast of St Loneliness'. This sense of being isolated from the community is captured in the lines 'I street-walk at night / Looking in the windows / Of other people's houses / Assessing their Christmas decorations, / Marking them out of ten'. Yet an invitation from a friend leads to companionship, as the friends review their memories of the past. The poem becomes a Proustian search for lost time.

Another Christmas poem that recalls a disturbing event is simply called 'Xmas', by Amanda Bell. This poem reminds me of all the people I know whose Christmases were marked by illness or bereavement. It is printed in the form of a Christmas tree, and the speaker recalls one Christmas Eve when her father suffered a 't.i.a.' (TIA: transient ischaemic attack). She was so 'triggered' that she felt that she 'could power /

each decoration / on the tree'. The paramedics set to work beside the food and wine that 'spilt as glass slid from his grip'. He is described as having 'one hand clawed & face screwed up', as the family figure out where they can find a hospital's Emergency Department. The event prompted the thought that 'This dark night of the year might always be the last', leading to family members 'fiercely forging / memories by the flames of table candles'.

A final example of a poem that conveys a negative image of the season is 'Christmas in Kinsale' by Derek Mahon. Described as 'Holed up here in the cold gardens of the west', the speaker in the poem is a lone figure carrying out rubbish in a gloomy landscape. Among objects that are 'wet and dry', the trash includes 'cardboard and the ... / remains of rib and chop, warm cinders, ash'. All of this reminds him of a dream he had of 'the white islands' of the Greek Cyclades that appear to urge him to go to Greece and to leave his present abode and the uninviting environment of a cold Irish winter.

So the images of Christmas in the work of these poets are not uniform, and readers may wonder whether the joyful, communal Christmas reflected in Kavanagh's poems can ever be recaptured. Possibly. I was moved by the effort made by a curate in a local parish to engage people in a communal sharing at Christmastime. At Mass he welcomed parishioners, visitors from outside the parish, visitors from other Christian and non-Christian faith traditions, and visitors who did not believe in God but who wanted to be part of the community's celebration of Christmas. Envisaged in this inclusive way, the season can retain its special bonding potency.

SOURCES

All of the texts mentioned in this essay can readily be found online.

THE CHRISTMAS GIFT

Mary Hilary

Lamplight shone on the tall, athletic figure standing huddled in the snow. The light fluffy flakes had already adorned Gary's coat with streaks of a darker shade, and his hair was dusted with glistening white jewels that settled on his curls and melted on his face, making him cold and irritated. He was angry, frustrated and impatient. He cursed the night air, the evening, and the bus for being late.

In the pub nearby, his friends and team-mates were celebrating their triumphant win in the mini-league. They were on their way to the big league and this cup was theirs. He was proud, content that he had led this team to their first success, working, training, sweating for months for their victory. The young team were all together for the first time to celebrate. They had a double celebration to enjoy, winning the mini-league and Christmas. It would be a long night for the excited victorious players, tasting success for the first time.

He muttered darkly under his breath, 'I should be there with them, instead of here'. He slumped against the bus-stop, waiting, with his eyes glued to the door of the pub. He had promised his mother that he would visit his granddad in the local nursing home that evening. 'Why this night above all nights?', he thought glumly, and sighed loudly.

The pub door opened briefly to let someone in. As the light flashed onto the speckled pavement, he heard an explosion of loud raucous laughter, music and the clinking of glasses. 'I should be there,' he muttered again to himself, and knew that his team were waiting for him. He lowered his head against the sleety sharp breeze and thrust his hands deeper into his pockets. As he waited, his fingers closed around the medal.

His face was turned towards the pub for so long that he didn't hear the bus approach from the opposite direction until it was almost beside him. Its door opened and the young driver gave him a sideways glance. Then his eyes lit up and he smiled broadly and said, 'Gary, the man of the match. Congratulations! Did you hear me shouting at the lads? It was terrific. Well done!' Gary nodded, then hesitated, a half-smile on his face as he turned slowly, with one foot on the bus and the other on the footpath. Seconds passed; he took a final look at the pub and then quickly jumped on board without a backward glance.

He sat with his eyes closed on the journey, his dejected face reflected in the window. 'Why don't you visit Granddad tonight, Gary? You haven't seen him for a long time, and he would be delighted to see your medal.' The voice echoed in his head as he recalled the stilted conversation with his mother, who had pleaded with him at supper that evening. For some reason she was insisting that he visit his granddad, and it was the one thing he wished she wouldn't ask of him—not today, not now. He had gone silent, quietly fuming, and said under his breath, 'Maybe, Mum; I have to meet the lads for a celebration, so I'm not sure I can fit this in today.'

The bus deposited a still-disgruntled man at the nursing home. He trudged up the path and was met by the mature, big-framed Matron, who asked his name. 'I'm Mr Culleton's grandson, Gary,' he replied. He wasn't a frequent visitor to his granddad, and for a brief spell he felt the Matron's eyes on him, as if discovering the guilt he had begun to feel.

The smell of the place sickened him. The polish, the smell of old slippers and disinfectant wafted up to his nostrils, and he braced himself to carry on down the varnished floor past the empty chairs at the side of the corridor. He followed the Matron, who walked briskly before him down two flights of stairs and along another corridor. Without looking back at him she said quietly, 'Your Granddad was talking about you all day today.' At last they came to the room; the Matron opened the door and, still without looking at Gary, walked inside. 'He's here, Mr Culleton,' she said. 'He made it.'

Gary entered slowly, his eyes adjusting to the darkened room. The television was off and a small light on the bedside locker highlighted his granddad lying on the bed, a sunken figure with his bones showing through his flesh as if his skin was two sizes too big. There was no noise except for the sound of his laboured breathing.

The old man turned his head and his eyes took a while to register the identity of his visitor. He smiled when he recognised the young face and patted the bed, saying in a weak, breathy voice, 'Great game, great game, son! They allowed me to sit up and watch you on the box.'

An air of peace came into the room and the two men sat together, two generations apart yet united in their love for the game they both lived to play. They talked of strategies, training, fitness and referees. They spoke of the new rules and the safety helmets and the nutrition that was a vital part of the clubs' programmes for young players. Granddad smiled and said, 'I would like to see the new clubhouse someday but it doesn't look like it now in this weather.' Gary nodded, knowing it would not happen but wanting to keep the hope alive in the old man's heart. 'I'll bring you down when the renovation is done, to see the new showers, gym and car park.' Granddad softly whispered, 'Gary, that will be something to look forward to someday.'

Gary took his granddad's pale, creamy, cold hands in his warm strong fingers and then reached down into his pocket; taking out the medal, he placed it in the old hands. His emotions flashed before him in that moment—from anticipation at meeting his team and elation at reliving the victory to anger at his mother's insistence that he visit his grand-dad—and then a sudden deep reverence overcame him as he watched his granddad's face light up when he tenderly and shakily grasped the medal and sat up slowly in the bed to see it more clearly. The old man beamed as he fingered the medal and turned it around many times in his gnarled hands and chuckled. 'Gary,' he said, 'the last time I held one of these was before you were born, and it is right good to see one again in the Culleton family.'

The old man lay back again on the pillow and sighed, going back in time in his thoughts. 'Did I tell you it was a great game, Gary, great game, and I saw you twisting and running and diving like it was me out there.'

There was silence for a while, and then the old man frowned. 'Wait yet now, Gary, your mother said you would be celebrating with your team-mates tonight?'

Gary smiled at him, stood up, took off his wet coat and put it on a chair near the wardrobe. He sat quietly beside his granddad and stretched out his legs, saying softly, 'You're all right, the lads can wait a bit longer. The Culletons have the medal back. A very, very, happy Christmas, Granddad.'

WHERE JESUS WALKED

Max McCoubrey

Travelling on the road from Baraachit, a rural town in southern Lebanon, I looked at my radio producer, Kevin Hough, and smiled. It had been a rough trip so far, and on this, our last evening, we were both looking forward to a change of pace. Kevin and I had been friends since our school-days and were united in a love of music, communication, each other and fun. Through a circuitous route, we found ourselves working together in radio. RTÉ had been invited to visit the Irish peacekeeping forces to record their voices for a radio programme to be broadcast on Christmas Day. My link with Kevin was an unbreakable bond. When our boss spotted it, he asked us to go on this unique assignment, knowing that we would both enjoy it and would mind each other in war-torn territory.

Wearing our identity tags, flak jackets and bulletproof vests, we were driving past houses that clung to the cliff edges around us. Below us the rocky terrain fell away into a gorge, carved out long ago by a fast-flowing stream. We were on our way, with our recording equipment and an army escort, to Tibnin, a Lebanese town spread across several hills east of Tyre. It was December 1986.

The talk in the truck was about how near we were to the area where Jesus had once lived, and to the river of Galilee, where His miracles of walking on water, calming the storm and feeding the 5,000 had been performed.

On this, the night before our return to Ireland, our hosts had arranged an informal evening. The soldiers had relocated a piano and it took centre stage. There were songs, stories and a quiz on the running order. Morale was at an all-time high.

Alex, who had been our assigned driver all month in an AML90 tank, took me aside a few hours into the evening.

'One of our guys, Eamo, lost the toss of the coin at the start of the day, and is now on lookout duty,' he confided as he poured me a cup of tea. 'He's on his own in the station all evening. He would love to have been here for this gathering.'

'So you tossed a coin?', I asked.

'Yes, and he lost.' He handed me the container of powdered milk.

'Would I be allowed to say hello?', I wondered.

Alex thought for a moment, and then went to talk with his commanding officer. He came back looking very happy.

'Yes, we can go and see him only if I can relieve him of his duty when he talks to you, and I am willing to do that.'

The rope ladder to the lookout post was long, thin and freezing to the touch, but we made it to the top and into the small area designed for maximum vision of the war zone. Eamo was there, face blackened, staring in silence into the ebony evening. Alex introduced us and then took over duty, to give us an opportunity to talk.

To say that Eamo did not avail of this chance was an understatement. He continued staring ahead, completely ignoring my presence. I decided to break the silence. Maybe that was what was expected of me. I didn't know.

'I'm Maxi,' I said quietly, watching carefully for any sign of recognition from the blackened face. All of his troubles were engraved on it. I read only disappointment, heartbreak and sorrow, but I kept going anyway.

'I am here to record the voices of the troops for a radio broadcast to be transmitted on Christmas day in Ireland.'

'Yes.'

He said it as if he was ticking an item on a shopping list. There was no warmth, no interest, and no response except what was expected of him in the capacity of a soldier in the service of his country. His expression never moved, even though his lips did, just long enough to form the words.

'I'm a singer,' I added.

His next movement was a blink of the eyelids. They cleared the way for more vision from his deadened eyes.

'Really?'

The silence hung. There we stood, the three of us, watching the bombs in Beirut lighting up the sky with their amber talons. Great explosions ripped into the quiet, bringing an afterglow of ribbons which turned our faces pink, purple and grey before they dissipated into the enveloping blackness. Eventually Eamo spoke.

'What's with the stage name, Maxi; where did that come from?'

'Maxi is not a stage name,' I responded to the welcome question, 'it's a nickname. The way yours is Eamo. That comes from Eamonn; well, mine is from the initials of my surname. My full name is McCoubrey, and the initials are McC. The girls in school called me that, when they found it difficult to pronounce my name—it's from Northern Ireland— and it stuck. I like it now.'

Another explosion hit the land where Jesus had walked. This was the biggest one yet, and it was followed by a barrage of bullets and an air-raid siren. Underneath my feet, I was surprised to hear the beauty of Kevin's piano-playing in the billet I had just left, adding an unexpected audio to the mortar-firing and battle ambience. He was playing the opening chords of 'Joy to the World' with all the strength he could muster. He must have heard the sounds of war too, and that, I knew, would be Kevin's first reaction. He was a man who believed strongly in thinking positively, especially in these extraordinary circumstances.

Kevin's tenor voice then led the troops in a chorus of male vocal power, all of them determined to drown out the sounds now trying to dominate them. Some harmonised and even the tone-deaf made their contribution, while the rest used their spoons in an attempt at percussion.

I marvelled at the massive contrast of activities in such a small area. The forest of cedar trees on the horizon had caught fire and javelins of

Max McCoubrey and Kevin Hough, Lebanon 1986. Image courtesy of the author.

putrid purple smoke were making their way skyward. There was a crackling of burning wood almost as strong as the ricochet of bullets.

Eamo spoke before the next hail and broke into my thoughts. His voice was now younger and more mellifluous.

'My insurance man back home was called McCoubrey, a real gentleman, always gave me time when I was a kid. I called him Mr Mack; I couldn't pronounce his name either.'

Beneath us, Kevin began the final music of the evening; all the voices within hearing distance were singing 'Oh Come, All Ye Faithful'.

I looked closely at Eamo's face. 'That's my dad!' I touched his frozen hand. 'I am Mister Mack's daughter.'

The disappointment left his drooping shoulders and a ray of recognition graced his tired grey visage. A face that had been unhappy suddenly became home to the widest grin this side of Bethlehem. His eyes were warmer than the fire consuming the cedar trees, his smile wider than the landscape view we had of the territory at war. He instantly reached out to shake my hand.

'Thank you for making the journey to bring our love to our families; it means so much to us when we can't get home and spend the holiday with them.'

My jaw dropped at the sudden change of heart that my father's name had brought to the sentry.

'You are most welcome,' I answered, and felt my heart skip a beat. 'Have a lovely Christmas.'

'You too,' he beamed. 'Later, may I take a photo of me and Mr Mack's daughter?'

'Only if you join in with me on the chorus of that lovely hymn,' I suggested.

'Deal!'

CHRISTMAS AMONG THE
TRAVELLING COMMUNITY

Salvador Ryan interviews Nell McDonagh

What are your earliest memories of Christmas while growing up within the Travelling community?

We loved Christmas. I have great memories. Christmas was always the most important celebration in our family. My earliest memory would be when we had just moved into a house in Mullingar (I was only about six or seven) and my mother, like many Travelling women of her age (reacting to being referred to as dirty …), went overboard in cleanliness. There was white tiles in our sitting room, and you weren't allowed use the sitting room. But Santy Claus had come down the chimney and my father was wearing a pair of wellington boots, and he had walked on the soot of the fireplace, right across mammy's white floor, to the end of my bed and the gifts were left there. And I remember my mother didn't appreciate Santy too well.

But Christmas for Travellers, even when we were on the side of the road, was the most important time of the year. It was probably the only time of the year you got to meet your relatives. Like, I remember, we were camping and Christmas was the one time of the year that you'd arrange to meet. But you'd always leave the countryside, and your country camp, for a couple of days until Christmas was over, and you'd go into near the town because the begging or the hawking that the women had to do—and don't forget, these women hadn't a 'nuck' [a Cant word for a penny]—

everything my mother and my grandmother had, they had to beg for. And in order to make Christmas special they always camped in or near a town so that the beggings would be good. Now you probably wouldn't get Christmas Day until that night or the next day because the women had to wait until the farmers and the townspeople were finished their Christmas dinner to get what was left over. So we depended on your mother finishing her Christmas dinner with your family and then whatever she had left over she would give it to Mam. It was also the one time of the year that the women were allowed to get a bottle of stout. So the women would go in on the Christmas Eve when they'd be hawking the houses or the shops, begging all day, and then they would go into the pub, and they'd be let in and they'd get one bottle of Guinness. And there used to be a woman outside Carnaross in County Meath here, that was a notorious good camp for Travellers, particularly for my family, and this woman (a country woman) every Christmas Eve … she would have known, we'll say there was five or six families camping in the area, for the five or six married women that was in the camp, she'd bring them down five or six bottles of Guinness. And this was the greatest present ever. So when the children was all fed, and when the men were all fed, then the women had time to drink the six bottles of Guinness together. That was very precious time.

What kind of preparations did the Travelling community make in advance of Christmas?
I never ever saw my grandfather without a suit on at Christmas, and he walking round the camp. If you got a good pair of shoes during the year, you'd mind them and you kept them for Christmas. The women kept their good skirts or their good aprons. The custom was that it was such a special time, such a spiritual time, that you wore your best. My grandfather never, from Christmas Eve morning until right up after Christmas, he wore the suit; always wore a tie; because it was Christmas; so the celebrating side of looking your best out of having nothing was of vital, vital importance. You met your family; you mightn't see somebody for a year before that; so when they came, there was always extra bread baked; there

was extra grub cooked out of nothing. The women for weeks would have been going to the likes of your mother and they'd be saying 'My family is coming up from Carrick-on-Shannon', or my family is coming from this place or that place; so, the women in the house would be putting their name in to get an extra bit of grub, to celebrate and have a party; and you'd be going to the nuns or to the priest's house, and you'd be saying 'My mother's people are coming up from Mohill, Father; they're all coming up and it'll take nearly them two weeks to get here'. So you'd be watching the priest to maybe get an extra two shillings, or whatever; or a half-crown; and that was always to supply the food and drink. And the parties and the storytelling went on for days.

Were homes decorated for the Christmas? And how were they decorated?
It would depend. The most important decoration you could ever have was the red candle. Do you remember the big, long, red candles? And my granny actually—wherever she got it, I don't know—but she got a star, like a massive big star, and my grandfather had a light, a torch, on his bike (this was only used during certain really dark evenings), but for Christmas she used to put the light of grandfather's bike into the star. You could open up the bottom of the star; and it would light up, and it was hanging on the wagon, outside the wagon. You'd see this star for miles down the road coming up towards the camp. And Granny minded that star—oh, for God's sake, she had it a lifetime. That, and the candles. The most precious, precious decoration you could ever have on the wagon. And even those that couldn't afford wagons always had to have a candle. From early November, you'd be up in the houses asking the people would they get you a candle, would they keep you a candle, would they give you a candle. And you'd look so forward to getting a candle.

Was the tradition of lighting the candle connected to making sure that there was a welcome for the Holy Family if they were passing, and looking for lodging on Christmas Eve?

Very, very much so. And if you were lucky enough to own a wagon, and you didn't have a star like Granny had, your tilly lamp would be lit. They were called storm lamps because of their strength. You could see this tilly lamp, maybe from about a mile; it was like a star in the sky. You always lit a candle, or you left a lamp lighting all night if you could afford the paraffin oil, for the Holy Family (Mary and Joseph and Baby Jesus) if they passed through. And if you were praying for an extra blessing, if a child or an adult was unwell, you'd believe because Christmas was a time the Holy Family visited you, that when they saw the candle, they knew that you needed help by seeing the candle lighting, or the tilly lamp lighting, so they passed through your home and they'd help the family member that was sick. And we didn't have photographs; you wouldn't have had photographs; but if I had a cap belonged to my grandfather, or an apron belonged to my granny, and they needed extra blessing, you'd leave them out beside the lamp so the Baby Jesus and the Holy Family knew that I needed prayers for my grandfather. They were so simple, but they were so reverent.

Tell me about going to Christmas Eve Mass.
If you were lucky enough, you'd go and, maybe, get a child christened at Midnight Mass. And they would walk, or travel in their pony and car a couple of mile. I remember years ago we camped in a little place called Killala, a rural area outside Dundalk. And there was a little church called Killala chapel. And we were all brought to Midnight Mass. And it was pitch black. And you'd maybe have one fellow in the front that would have a light (the others wouldn't) so they'd all stay behind each other. Don't forget there wasn't much traffic on the roads. And we'd go to Mass. And one of the women had had a child. And the child was brought in to get christened at Midnight Mass in Killala chapel. And we'd go on down to the church. And nobody was hurrying. And they were shaking hands with all their neighbours, the country people; and of course if I saw your mother again, and she was a special friend, and I knew she was going to give me an extra bit that day when I went for my Christmas dinner; and

they were so welcoming; they'd say 'We're having our dinner at twelve o'clock; come up to me at one o'clock and I'll have it all ready for you'. Or some of the country people would actually bring sweet cake or little bits to the Mass with them, and they'd leave them outside the chapel so that when you came out from Mass you'd collect your little box of grub, or your bag of beggings off them, and put them up on the pony and car. And there was always a bar of chocolate for the children at Christmas. You normally went for a longer camp at Christmas because it was too dark to move. So we could be three months at that camp because we were waiting for St Patrick's Day and everyone went then. So I'd built more of a relationship and your family knew early October, without fail, we were coming to camp near you. You could set your watch that every year we were arriving in October. So we got to know each other.

Were cribs popular among the Travelling community—were they to be found in homes?
They wouldn't have had a crib as such; however, there used to be men (the tinsmith men) who used to make little figures, and you'd get a bit of straw … you always got into the chapel (Mass was of mega importance—if you were dying on your deathbed, you had to go to Mass on a Christmas Day). But the men used to go maybe two weeks before Christmas, and when the crib would go up in the chapels, they'd go in and get a bit of straw out of the crib 'cause that was considered really lucky, and many Travellers believed that it had particular cures. Like, if you had ailments of continuous sickness or bronchitis or anything, you always put a bit of straw from the crib inside your jumper, or inside your vest, and the children in particular. So the men would go to the chapel, get a bit of straw, bring it back, and put little figures that they'd make out of elder bushes. The elder was very easy peeled. And so they'd peel it and shape it into little figures of a man and a woman (Joseph and Mary) and the Baby Jesus.

How important a figure was Santa Claus when you were growing up?

In my home, being the only girl, Santa was in my life until I was about fourteen or fifteen years of age, which is really unusual. My father would've been considered a fairly well-off man insofar as he came from a small family, and the three men had all trades (one was a tinsmith, one was a hawker, and one was a wagon-maker) so they all had a few extra shillings. So Santa always came. It was always a doll. Every year without fail, everybody got a doll; a doll for a girl and a gun and pouch for a boy. And that was right across the board. Or a cowboy hat. And the mothers would try to make little rag dolls for the girls. So even though it was very hard times, and the time we were growing up it was very much on the gift of love and the gift of making an effort, and if my mother or Granny went to a house and got the leftover turkey, or the leftover goose or whatever, they were so appreciative of that. You'd be praying for the woman; you'd be almost on your knees thanking them for the gift of food. And particularly a bit of extra grub. I mean, you never got a sweet cake, a Christmas cake, only if somebody in a house gave it to you coming up to Christmas; because you couldn't afford currants or anything. Women would make ribbons for your girls' plaids; or the older girls would get a pocket, their first beady pocket for Christmas; the young married women would get a beady pocket or, if they could afford it, a rug or a shawl.

Christmas was very much on the religious side of the belief in the teachings of the Church. It was very much on the Catholic faith. As I said, I've vivid memories of my brothers bringing me to Mass on the handlebar of the bike. And the pony and cart, and the cart getting washed, and polished almost, to bring down to the door of the chapel. You'd be all going down, and your hair would be all plaided really well. You wore your good shoes. You were always in your good wear for Christmas, and particularly for Mass at Christmas. It was such a happy time. Even in times of awful weather. I was born on 14 January in the back of a tent. But my mammy and daddy always told us about Christmas before that—my mother was very much confined to the tent—but the women and the neighbours, the country women, who got to know her, used to come up at Christmas and give her extra little gifts, or extra food. It was a hard time, but a very, very special time.

And, on Christmas Day, ye would sit down for the dinner later in the day after the women came back from going round the houses?
Don't forget, the women had to go out in the country, as it was called, so the women had to get ready. You were always ready a couple of days in advance. You'd have everything organised for where you were going. So you had to wait until the country people were finished their dinner. So if it was a couple of mile up the road, I'd bring the pony and car up, and your mother would have it all packed for me and ready to bring it home. So we would have always had dinner, definitely. You'd get fried bread with onions that morning before you'd go out. There was never any meat for breakfast that morning because it was always kept for the Christmas dinner. So you'd go out in the country. It could be twelve or one o'clock (dinners weren't as late that time) and you'd collect the food. It was already cooked.

Who would gather together for the Christmas meal? Would it be the nuclear family or wider family?
Anybody on the road. So if there was four or five families, the men would always be served and, this is something that has been continued (but maybe not as much now), the men would all be at one fire, and the men would be all served first; and then the children would be served; but you'd serve everybody on the road. The women would cook together, and serve it together. And don't forget we wouldn't have had access to, like, plates or cutlery, or whatever, so it could be the lid of a pot you were getting your dinner on; but however you got it, it didn't make it any less special. You could have five or six children eating out of the one lid of a pot. The women would boil the spuds and you'd get a piece of white, calico cloth, like an apron, and you'd spread that out, and you'd strain the spuds and put them out on top of the cloth. And the men just served themselves and the meat was always on a separate plate for themselves.

And where would that usually take place?

Outside. Outside or in a shelter tent. If the weather was really bad, you had a big shelter tent. So whoever would have a bigger shelter tent. Or you'd probably more or less go to the older family member, like Granny. Theirs was the fire we'd all go to. The tent would be all bits of balloons, or whatever they got; any bits of rags; like a May bush; tying up the bits of colour. And the fire would be lit. And you could be in there till all hours of the morning singing songs and telling stories. It was a celebration. And the best that you could do. So if it meant coming into a shelter tent, that was your castle. And you cooked your food. And you shared everything and because we got it late (you'd be waiting for the women to come back to the house). Of course the food wouldn't just be for today, Christmas Day; it would be tomorrow and the next day. Stephen's Day was always a day for the men; they always kept an extra few bob, and they'd go to the pub. And the women would have that time for themselves; even though we didn't go to the pub, it would be very much a women's day.

And what sort of stories would be told around Christmas?

Christmas was so important for family. And I think before it was even trendy—people now coming home from America or coming home from Australia—well we were coming from the four corners of Ireland—to meet your family. So that was a big celebration. And you'd hear all the stories about people camping over in Galway, or you'd hear about the people below in Waterford or Cork, telling the stories of what was happening in the area, who had a child (this was in the time before mobile phones; and no electricity), who had a baby, what was the baby's name; who it was called after; who had got married; who had died. One of the stories from my own family that Daddy always told was when my grandfather had a sister who died in childbirth (she was sixteen) and she died around September or October, but they didn't know until they met at Christmastime, and they were camping around Kingscourt, Co. Cavan, and when they arrived to Navan to tell the story that Daddy's aunt Julia had died (she was just sixteen) Daddy's uncle Tommy got such a scary fright that he actually jumped into the Boyne river because he was in such pain and shock at the loss of his beautiful sister.

But around Christmas, they were always making good stories out of sad stories. You always spoke about the likes of Mrs Hyland, who would give this gift to the women. You'd always know, the Travelling women used to sell swag; they'd have the holy pictures that they'd give to the women in the houses that were good to them. So it always meant good memories. My father had a story. My Granny was begging in Navan on Christmas morning; after Mass she went begging; and a woman in a house gave her a tin of peas, and they had never, ever, ever, seen food in a tin. And they were so afraid when my grandfather was opening the lid of the tin, with the clips, they actually wouldn't eat them; they thought the woman was trying to poison them. My granny talked for years afterwards about the (missed) opportunity to taste peas in a can; he'd never tasted them in his life; no food from a can; they thought it was a plan to kill all the Travellers.

Tell me something about the practice of gift-giving among the Travelling community at Christmas. Were there certain kinds of gifts that were particularly popular?

If you didn't see your relative for twelve months beforehand, during the year the women would make aprons, and they'd decorate them with buttons or make a pocket. Or get hair slides. And they'd keep them. Or if I went out in the country and a farmer's wife gave me a pair of wellington boots, and I got another pair of shoes off somebody else, well I would keep them for my sister that was coming up from Carrick-on-Shannon, as a gift for Christmas. So if I got two pair of shoes (I only needed one) the other one was kept for a relative who came on a special occasion, who I mightn't see again for a couple of years. So gifts were exchanged. The men could make mouth organs; some of the tinsmiths. They were powerful men. They could make a mouth organ. Now not every man could make it. Some of the men could. So if you had someone in your family that could make a mouth organ, he could make five or six for the children coming up, or for the men coming up to visit, and you gave them as a gift. And hair slides. Hair slides was a big one. You'd gather up bit of ribbon. Or you might get a bit of red cloth off your mother during the year, so then I'd sew on little bits of silver. And if you made paper flowers, at Christmastime you melted candle wax and you dipped the paper flowers in the wax, which made them last much longer. So they were like plastic flowers, but they weren't. So you'd make a big bunch of them if someone belonging to you was coming up. When I think back how simple a thing that made people so happy. The women would go off back home with a big bunch of paper flowers, some hair slides, or a packet of hair clips, and they were so happy. Or maybe I'd gather up buttons during the year for a beady pocket, and I'd keep a couple of buttons and I'd give them to my sister, or my aunt, or my cousins who came up, and then you'd meet them two or three years later and they'd have the buttons sewed on to the pockets, and they knew; they could say 'I got that off you when we were camping at Carnaross'. So they always knew where they got the stuff from.

What games were played at Christmastime? Were there particular games or activities associated with Christmas rather than other times of the year?
Because people were in good humour and you met people you wouldn't have seen in a long time, so when they came to visit, everybody came, children and everything. The actual adults used to have a game. It was called Tip the Coal. It was very unusual. You'd all turn your back and I'm the one that's on. So I'd get a stick and I'd take a coal, and I'd tip the stick on that coal. Then he'd turn around and he'd have to guess which coal it was. And, Jeeny Mack, when I think of it, we must have been so simple! It's sort of harmless. But the most interesting game which I used to love, and older Travellers used to use it ... we'd a man here who worked on our Living History project, and he was a man in his eighties when he died. And they had a powerful game, and you used it particu-

larly with the visitors who came at Christmastime. It was who could tell the best lie, or make up the best story. So you were camping with me all year and I could tell you a story about the mare foaling and it being stolen by the fairies, or whatever. Now Travellers had awful superstitions about fairies and all that. This could go on for hours and hours, and everybody would be involved, men and women. But you didn't show any emotion or start laughing. That was part of the game. So it was very much an adult game in the sense that, like your granny and grandfather and all took part in this game. You might have a woman saying that she was hawking the houses one day and the woman of the house gave her a fifty pound note. And the woman had got this back from America or something. And they'd be all saying what did you spend it on? Or there'd be suspicions because you got a new cover for your wagon during the year. There was particular families. The Keenans were natural storytellers. My grandfather's people were related into them. So they could tell you a story; like there used to be a famous story of two brothers called Martin and Michael Keenan. Martin lived in Manchester and he used to come at Christmastime. And Martin was telling a story to an audience of about twenty people in this shelter tent, and he was telling this story about a horse; that he'd bought a horse during the year and the horse could talk; he was so well trained the horse could talk. And he said to his brother Michael, 'And isn't that the truth, Michael?' and Michael would say 'Yeah, I was there!' and Michael would confirm the story. There was stories told about farmers giving you a full cow, or curing this cow for you, and this is where all the food came from, but sure they were made-up stories, and they involved the children as well. And the children would go along with it. The stories were used as a form of celebrating, and of respecting and welcoming the people that came to you. It was about making your stay in my camp a memorable one and a good one.

How were the dead remembered at Christmastime? Were there particular practices associated with remembering loved ones who had passed away— visits to the grave around Christmas, or remembrance at meals?

You'd always visit the dead at Christmas. Whether it be Christmas Eve or Christmas Day, there was some time that you went and you visited your dead, and you'd put fresh flowers on their grave, and you'd clean and wash their headstones. And you'd always remember the dead by getting prayers said for them. Or if you had a picture of them, you displayed it at Christmas. You minded the picture, but you took it out at Christmas to remember the dead, to be inclusive of the dead, and to make sure they were still part of the family.

Was the practice of 'hunting the wran' on St Stephen's Day popular among the Travelling community?
That was probably the best day. You all went out on the 'wran'. The children were brought into the town (they never got into the town); you'd all have soot off the fire, and the *gríosach* they called it (you know the coals with the burnt sticks) and you'd cover your face with black and designs, all crazy-looking, and an inside shirt, or your mother's shawl, and particularly if you had a family where there was a good singer. And girls were allowed into pubs on Stephen's Day; and my aunt Nelly would be singing like a nightingale; and the people in the country pubs were always very kind; they were very, very kind to Travellers; and they really and truly made it very special. Like there was no such thing as discrimination at that time. I was never aware of it. My mother never spoke of it. My father never spoke of it. Like the reality was, we were camping on the side of the road; we had nothing; the people who had it shared it with us. So the men would all go to the pubs and spend most of the day in there. The children would be brought out on the wran. And we'd be going singing. And you'd get a fortune. And there were families like the Keenans who were remarkable singers. And the men would go out on the wran before they went to the pub. And they'd be brought off singing and entertaining in the pubs. And then you came home. And the men would take a few pound and the women would be counting the pennies. And the grandfather used to say 'Well I can get one box of tin out of this'. Or you might be able to get enough stuff to make a new chimney for

the wagon. The better singer you were … and that you'd have no shame. You weren't allowed to have shame. So they'd say to you 'Now, put your shame in your pocket, and go in there and sing', whether you could sing or not. You were made sing and tell stories; and dance. It was great entertainment for the people living in the town. You couldn't have shame. You wouldn't have survived if you had shame, or were shy. The louder you could sing, the better. And you'd go round with a saucepan and you'd fill up the saucepan with pennies and ha'pennies and shillings. It was an income. It was like a couple of month's beggings. And the women would spend that day … it was very much a sit-back day for the women.

Can you tell me a little about your memories of New Year's Eve celebrations among the Travelling community? How important was this celebration when you were growing up?

New Year's was important because it was the start of the year. And there was some strange customs around it. Like, a woman couldn't wash her hair on New Year's Day. You didn't wash your hair. You didn't wash clothes. The first person into your sheltered tent or wagon at that time had to be a dark-haired man. There was a belief that Jesus was a dark-haired man, so because of this he's a representative of Jesus coming into your home, to bring you luck for the start of the new year. I remember my mother used to send my brother (he'd really pitch-black hair); and she'd send him out the back door and walk the whole way round the end of the lane (because we lived in a little terraced cottage and there was no side entrance); so he was made walk all around the end of the lane and come in the front door just in case another man came in in the meantime and he wasn't black-haired.

You didn't argue or fight. And if there was any feuds to be settled, or any arguments to take place, you'd air your dispute, shake hands and go to the pub. But you never, ever, were allowed to use a curse or bad language, or to use anger on New Year's Day, because if you did, you'd carry it with you for the whole year; and you'd carry bad luck with you for your family. We didn't have New Year's Eve celebrations, but the dawning of the morning on New Year's Day was always important.

And if you were in the countryside, when you saw a new lamb, a baby lamb early in the new year, the direction that the lamb was facing in was the direction you would be going for the rest of the year. If the lamb I saw was heading towards north, then we were going to be travelling north-ways for the rest of the year.

What memories do you have of the celebration of Little Christmas, or Women's Christmas on 6 January? What did it mean for Traveller women on this day—were there particular customs associated with marking this day?
It was always a day you went to Mass, whatever day it fell on. So it obviously meant something. I don't know if it was a … don't forget we came from a very patriarchal community … so I don't think the whole idea of Women's Christmas was actually conceived by Travellers at that time, but I know it was always marked by Mass. And because the country women would be at home on that day, and they'd be getting looked after, so they were more generous; so your beggings on that day were always better than they were any other day. Because the women were in good humour. They were getting looked after and they were getting extra food; and the men were doing that; so the country women would give the Traveller women (they probably felt sorry for us, of course), so they were very good to us on that day. We knew what day it was. The Travellers knew what day it was. But we also knew that the country women were kinder and more caring on that day.

How has the celebration of Christmas among the Travelling community changed over the years?
Massive changes, not for the good. It very much brings out the divide between the rich and the poor. I work as a family liaison officer for severely disadvantaged families and I see it now. If you have money, you literally could be in Disneyland in some of the homes you go to. And your wealth and your position in society is shown on Facebook by the

Louis Vuitton gifts I get. And then you go to people who have nothing to eat, only are depending on food from other people, from the Vincent de Paul or whatever. So they're completely ostracised. You would never see that in my father's day. When we were growing up there was no such thing as a rich Traveller; there were some Travellers more wealthy than others; particularly, the more traditional Travellers were the more wealthy ones. But then everybody shared. The beggings the women got on Christmas Day were shared. It's not like that now. Now it's all to do with your place or standing in society. If I can show on Facebook or social media that my three daughters got Louis Vuitton bags, or all these very expensive things, and then you go to other homes where the children are wearing their school uniform on Christmas morning because they've nothing else to wear. The divide between rich and poor is gone to an extreme now. And it's tragic really. It's not for the good. And that's where it now manifests itself in mental health issues like suicide. I mean, I would imagine, we're all Travellers, and we should share and look after each other; but that doesn't happen now. People have lost what was at the very core of who we were, which was kindness and love. And it wasn't just for Christmas. Of course there was extra at Christmastime because it was a really special time; we were brought into the town to look at the lights; you were brought into the town to look at shop windows; now I wasn't getting anything in the shops, but I saw the shops and that made me feel as good.

Any concluding reflections on your memories of Christmas in the past?
It was a time when men and women were more equal. The men would make sure the children got a pair of wellington boots. I remember my husband Michael telling us a story, and Michael came from a very large family. You got a new pair of wellington boots at Christmas. You might walk bare-footed all the rest of the time, but you got a new pair for Christmas. Women got new shoes. It was a time of mutual respect. And it was a time when the elderly were treated with so much love because their stories were invaluable. So it was very much a time for everybody.

'I THINK SANTY
IS MY DADDY'

Denise O'Meara

During my childhood in the 1990s, the local bazaar in Riverstick, Co. Cork, was a good sign that Christmas would soon be here. The bazaar was hosted to generate funds for the local hall, and involved the sale of raffle tickets and a big wheel, spun by the late Paddy O'Donoghue, to reveal the lucky winner. The winner had a choice of prizes, including fresh turkeys hanging by their feet from a rope on the stage, hams, bottles of whisky and brandy, tins of sweets and biscuits and toys. I remember children winning the prizes, and about to select the toy, only to be interrupted by a parent coming thundering up on the stage, prising the toy out of their hands and insisting that they take the more valuable turkey or brandy.

The bazaar was an opportunity to meet Santa, and on at least one occasion Santa arrived by helicopter from Cork Airport, landing on the GAA pitch. I still remember the wind generated by the propellers, and poor Santa trying desperately to exit the helicopter while attempting to keep his beard and disguise intact. On other occasions he arrived by tractor, fire engine or horse and trap, and he sometimes arrived a little the worse for wear if he attended the pub on his way.

During one of our visits to Santa, my father did not join us, as he was going to a card drive to play forty-five, or so we were told. Forty-five is an old trick-taking card game that has many different names throughout rural Ireland. I remember thinking that something was a bit off about Santa; when my mother (RIP) asked us what we thought of him, I said, 'I think Santy is my Daddy' and burst into tears. My sister Julie and I had to be ushered out a side door so as not to upset the other children. My poor mother spent the journey home convincing us that the real Santa was busy that day and had asked my father to help him out.

The 8th of December was a big shopping day for country people, particularly farmers, and we either got or took a day off from school to head into Cork City. My father also came with us, and he would have all his jobs completed on the farm before we left to beat the crowds. He used to separate from us to visit the English Market, and return with a white plastic bag filled with tripe and drisheen. Tripe is the lining of a sheep's stomach and drisheen is a blood pudding. That evening, he cooked the tripe and drisheen in milk and onion. He thickened it with cornflour and ate it with bread. The house used to stink of it.

The excitement would really kick off when we put up the Christmas tree. It was usually bought in Tony O'Neill's filling station in Riverstick. It was a decent shop at the time, selling everything from penny sweets to Japanese imported cars, a car well suited for carrying bags of nuts from the co-op, ferrying children to school and driving through fields. The Christmas tree was stood in a mineral-lick bucket filled with sand, and the bucket wrapped in Christmas paper. The tree was decorated with coloured baubles and tinsel and multi-coloured fairy lights, which only ever half-worked and required bulbs to be replaced and multiple rounds of obscenities to untangle them from the knot in which they had been put away the year before.

In the days leading up to Christmas, the turkey was bought if it hadn't already been won at the bazaar or a card drive. Cleaning out the turkey was mostly a job for my father. The removal of the gizzard was the tricky bit because the meat would be destroyed if you burst it, but I'm sure it was burst on more than one occasion to much annoyance. The sinews were always the most difficult to remove, requiring another bit of swearing to help loosen them. The turkey giblets were retained for giblet soup, my mother's speciality, prepared by boiling the giblets with a chopped onion, carrot, leak and celery, and seasoned with a fresh sprig of thyme. Potato stuffing was another important element of the Christmas dinner, prepared by mashing cooked potatoes into softened onion with butter and thyme, adding the mix to an ovenproof dish where it was forked to shape the surface, and placing it in the oven before the dinner so that the top became nice and brown and crisp. My mother said that my grandmother also made stuffing like this, as I do now.

On Christmas Eve 1997 there was a bad storm that swept through Munster, taking trees and electricity and phone poles with it. On our farm, some trees were knocked and a few galvanised sheets blew off the shed, but for the most part we escaped major damage. We did lose our power, however, along with thousands of others that year. There was a lot of preparation required on Christmas Eve for the Christmas Day dinner, and a gas bottle with stove top—which was usually reserved for heating cow's beestings (colostrum) for new calves—was brought in from the yard. The ham and potatoes were all boiled using that, and we toasted bread on an open fire to make ham sandwiches. Later, toasting bread on the open fire became a new Christmas Eve tradition, either before or after Christmas Eve Mass.

It was Fr Joe Coughlan who first allowed altar girls to serve Mass in our parish, and many girls took up the opportunity, including Julie and me. Fr Joe also reintroduced the Christmas Eve Mass; after a few attempts at an actual Midnight Mass, it was renegotiated to the more amenable time of 8pm, but retained its midnight title. Fr Joe was a bit of a revelation in a parish that was used to more traditional priests. During one of the Christmas Eve Masses, I remember my late cousin Gearoid taking more than an acceptable sip of the altar wine. Gearoid was obscured by the low lighting and candles used to create a festive ambience for the occasion, but the laughter and kerfuffle surely gave the game away.

A Christmas candle was placed in the window at home; it was always first lit by the youngest on Christmas Eve, and anyone could light it after that until 6 January, when Christmas officially ended. We made a candle display in mosses and gathered bits of greenery from the hedge-rows—or ditches, as we called them—and included red berry holly, ivy and any garden flowers currently blooming for the occasion. Historically, the candle in the window was to welcome strangers roaming the countryside, although if someone came roaming in my childhood they were more likely to have had the guards called on them than to be welcomed in, but in the 1800s and well into the 1900s this was common in the Irish countryside, and the candle light represented a charitable and good Christian household.

There were visits to various houses and relatives over Christmas, and all involved a game of cards, usually forty-five—a relatively easy game to learn but difficult to master, or so the more professional players would have us believe. We received an education in card-playing during these games; even if a game had been well won, it was discussed with a level of critique rarely seen after a county game. I still love a game today, when I get the chance to play.

GRANNY'S POTATO STUFFING

Clodagh Tait

When we were children, our Cork grannies were distinguished from one another by their special attractions. 'Granny with the stairs' had stairs; 'Granny with the swings' lived up the road from the playground in Schull, which along with swings had a slide, a seesaw and a very fast roundabout whose memory still makes me feel queasy. This granny was Mary (May) Sweetnam (née Wolfe). She and my granddad William had retired to a 1960s bungalow in Schull, a few miles from their former home and farm on the rocky slopes of Mount Gabriel. The house has a stunning view of the harbour towards the islands, though when he was complimented on it once my taciturn grandfather, a man more inclined to see beauty in a herd of healthy bullocks than in picturesque vistas, commented ruefully, 'Huh! Nothing but bloody water.'

I don't imagine that Granny had much time to contemplate the view, at least not when she had visitors. She was a slight woman and seemed to be constantly in motion, somewhat hunched at the shoulders like an athlete dipping towards the finishing line. She hardly even sat at mealtimes, instead hovering behind her guests, waiting for space on their plates so that she could load on more food.

Her generous hospitality is recalled in my, my parents' and my brothers' households every Christmas as we sit down to 'Granny's potato stuffing'. It's termed 'stuffing' but we don't usually stuff it into anything, though technically you could. The recipe that is still referred to is a piece torn from a letter (on the inevitable Basildon Bond blue notepaper, now spotted with age) from Granny to my mother. It is written in a conversational style, and the measurements are impressionistic, originally reliant on my mother's understanding of the size of 'my big pyrex dish' and the (ceramic) cup used for measuring the flour. However, it can easily be scaled up or down according to the receptacle (pro tip: you want the biggest one you have, as you can never have too much potato stuffing). How wet it's made depends on the preference of the maker. My mother makes a wetter mixture which my father always says 'sticks to the insides'; mine is usually drier. Either way, it is excellent reheated with leftovers, or even carved into chunks for a turkey sandwich. The 'gravy' referred to is the sediment from the roasting tin in which you're cooking your goose or turkey, and it makes the top nicely golden, but vegan alternatives can be substituted, and of course it can also be made gluten-free. Vegans will prefer the margarine specified here, but otherwise butter is a good option. I note potato stuffings online that include things like sage, celery and parsley, which sound nice but are not The Same.

POTATO STUFFING

I mash potatoes and put them in a pyrex dish. When hot put a slice of margarine in to the hot mashed spuds, pepper and salt and chopped onion. I get about one cup of flour in my big pyrex dish and sift on top of mashed spuds and wet it with milk, you would need to wet it fairly well and stir it up, then I would put a few dessert spoons of chicken gravy or turkey gravy on top and stir it nice and wet and put one spoon on top and rub the spoon on top and it will bake brown and soft. This is my old way, and I'll have to make a lot for Christmas for they do not like bread stuffing.

CHRISTMAS IN ROME

John-Paul Sheridan

Four particular Christmases from my younger days will forever be etched on my mind. Between 1986 and 1990 I was a student at the Irish College in Rome, the last of the Continental colleges which had served the Irish Church over the centuries. There was a rule at that time that seminarians were not permitted to return to Ireland for Christmas, and so I spent the Christmases of 1986, 1987, 1988 and 1989 in Rome.

In settling down to write this piece, I was very much of the same mind-set as Dylan Thomas in his *Child's Christmas in Wales*: 'I can never remember whether it snowed for six days and six nights when I was twelve, or whether it snowed for twelve days and twelve nights when I was six. All the Christmases roll down towards the two-tongued sea.' All these Christmases are rolled into one. The stories and reminiscences are melded together into a single memory of a time when I was a seminarian, and for the days leading up to Christmas it was a little easier to be one. There are strong memories that come back to me from time to time on hearing a carol or a piece of music. Although it has been a while since I was last in Rome, strong memories are evoked when passing through streets and squares and churches. Former classmates and those who were in the college in the 1980s will have their own memories, which might differ from mine. We have both the ability and the habit of sifting through our memories, leaving the difficult ones aside and the happier ones to the fore. This is what I want to remember in these few lines.

The season of Christmas began in the city with the celebration of the Feast of the Immaculate Conception on 8 December. The pope would come to the Piazza de Spagna to venerate Our Lady before the statue there. On the occasions when we went along it was difficult to see anything, except when a wreath was hoisted up to the statue, a tradition maintained by the firemen or *vigili del fuoco*. From time to time there was the music of shepherds who would come down from the Castelli, the hill towns around Rome, to play their bagpipes. There was usually an invitation to refreshments in the convent of the Poor Servants of the Mother of God, who lived just off the Piazza de Spagna, at the Mater Dei convent. Having been in Rome since the 1880s, in those days they ran a girls' school. There were many Irish sisters among the community, whose names I've forgotten but whose hospitality I have not. After this there was the walk to the Piazza Navona, where the Christmas market would now be open. I took particular delight in all the accoutrements available for the construction of a crib. You could buy bark and cork and greenery and a huge variety of accessories to equip your manger scenes. This was a very popular tradition with the Romans, who would decorate their homes with the manger scene, usually adding to it every year, making the simple scene in Bethlehem into a huge tableau. It was in these markets that I first began to collect the figures for a crib that still comes out every Christmas.

The crib was important to the Italians. In the 1980s you were more likely to see the manger scene in a shop window at Christmas than the usual decorations. The city didn't seem to have the same level of commercialism as found in Ireland. In fact, Rome was a city of cribs at Christmas. Every church had one, and there was a tradition of a 'crib crawl' to see some of the best. Some were quite elaborate, consisting of many different scenes with a cast of hundreds. The biggest was the one in St Peter's Square, but by far the most elegant, detailed and sumptuous were the Neapolitan cribs which could be seen in some churches.

Classes at the Gregorian University had a fifteen-minute interval between them (enough time to grab a coffee from the bar), and in these intervals coming up to Christmas the various national colleges and religious congregations would sing native carols and songs in the large, two-storey-high atrium immediately inside the doors. Students would stand around and listen, applauding enthusiastically when it was finished. The Irish took their turn, sometimes supplemented with students from the other Irish houses: the Irish Franciscans at St Isidore's, the Irish Dominicans from San Clemente and the Irish Augustinians from San Patrizio.

On the occasion when an invitation was issued by the British ambassador to come to a party on one of the Sunday afternoons before Christmas, we would sing carols, accompanied by students from the Scots College, the English College and the Beda. Other invitations were extended over the years, finding us in all sorts of places, from convents to colleges. In those years there was an excellent tradition of choral music, along with some superb singers.

In the Irish College the usual preparations took place. A tree was purchased, the decorations were put up and food preparation was begun. In those years the Sisters of St John of God were in charge of the house, and I remember them with fondness. Their contribution to the life and soul of the college was immeasurable, and they made the Christmases away from home a little less poignant.

The Advent Service was always a big night, and it fulfilled two functions. Liturgically, we were in the season of Advent, and so we celebrated as such in the college chapel. At its conclusion, the choir would process to the stairs at the entrance hallway, followed by the congregation. A carol concert would ensue. This would be followed by another procession—to the refreshments.

At Christmas there was the vigil Mass with the college community, after which Santa Claus would come to the first-years. This included all who were experiencing their first Irish College Christmas. One or two students also organised a Secret Santa or Kris Kringle, so as to make sure that everyone received a gift at Christmas (the Italian postal service was not very reliable, and sometimes the parcels from home hadn't yet arrived).

It was a tradition to attend the *Urbi et Orbi* in St Peter's Square on Christmas morning. The Irish flag was brought along, not so much to let the pope know that the Irish were there as to let families at home know where we were in the crowd. We would then return to the college for Christmas dinner. At that time, and without the benefit of mobile phones, families would sometimes ring during dinner. There was a hush, all eyes waiting to see who would be called. Then the walk to the phone, taking it outside for some privacy, and the inevitable tear-strewn face (at least in my case) that would return with the phone a few minutes later. Dinner over, a quiet restful afternoon was the tradition. In the evening the community would gather for some entertainment in the common room. Staff would be there, along with the sisters, and songs were sung, and poems and monologues recited.

The following day, students were allowed to leave the college—customarily for somewhere in Italy and usually for as little money as possible. Others went further afield, and there would be stories to be told on their return. I only ever went away once; I wasn't very adventurous.

I came from a family that had few enough traditions or rituals around the Christmas season. We were certainly not the sort who stood around the piano singing carols. Apart from the alternating venue for Christmas dinner and the cousins' party on St Stephen's Day, the season passed off without much incident. In the years since ordination, there have been a variety of Christmases celebrated—one in Chile, several in New England, and the remainder with parish and family. But none can compare to the 'Roman Christmases' and the variety of festivities, rituals and traditions that were part of them; neither do any hold such memories.

EMIGRANT CHRISTMAS: CLINGING TO TRADITIONS IN SOUTH KOREA'S ENGLISH-TEACHING COMMUNITY

James Hendicott

I t starts to feel like Christmas about two weeks out, which, in my own slightly grouchy opinion, is just about right. Thick snowflakes settle around frigid Seoul's scenic sights: the stepping-stone-filled Cheonggyecheon urban stream is lit up in icy, glistening lights, and both the skyscrapers and the wood-framed traditional palaces take on a foggy, cold complexion. Squares in the city's heart contain ice-skating rinks and snowmen, and commercials start to contain snowballs or reindeers or Santa characters that always feel different, like our own cartoons overlaid with a light manga influence.

Of course, celebration isn't easy. After all, while some of the Irish residents in Seoul's vibrant, English-teaching expat community miss home, you sense that most are almost too busy. Working hours stretch from dawn to dusk, an odd schedule where in the middle of the day we're unleashed into a vibrant but bitingly cold December city, where food carts draw us in with their cooking steam and the challenging peaks around the massive Han River Valley call out.

It's at the weekends when life comes alive, though, if truth be told, we're out almost every night. Seoul is a young person's paradise: the things that appeal in your mid-20s are all cheap to the point of it feeling like a waste not to do them. We eat out every night because, well, everyone does, and costs are comparable to going to the supermarket. Falling into a tiny apartment at 11pm just to sleep, after indulging in BBQ and kimchi accessories, is just a part of the routine.

That routine slowly breaks, as I say, about two weeks out. The classes are no less intense, and the nightlife no less ferocious either, but our neighbourhood of Haebangchon is starting to soak up that sparkling feel. Some, the lucky few, even have families visiting. As recalled by Galway native and long-term resident of South Korea Phillip Brett:

> In the beginning, Christmas was almost a battle. With only the 25th as a day off, it felt like a constant struggle to balance celebrating the day in two countries. Christmas with chosen family in Korea, and video call Christmas with family at home. It would typically involve multiple Christmas dinners scattered over the days leading up to the 25th, and there would always be a live music show to go to on either the 24th or 25th. A number of times I'd come out of a show after a few drinks and dancing, to jump straight on a video call with family for the walk home, and then open presents together.

Haebangchon sits in a surreal gap between what you might call the 'real' Seoul and a hazy mishmash of cultures heavily influenced by the gigantic American military barracks that sits just over the area's back gate, a defensive remnant of the Korean War that still spills too-young GI-Joe soldiers out into streets adapted to hold them.

Our preferred bar is more local, to the point where cheap soju and watery beer—Korean beer always feels watery—are its core offerings. At Christmas it becomes bustling: half-celebration and half a search for connection in a time when being far from loved ones is particularly acute.

There are a few little glittery decorations and spicy table food, and one night, when chatting about Christmas back home, we're thrown out for putting 10,000 Won in the jukebox and lining up The Pogues' *Fairytale of New York* ten or fifteen times in a row.

Some tell stories of the teenagers who come round and sing on St Stephen's Day and ask for money in small Irish rural towns, but the closest we can come to recreating the feel of Christmas is in searching out its food. The local Tesco—yes, Seoul, bizarrely, has a single large Tesco—has *panatone*. Italian sugary bread is not an Irish staple, but we hand it around eagerly and then try to convince ourselves that the sweet street-side omelettes that seem to appeal when they're cooked on the hot BBQ plates at 4am have something of a Christmas feel to them, like ham cooked in a vat of sugary Coke. Phillip Brett adds:

> I remember one year in particular where I took advantage of the day off to catch up on laundry and house chores before settling in for mulled wine and video calls with family at home in the evening to open presents together, then straight into work the next morning, eight hours after the call ended.
>
> As a child, Christmas morning was the rush of excitement to open presents, whereas time zones demand I hold off till about 9 or 10 at night to match the family schedule. As a holiday that relies so much on tradition and familiar faces, the inconsistency of life as an immigrant makes it tough to build new traditions of your own.

In truth, Christmas here is narrowed down to just one day. After all, how many days off can you have for religious holidays in a society that's split almost equally between three different religions? On the 24th, after our last class, late in the evening, we head out for food and exchange small gifts, but the usual sense of anticipation is tinged with a piercing sense of absence.

Two teachers from Scotland host Christmas Day. We've splashed out on Guinness—€5 a can on import—but nobody can find anything close to a turkey, so a big meal of Korean-style ham is the order of the day. Long working hours put aside for the day, Seoul's normally wild and slightly vapid weekend party culture gives way to a day that centres around being there for each other. Hailing from differing corners, we each leave for the privacy of the bedrooms to take calls from home as the night wears on.

The perverse side of the loneliness of Christmas far from home is that we all choose to be there, to varying degrees. Okay, there's little holiday to be had, but life as an immigrant in a country of relatively few immigrants is a lifestyle choice, and one that most of us choose to cling to with a sense of adventure. Some days it can feel like an extended holiday, like travel that funds itself. Other days, like Christmas, local friends are set aside and you cling to those who make you feel like you're back home, even if just for a minute.

The result is that life is turned on its head: the everyday, at least for a while, is fantastically weird and wonderful. Weekends are spent exploring little villages or climbing hills, while every day in class brings new insight into Korean culture. If you order the wrong thing in a restaurant, you'll get soup containing fish brains, or sea cucumber, or a side of the dreaded silkworm larvae.

And then comes Christmas, normally a celebration but now a time when thoughts turn to home and what everyone misses. The one time when, if we could, we'd probably all jump in that teleporter and arrive in time for Christmas dinner and to sit around the fire at home, happy to find ourselves the subject of one of those beautiful videos of people who unexpectedly come home and make their mothers weep. But we can't, because part of it all is that we have to work in the morning, so instead we form another family and we simply get through it, incorporating a little bit of happy nostalgia where we can.

After all, emigrant life, at least in Seoul, is about lifestyle and exploration and the excitement of living in a world that can feel incredibly alien, about trying to get by in a language that has only three tenses but seven structural levels of formality. Christmas is just one day, and it's a day when our minds are forced back home again, a homesick corner in amongst a life purposefully less ordinary. It's hard, but we'll take our adventure. Most days.

THE WELCOMED GUEST: CHRISTMAS IN CZECHIA

JP Ryan

Christmas was the great conjurer of magic. It punctuated my childhood with happiness and hope. It's not that we had much as a large family, but we had far less beyond this festive season. The Christmas tree was a luxury beyond our dwelling in early childhood. Its arrival in later years complemented the traditional fairy lights around the front cottage window. Invariably, it was a no-fuss approach to getting into the spirit of things – but with a delightful assortment of colours nonetheless. And to add to the excitement, some blandly toned balloons and crêpe-paper decorations pinned to a tatty ceiling. Despite its simplicity, it was a visual showpiece that evoked inner warmth and excitement. And in keeping with visual showpieces, there was little to rival the colour TV that came from the rental outlet at this time of year. For those few short days over Christmas, it replaced the black-and-white monstrosity sitting on the corner cabinet. Without doubt, we wallowed in the opulence of Christmas in colour before this modern marvel was returned to the TV store after the festivities. It was an age-old tradition that never failed us, and we were gifted with parents who never let us down, even in their struggles, at this time. So with very little in terms of material gain, what more could we have needed? In short, Christmas was always a welcomed guest in our home.

While my inevitable departure from childhood came with the stark reality that everything is transient, that unremitting inner glow always upheld its duty at this time of year. Now, in fatherhood, so far away from my homeland and the traditional Irish festive pageantry, my early Christmases awaken and often run like a slideshow in my head. That sense of home, family, the excitement of an unexpected snowfall, the array of coloured lights in our small town, the gifts, the annual TV shows, midnight Mass and, in later years, the pub atmosphere and friends. It's all there, fossilised for reflection and fused with the excitement of new senses in a foreign land that we have tried to make our home.

Of course, an Irish Christmas was not without its Catholic iconography predominant in the household of any conventional family at this time—the crib and the Sacred Heart, centrepieces of family life and faith. When I first arrived in the Czech Republic, I noted that the Sacred Heart in this part of the world was as elusive as Santa. I assumed that the Communists had run him right out of town and somewhere into the annals of history. To my surprise, however, he seems to have survived many tumultuous transitions throughout the ages and to date, instead of Santa, he appears to have re-manifested himself bearing gifts in the form of baby Jesus, or, as the Czechs would say, *Ježíšek*. Yes, after evening dinner on 24 December (Christmas Day in the Czech Republic), the bell chimes to announce the arrival of gifts under the tree from none other than *Ježíšek*! So as Irish children with an Irish father and a Czech mother, my boys have swayed cautiously from Santa to Ježíšek for fear of relinquishing their early traditional experiences that would possibly deprive them of extra gifts!

Like the Irish, the Czechs have their own steadfast traditions that they respect and play out at Christmastime. This, of course, includes their own selected foods and traditional fairy tales on re-run across varying TV channels. And a noteworthy addition is the visitation of three interesting characters to ensure that children are ready and well behaved for the big day. In schools, houses and pubs across the country in the run-up to the main event, the arrival of a unique trio is very evident: St Nicholas himself (*Mikuláš*), the Angel (*anděl*), representing 'good', and the Devil (*čert*), representing the 'bad'. I suppose that the most notable

357

part of the tradition is the reaction of children to their arrival. They must offer a song or poem to the trio. A brief assessment ensues to ascertain their behaviour throughout the year. A good child is rewarded with treats from anděl and a bold child is given a sack of potatoes or coal, or taken to hell in čert's sack as the ultimate penalty—albeit I have yet to witness 'a bold child' in the mix. I have, however, witnessed several scared children in the presence of the *čert* and, anecdotally, I have learned from adults that this fear is often a concrete memory for them, tantamount to mild trauma!

In all of this, it might be worth flagging the irony of my comparisons and observations. While a godly Irish tradition becomes more diluted and commercialised, and leans into the Americanised version of Santa, an ungodly Czech nation holds on to the tradition of Jesus and their accompanying customs that mark this important annual event. And all of this despite stepping from the shadow of communism not so long ago!

In any case, the endearing magnetism of it all still draws me in, and my mind is always besieged with warmth and reflection as we approach this time of year. It's difficult to quantify that sense of magic, too. I tend to conform to the notion that magic is not so much about getting more as it is about getting just enough to buy into the illusion. And what about hope? Well, isn't that an empowering concept woven into the very fabric of the sacred Christmas narrative? And its omnipotence is there to be distilled and interpreted in many ways for each person. But make no mistake—this spellbinding time is a blessing denied to many, and I often fluctuate between the novel fantasy and the sobering reality that Christmas is not a fairy tale for all. In essence, as a father of children who are not holding back on tossing their innocent years aside, I often question how long its charm will endure. It wasn't so long ago when my firstborn, barely on his feet, gently jabbed the tree trinkets in bemusement and silent wonder as he cast his tiny gaze around a room of festive resplendence. It was equally only like yesterday when he and his little brother gently rounded their soft new lips to utter that ubiquitous and universal Christmas mantra, 'Ho, Ho, Ho!' So, if I've learned anything in my almost 50 years of existence, it's that everything is subject to change and my feeling on Christmas might be no exception to this truism. But there is always the last stop that I have come to know as hope—and a pinch of sadness, if I am to be honest; for how can we truly afford ourselves the well-rounded flavours of happiness and hope without a pinch of this in the mix?

THE WELCOMED GUEST

Christmas came
wrapped in winter's snow,
seeking refuge in countless hearts,
taking new steps on old roads
and old steps on new,
through villages abound,
and the smallest hearts had the biggest rooms.

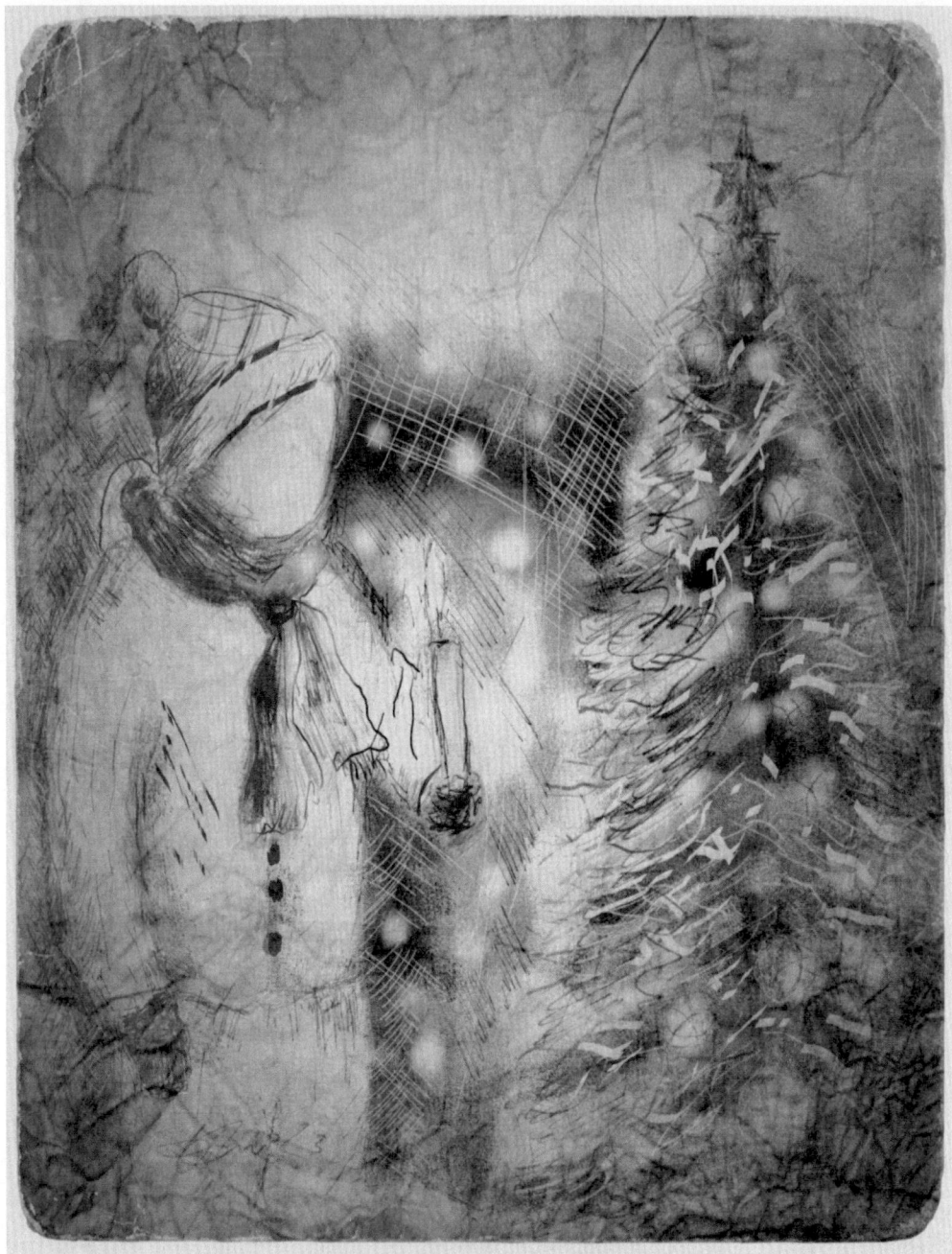

The Caroler. Image © JP Ryan.

CHRISTMAS, PRISONER AMNESTIES AND TEMPORARY RELEASE

Keith Adams

In 1979, during Pope John Paul II's visit to Ireland, the Minister for Justice recommended that 68 prisoners be released to mark the occasion. The persons released in this amnesty were deemed 'unlikely to be dangerous to the public' and were all due for release later in the year. Nevertheless, always sensitive to public ire, the Minister for Justice also recommended that the group of prisoners should not be released until the third and final day of John Paul II's itinerary—Monday 1 October. In a memo to the government from the Department of Justice a reasoning was provided:

> It is considered that it would be unwise to take the risk of releasing a large number of offenders during the first day of the visit when Dublin's dwelling houses will be virtually empty and releases on Sunday would pose staffing and transport problems.

In the past, other occasions—usually major religious events—also led to more general prisoner amnesties being granted. Prisoners were released to celebrate the Eucharistic Congress in Dublin in 1932, the Holy Year of 1950 and the canonisation of Oliver Plunkett in 1975. O'Donnell and

Jewkes considered the practice to be 'motivated by a sense of Christian charity and belief in the power of redemption', yet it was moderated by a concern for issues of a more practical nature. In this case, fear of burglaries in the empty homes of Mass-goers at the Phoenix Park led to the prisoners being released at the last possible moment.

GROWTH IN TEMPORARY RELEASE

Temporary release for prisoners was legislated for in Ireland under the Criminal Justice Act 1960. Prisoners were increasingly either released for short periods during their sentence or fully released before their sentence was complete. They were also permitted to leave prison to join their families for Christmas. The periods of release granted to these qualifying prisoners at Christmas varied from a few hours to up to seven nights.

In a Dáil debate in December 1962, in response to a question about Christmas release, then Minister for Justice Charles Haughey said that he would consider 'granting temporary release to a number of well-conducted prisoners to enable them to spend the holy season of Christmas with their families'. Furthermore, when exercising his decision-making on those to be released, he would take into account 'the nature of their offences, the previous record, the home environment, the good conduct and industry while under sentence and any factors which, in my opinion, will lead to reform and rehabilitation'. On 10 December 1964, the 16th Anniversary of the Declaration of Human Rights, Brian Lenihan Snr announced his intention to honour Christmas by releasing 40 prisoners with short sentences remaining, and granting ten days of temporary release to 35 more prisoners.

The practice of temporary release expanded in the 1970s. Alongside mass releases for events like papal visits, regular amnesties also occurred at Easter and Christmas across the prison estate. When trying to make sense of Irish civil servants' scepticism about the utility of the prison,

Louise Brangan argues that this uncertainty was rooted in Ireland's traditional and conservative social order, which prioritised the values of community and family. She continues that, while other countries were focused on progressive individual rights, Ireland was a 'nation largely defined by its communitarian Catholic culture, where family life was paramount to the national order'. These communitarian ideals led to the prison being understood as detrimental to those conservative values of family and community. Prisoners were viewed firstly as people within social networks rather than as individual offenders in isolation. Thus temporary release at Christmas (and Easter) was a key practical outworking of this understanding, and a defining characteristic of the prison system in the Republic of Ireland in the 1970s. Compared with today's increasingly restrictive criteria, few crimes or lengths of sentence disqualified a prisoner from qualifying for temporary release.

DECLINE IN CHRISTMAS TEMPORARY RELEASE

Over the past quarter of a century there has been a precipitous decline in the granting of temporary release for prisoners at Christmas. On average, between the early 1960s and the mid-1990s, more than one in eight prisoners were allowed home for Christmas. The zenith of this policy was seen in 1995, when 390 prisoners were granted temporary release; this equated to 18% of the prison population.

Since then, numbers have fallen despite a rise in prison populations. In 2000 there were 270 Christmas releases (9%), and by 2008 this was down to a low point of only 107 (3%) prisoners being granted varying periods of temporary release for Christmas.

Discounting the two years of Covid public health restrictions, when fewer prisoners applied for Christmas temporary release owing to the strict isolation protocols upon return, the number of prisoners granted Christmas temporary release has remained low in proportion to the rising prison population. The Department of Justice has endeavoured to explain that this trend is the result of the unavailability of suitable prisoners. O'Donnell and Jewkes conclude that this explanation is unsatisfactory, as there has been an increase in both long-term prisoners and those in for short sentences for minor offences. Most could be assessed as low-risk and could continue to be released as before. So, if the official account lacks credibility, what may explain the downward trajectory?

CHRISTMAS RELEASE, AMNESTIES AND PENAL SENSIBILITIES

Amnesties and temporary release at Christmas provide us with some insight into the values and priorities undergirding a criminal justice system. On one hand, the decline in Christmas temporary release since 1995 may map onto wider trends within the Irish 'punitive' turn, as more restrictive regimes were established based on security and control rather than rehabilitation. On the other hand, the swift decline also presents us with evidence that how prisoners are understood within society, and by policy-makers, has changed. In the 1970s, when amnesties and temporary release were granted liberally, prisoners were understood to still

Prisoners Granted Christmas Temporary Release, 2005-2022

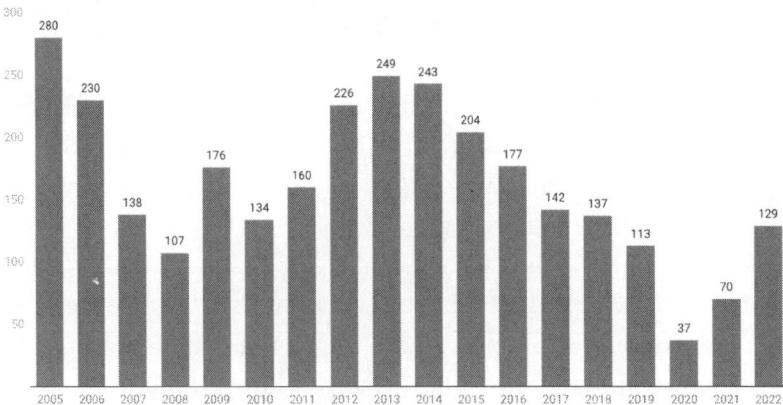

Fewer prisoners applied for Christmas release in 2020 and 2021 due to the isolation protocols upon return to prison and the higher risk of infection in the community than in prison.

Chart: Jesuit Centre for Faith and Justice • Source: Irish Prison Service • Created with Datawrapper be members of society. The ever-present Irish Catholic conservative virtues of the stable family and the traditions of community provided the rationale for prisoners to be temporarily released for baptisms, weddings, funerals and the serious illness of a close relative. Their social identities had not been diminished by the criminal justice system, as they could return to their families at key intervals during the sentence.

A brief gendered analysis may also be instructive here. Prior to committal, female prisoners are more actively involved with their families and have more care-giving responsibilities than their male counterparts. Often their offending is related to providing for others' needs. If the values of maintaining the family unit and preserving communal ties have endured within criminal justice policy-making, then we should see a higher proportion of women granted temporary Christmas release than men.

PRISONERS GRANTED CHRISTMAS TEMPORARY RELEASE, BY GENDER

Year	Male	Female
2009	168	8
2010	131	3
2011	151	9
2012	217	9
2013	243	6
2014	229	14
2015	199	5
2016	174	3
2017	141	1
2018	136	1
2019	113	0
2020	37	0
2021	70	0

A breakdown of the Christmas Temporary Release figures by gender was provided by the Irish Prison Service. Table: Jesuit Centre for Faith and Justice · Source: Irish Prison Service · Created with Datawrapper

In reality, few women are released to their families for Christmas. In the six years from 2016 to 2021, a total of 671 men were granted release, while only five women were able to go home for Christmas for even a few hours. Other dynamics may be at work here, such as ostracism and personal shame so that applications for leave are not submitted, but those women in Limerick prison and the Dóchas Centre (Mountjoy female) are not having the opportunity to preserve community ties and familial obligations in a season when these connections are most eagerly sought.

More research is needed to understand the causal factors here regarding why women prisoners have less access to families and children at Christmas. The practice, however, of offering amnesties for Easter and Christmas recognised that these were major occasions in Catholic Ireland when the entire family usually reunited—and in Ireland that could include family members who were imprisoned. In our present multicultural Ireland, other dates in religious calendars, such as Eid-ul-Adha, merit the same temporary release.

In place of people with social ties which bind them to a community outside of the prison, prisoners are now understood in relation to their offences. Louk Hulsman, a Dutch criminologist, describes this process as being 'separated out', whereby the offending incident is the sole means of understanding the individual, isolated from 'his environment, his friends, his family, the material substratum of his world'. This process seems even more acute and painful for women in prison at Christmas.

SOURCES AND FURTHER READING

Louise Brangan, 'Pastoral penality in 1970s Ireland: addressing the pains of imprisonment', *Theoretical Criminology* **25** (1) (2021), 44–65.
Louk Hulsman, 'Themes and concepts in an abolitionist approach to criminal justice', retrieved from *Loukhulsman.org/Publication* (1997).

Christmas card with image of open prison door, Mountjoy prison, Christmas 1941. The inside message reads: 'Though our cells are cold and cheerless / As the manger in the stall / Yet our hearts are warm and glowing / For our friends beyond the wall / May your dearest wish be granted / By the Christ Child on this morn / And our country's bonds be sundered / Ere the coming year is worn'. © National Museum of Ireland.
With special thanks to Liam Doherty and Clodagh Doyle, Irish Folklife Division, Castlebar.

Ian O'Donnell and Yvonne Jewkes, 'Going home for Christmas: prisoners, a taste of freedom and the press', *The Howard Journal of Criminal Justice* **50** (1) (2011), 75–91.

CHRISTMAS IN HOSPITAL

Patrick A. Williams

The joy of Christmas is communal—from the gathering of the community at Christmas Mass to sitting down for dinner with loved ones or the annual return of friends from faraway places. This is a time to be with other people and to celebrate common experience. Before there was Christianity, there were community gatherings at the darkest time of the year, to look forward together to the coming spring. Religious or otherwise, the common thread in many Christmas experiences is togetherness.

Disease does not form part of this picture. The experience of illness is interior, lonely, unique. We can feel joy together but cannot feel one another's pain. To be ill at Christmas is thus to be largely excluded from the joy of the season, but this is a situation in which many find themselves each Christmas. People break their hips, catch pneumonia or suffer strokes and heart attacks more often in December than in June. Winters in the northern hemisphere are marked by a proliferation of infectious diseases—the 'flu, the common cold, the winter vomiting bug, not to mention Covid. And so each Christmas week, under the tinsel-hung striplights of hospital wards, an unlucky few stare glumly from their beds as the realisation sinks in that they won't be 'home for Christmas'.

Hardly anyone likes to be in hospital at the best of times, and Christmas in hospital is far from the best of times. Some of the saddest sights I've seen in hospital have been at Christmas. One Christmas Eve in the Emergency Department, as we prepared to carry a girl in on a stretcher from the ambulance, I noticed the emergency nurse stash her Santa hat in her scrubs pocket to respect the moment. Another day I saw Christmas dinner being wheeled through the cancer ward past patients only able to eat through tubes. There was the recently divorced man who asked in a whisper not to be discharged on 23 December so that he wouldn't have to go home and face a first Christmas alone. On another Christmas Eve I admitted a kindly woman of advanced years who, delirious and unsure where she was, became upset and agitated. I called her son so that she might hear a familiar voice on the phone, only to hear how relieved he was at his mother's absence and the burden it removed from him. To be hospitalised at Christmas can be scary, lonely and at times unreal.

Unpleasant it may be but it is also mercifully rare. Most people are healthy enough most of the time that they don't need to think about hospitals, least of all at Christmas. So, the people with most experience of Christmas in the hospital are not the ill but the staff who work on Christmas Day year after year. A Hallmark tableau of Christmas at home with carols and a turkey in the oven does not accommodate those who have to work cleaning hospital wards by night.

Hospital staff are not the only people who have to work at Christmas, of course. Many people eat out in restaurants or stay in hotels at Christmas. Many shops stay open and some public transport services run on Christmas Day. All of these services have staff and customers, and yet there is something different about the hospital at Christmas. The business of health is different from any other business. The hospital 'customers', unlike those in a hotel, have not chosen to check in, and the services that the staff provide are of a different order from their counterparts in a convenience store. More so at Christmas than at any other time, the hospital is unique for the connection between staff and patients—the sick and the healers bound together.

Medical staff usually get the Christmas roster in October. There is a collective intake of breath as the email is opened on a hundred phones, everyone fearful of seeing their name next to that date. Of course, some do not mind working at Christmas—those who come from different faith traditions, for instance, or those who live far away from their families. Many of my colleagues choose to work during Christmas every year, as for them it holds no special meaning. I often think how lonely it must be to see the excited preparations of the hospital and be reminded of family far away.

The most visible of these preparations is the spread of decorations around the wards that starts as soon as Hallowe'en is over. At first glance these may seem incongruous or insensitive: a hospital is a place of pain and grief, and decorations may seem to trivialise the environment. Indeed, those areas where life and death are closest—the resuscitation rooms and the euphemistically named 'family rooms' for grieving—are left bare. Christmas cheer can only lift so much. But the rest of the hospital, staff and patients alike, take joy and comfort from gaudy fairy lights, tinsel and piped carols. In Christmas 2021 I was working on a Covid ward as yet another wave of infection spread. All our patients were on ventilators, staffing levels were low and the hospital was filling up. But on the day when the ward sister found time to put up the tree with a figurine for each staff member, we all stopped to admire it. It stood, talismanic in the centre of the ward, raised on a desk so that it could be seen from the patients' rooms. No matter how hard things got, it always lifted my mood to see it out of the corner of my eye. It reminded me that the world could go on and that, despite the dark circumstances, we could retain the capacity for joy.

It was not just decorations that lifted our spirits. The Christmas dinner that I saw passing through the oncology ward came to our ward, where it was delivered to patients who could take breaks from their ventilators. The staff had Christmas dinner in socially distanced shifts in the common room, replete with cake donated from a local bakery. We had a storeroom overflowing with presents, some from patients to staff and others from staff, bought with a communal fund, for the patients who had no visitors.

The human connection between staff and patients is foregrounded at Christmas. There is a sense of camaraderie, of shared experience. On the Covid ward at Christmas I encountered a strange role reversal in which a patient, unable to breathe without her oxygen mask, expressed sympathy that I was 'stuck here' with her instead of with my family. I was left speechless, wanting to point out that by any objective measure it was she who was worse off. She didn't see any irony in this, the sick commiserating with the well. She simply saw another person separated from family and friends.

None of this is to say that Christmas in the hospital is not difficult, despite the decorations, the carols, the cribs and the religious services. For the patients, there is little respite from illness. After dinner and before crackers, a man lies back on his bed, eyes closed. The nurse checks him; he has a fever. Years of repetition have turned training to instinct. Suddenly it's a day like any other day. She attaches a drip to his arm and calls the doctor. He is sent for an X-ray, his Santa hat receding out of sight as the porters wheel him away.

These are the rhythms of illness, the unceasing routines of the hospital, a building where lives are changed forever, daily—a cancer diagnosis, an amputation or a loved one's death. Each of these events is devastating, but each happens a hundred times over, every day. The extraordinary is rendered mundane.

It is empathy with others that enables us to navigate the experience. Staff and patients connect through recognising each other's circumstances. It is at Christmas that these circumstances come closest, and so it is at Christmas that the hospital is most human.

INCARNATION: DIVE DEEPER

Bairbre Cahill

‘Incarnation’ is a word that pops up in many a Christmas homily, but what does it mean? Christians believe that Jesus was ‘made man’—incarnated. And yet there is so much more to it than that. We need to dive deeper. Incarnation expresses God’s desire for relationship. Ronald Rolheiser speaks of incarnation as God’s desire to ‘have skin’. The concept of ‘deep incarnation’ takes that idea even further; every aspect of the created universe is gathered up into this understanding of God’s self-expression, self-gift and desire for relationship. The creative energy of God is recognised in rock and tree, ocean and sky, woman and man. We begin to realise that all of created reality can speak to us of God, and that God’s presence and power are deeply incarnated in all aspects of the world. Every atom plays a part. The clarity and completeness of this incarnation takes place in the person of Jesus. In him, the Word and Wisdom of God find fullness of expression. We are told in the Gospel of John that ‘the Word became flesh’ (John 1:14). The theologian Dermot Lane points out that when John uses the Greek word *sarx* he is being very clear. It is not simply that Jesus becomes a male, or even that he becomes a human being, but he becomes *sarx*—a living being. It is worth thinking back to Genesis, where God takes earth—the stuff of our flower beds and vegetable plots—and creates Adam. So, in Jesus, all of life, all that is living, is gathered up. This child in a manger has implications for all of creation.

The reason why the phrase 'deep incarnation' is coming to the fore is because it reminds us that we are ultimately deeply connected to all of creation. We cannot look at Jesus, his birth in a stable in Bethlehem, the life he led, his death and resurrection as events that only have relevance for our own personal relationship with God. Deep incarnation tells us that the whole of created reality is caught up in what happens in and through Jesus. Pope Francis reminds us constantly that if we are people of faith, that has implications beyond our own lives, our own families and parishes. Rather than succumbing to the notion that faith should only be lived in limited, private spaces in a secular world, we are instead invited to recognise that we live in a universe oozing with the presence of God. As Thomas Keating stated in his last poem, shortly before he died, 'Only the Divine matters, And because the Divine matters, everything matters'. Incarnation invites us into a radically different relationship with the world, a relationship where everything and everyone matters.

Take a moment. Look up to the sky. Look down to the details of leaf and stone and raindrop. This, too, is incarnation. Sit in the car in a busy place and look at the people passing by, this shared humanity. We, too, are incarnation. What do you notice in people's faces, their bodies? There are stressed and anxious faces perhaps, a body curled in on itself against the cold, rush, push, determination to get through and get home. Moments of tenderness, glimpses of delight. Now put Mary in there—hassled perhaps, heavy and aching at the latter stages of pregnancy, worried about what is to come.

How often do we ignore the human reality of Mary and Jesus? We are inclined to presume that incarnation is a well-ordered, well-dressed, tidy affair. In doing so we have surely stripped some of the power and passion out of it, whitewashing God's desire to be with us, domesticating it.

Someone said to me recently, 'My image of Mary is of a strong woman's work-worn hand'. How powerful is that! How distant from the plaster-cast statues! We need to reclaim the physical reality of Mary and Jesus. Mary laboured Jesus to birth with pain and sweat, a young woman without even her own mother to accompany her—only poor Joseph, who hoped he would know enough to help. Imagine Mary lifting a small, vernix- and blood-smeared infant to her breast, and in the days ahead struggling to establish breastfeeding, dealing with swollen breasts and cracked nipples like pretty much any other mother. And at the back of all of this, God's desire to be with us is finding form and shape.

Incarnation does not stop here. It continues to be evident in every moment and action of Jesus's life. Incarnation is his very way of being. It is God-with-us. Richard Rohr talks about how Jesus lives his life as a participation in the love of the Trinity, saying: 'His life embodied what God's love intends for the world and demonstrated the Spirit's power to transform, heal and make whole what is broken'. This applies to Jesus's teaching and healing; the way he connects with those on the margins of society; how he challenges those in power; the desire he has to break bread with people, to build relationships, to wash feet. It also applies to Jesus who is arrested and beaten, who is hung on a cross and laid in a tomb which cannot ultimately contain him. This, too, is incarnation. This, too, is telling us something about who God is and how God desires to be with us. What happens at Christmas is intimately connected with what happens on the cross and all that happens in between. The artist Sieger Koder captures this well in his painting of the stable where Mary tenderly holds Jesus and they are overshadowed by the beams of the stable in the shape of the cross, the letters INRI chiselled into the manger.

Incarnation, like creation, is messy. It involves depth, intimacy, power and pain. When we take the reality of incarnation seriously, it challenges us to reflect on what incarnation, embodiment, means in our own lives. After the experience of the pandemic, we are perhaps more finely tuned than ever to the implications of being embodied, that we do not exist simply as spirit. We are part of creation. Our bodies are God's gift. God's wisdom and beauty are expressed in the multi-faceted variety of humanity. We recognise more than ever the sacredness of touch, the beauty of physical presence, the power of tenderness. Yet the Church has been culpable in many ways of making people ashamed of their bodies. Too often the impression has been created that our bodies create opportunities for sin and are an obstacle in our relationship with God. Such an attitude flies in the face of incarnation.

Incarnation is an ongoing reality, beginning with creation and finding its high point, its greatest clarity, in Jesus Christ; but it does not end there. Jesus is the showing forth of the Word, Wisdom and Spirit of God. As Christians, baptised into the body of Christ, we are called to be the ongoing incarnation—the making present—of Jesus, his message, his values, his way of being. This cannot simply be about personal religious practice. Remember those words of Thomas Keating, 'Only the Divine matters, and if the Divine matters, then everything matters'. This realisation moves us in the direction of what Pope Francis—in *Laudato Si'* and now again in *Fratelli Tutti*—refers to as an integral theology. Quite simply, everything is connected.

That has huge implications for how we live our lives and our perception of what it means to be people of faith. In *Fratelli Tutti*, Pope Francis makes it clear that we are created for relationship, and that the living out of those relationships—with creation, with each other and with God—is the core meaning of life. *Fratelli Tutti* pushes us beyond our comfort zones and challenges us to recognise our connectedness with those who are poor and oppressed, those whose political or social views differ from ours, those who believe in God and those who do not. Together, through empathy and dialogue, we should seek the common good. For Pope Francis, it is very clear that this is what it means to be a Christian and to participate in the ongoing incarnation of the Word, Wisdom and Spirit of God.

Go back to that stable; pause for a moment and recognise the cosmic significance of this young Jewish woman cradling her newborn child. In this child all of creation finds its meaning and its fulfilment. This is more than an image for a Christmas card. This is a radical statement of our fundamental interconnectedness, and of God's desire for relationship with all. Deep incarnation reminds us who we are.

SOURCES AND FURTHER READING

Thomas Keating, *The secret embrace* (Center for Action and Contemplation; cac.org).

Dermot A. Lane, *Theology and ecology in dialogue: the wisdom of Laudato Si'* (Dublin, 2020).

Pope Francis, *Laudato Si'* (papal encyclical, 24 May 2015; www.vatican.va).

Pope Francis, *Fratelli Tutti* (papal encyclical, 3 October 2020; www.vatican.va).

Ronald Rolheiser, *The holy longing: in search of a Christian spirituality* (New York, 1999).

Gemma Simmonds, *The closeness of God: the art and inspiration of Sieger Koder* (Liverpool, 2013).

A CHRISTMAS CONFESSION

Salvador Ryan

This is a piece I wrote a number of years ago, having hastened to a Limerick coffee-shop immediately afterwards to jot down the experience.

So anyway, there I was, sitting in a queue of people, waiting for confession in the Augustinian church in Limerick. It's a favourite spot of mine anytime I'm in town, and whenever I go to confession at Christmastime I almost always go there.

Those who have ever had the experience of going to confession will appreciate how you might want to take a few moments beforehand to gather your thoughts—well, this particular morning, that certainly wasn't going to happen. Although there were five or six people already waiting when I arrived, with two priests hearing confessions the line was moving fairly fast. No sooner had I landed and begun to take a bit of time to myself than I got a dig in the ribs from an older man to my right.

'Howya?', he began, 'miserable day out.'

''Tis,' I replied, not anticipating any further exchange.

'C'mere, did ya ever hear the one …,' he began again (at which point I just knew that, whether I had or not, I was going to hear it now), '… about the priest in Cappamore whose curate got sick and he needed a hand to hear confessions around Christmas? So he called down to the monks in Glenstal (who weren't long in the place at this stage and a lot of them hadn't great English) and he looked for a bit of help to hear confessions in the parish …'

The confessional door swings open. Another penitent goes in. We collectively shuffle further towards the sacrament.

'Anyway,' says he, 'the parish priest picked out the one with the best English and 'twas he who landed up at Cappamore church to hear the confessions …'

The second confessional door opened and another penitent emerged. More bum-shuffling.

'Well, the monk was going on great guns until one fellow came in and confessed to making a whole lot of *poitín* illegally. Well, the Belgian Glenstal monk wasn't quite sure what this was, or what penance to give him, so he got out of the confession box and told yer man to wait in the church while he went to get advice. Over he goes to the parish priest's box and sticks his head in when there's a bit of a lull in proceedings …'

By this stage there's a glint in the older man's eyes as he warms to the tale and anticipates the denouement with no little glee. Meanwhile, yet another penitent emerged, and the confessional door clicked shut once more on a contrite soul. The older man is next in line, then me. I suddenly wondered whether he'd get the story finished in time.

'Well anyway,' he begins again, with more urgency this time, 'the monk gets his chance, and says to the parish priest that there's a man in the confession box who's told me he's made a whole lot of *poitín*—"What will I give him?". And the parish priest, recognising the individual in question at once, doesn't hesitate for a second: "Give him a pound and ten shillings and not a penny more"!'

And the storyteller erupted in guffaws of laughter and rocked back and forth on the pew like a Christmas toy. I laughed too, but with more restraint, being aware of some of the more strait-laced characters in the queue behind me.

Click. Another confessional door opened. The older man got up to go inside but, before he did, he leaned back to me and said, 'I'm going to tell that one to yer man inside … happy Christmas!'

With that, he skipped over to grab the door that was being held open by the last penitent, a middle-aged woman laden down with a shopping-bag full of festive purchases. And, finally, I was left alone with my thoughts. But no sooner had I switched back into a more serious mode than there was another 'click' and a confessional door opened (needless to say, it wasn't my friend's confessional box—he'd be there for a while yet!) and I was in. And, much as I would love to be able to tell you what transpired next, it would probably do neither of us any good.

CHRISTMAS COUNTDOWNS

Ita Callagy

Everything seems to have a countdown nowadays, marked (and marketed!) months or sometimes years in advance: elections, summer festivals, the World Cup, Hallowe'en and, of course, the biggest countdown of all—Christmas. The Facebook posts on St Stephen's Day often kick things off: 'Only 364 more sleeps to Christmas, folks … the countdown begins!'

Over the years, I too have been swept up by countdowns, but not quite in the same manner, especially at Christmas. Two of the most important Christmas countdowns for me occur not months or weeks in advance but within twelve to thirteen hours of each other, on Christmas Eve and Christmas Day. One of these countdowns is in a professional capacity, the other in a personal capacity.

Across the two decades or more of my working life, I can count on one hand the number of Christmas Eves I've had off—first in catering/hospitality and then in the media. The latter is where the countdown is most essential: those final ten seconds before we're going on air, typically at 22:59:50, and the countdown to off-air at 23:59:50. But it's another countdown, that on Christmas Day at the edge of the Atlantic ahead of the Sligo Christmas Splash, that I enjoy the most.

For over a decade, my Christmas Eves have been spent in churches or cathedrals around Ireland—in recent years Galway, Antrim, Dublin and Louth. I work with a production company which broadcasts Midnight Mass to the masses across RTÉ TV, radio and the web. Sometimes the

TV broadcast is just in Ireland, and at other times it's a shared broadcast across the European TV network (EBU).

EBU broadcasts are always a bit more pressured: scripts have to be provided not only for the Mass but also for the short pre-recorded video (VT) introduction. Everything from the live opening welcome in the church by the celebrant (typically featuring several EU languages) to the final blessing needs to be sent to various countries weeks in advance in order for EBU narrators to be able to translate it into their own languages for the Mass and the VT.

In the same way that Christmas is a time for bringing out the best china and cutlery, the VT is a chance to show Ireland at its best, especially the parish which is hosting the Mass. Typically it features communities working together for local charities, or parishes preparing to celebrate the birth of Christ.

While the early weeks of December are spent rehearsing in the parish or church, Christmas Eve is when it all really starts to take shape, and timing becomes essential. We arrive at the church and rig the cables for our cameras, our sound and our lighting. Often we help to rearrange pews in order to be able to see everyone who shows up (often people will stay at home to watch the Mass on TV and then pop down afterwards to tell others how wonderful it all looked or how great they sounded!). Sometimes the crew will have toasty (and tasteful—we are working in a church, after all!) Christmas jumpers on, and there's on-site treats for the choir and readers and celebrants, who may be stuck with us rehearsing the Mass for two to three hours.

The rehearsal is essential but slow. People need to be in place before they're due to speak, and for readers who are used to only approaching the altar at the end of the psalm as the choir sing a final line it feels strange to be walking up while they're still mid-chorus. For those tuning in from home (and for us behind the camera), however, those five seconds of silence and slow footsteps approaching the altar feel like minutes—and on radio the silence feels even longer.

It feels even longer again if the reader then starts to take out his or her reading glasses, fumbles with the reading, looks up and then begins.

An extra 30 seconds can be lost on those silent actions alone, and by this stage the radio listener has switched stations, assuming that the signal has been lost!

Hymns and soloists are stopped and started, those in the procession walk the church aisles umpteen times, and we rehearse and we rehearse and we rehearse again until we're sure that we have everyone in the right place at the right time doing the right thing—whether that's reading at the correct speed (not too fast, not too slow), processing at the right speed (not too fast, not too slow) and singing at the right speed (not too … you get it)—so that we can ensure that the Mass won't run under or over time.

While it's not ideal in live situations, occasionally things still happen too quickly or slowly, so that as we approach the end of the Mass we run the risk of coming in short or over. Short isn't ideal, but it's not too much trouble for those at the broadcasting end (RTÉ/EBU)—they can pad announcements or run a short ad or jingle, and the viewers won't notice anything unless they're running a clock themselves.

Christmas Eve 2019, Galway Cathedral.

Running over, however, is—if you'll pardon the religious pun—a cardinal sin, especially with the EBU. RTÉ can occasionally tweak their schedule to allow for 30 seconds or a minute or so over, but as the EBU signal could be going out across seven or eight countries, there's very little chance that they will all have that flexibility to allow the programme to continue, even if the Mass isn't finished—and even more so if it's an automated system which typically kicks in with no allowance for over-run. If the off-air time is given as the first stroke of midnight, that is when they will finish their feed, whether the final blessing has been given or not.

So it's in our best interests to rehearse until that won't be an issue, and while this means that our Christmas Eve crew dinner might get a little colder than we'd hoped, it's worth it every time to hear the director say 'Clean as a whistle, folks, well done' at the end of a broadcast as we hit 'zero—off air'. That countdown from ten at the start of the programme and the countdown to off-air at the end of the programme are the most nerve-inducing and relief-inducing countdowns of all.

Christmas has been a strange time for me since Christmas Day 1998, when fifteen-year-old me received a phone call to tell me that my nineteen-year-old friend Crónán McCarrick had drowned in an accident with his older brother Seán on Christmas Eve. It sounds dramatic to say that everything changed that day but change it did. I had seen him across the street at lunchtime on Christmas Eve and decided against saying hello to him as he was in conversation with others. Twenty-four hours later he was gone, and Christmas was, to borrow a line from Yeats, 'all changed, changed utterly'.

I spent the next few Christmas Eves at work, never in a mood to celebrate, and then a few solo in the UK, where I was managing a restaurant. Christmas 2006 was my first Christmas back in Sligo for a few years. It was also, thanks to my big brother and some Christmas pints, the year that I was talked into doing the Sligo Christmas Day Splash for the first time and the year that I caught some form of a renewed Christmas spirit.

The Splash is essentially a chance to run into the Atlantic at midday for a local charity, splash about whilst singing 'Jingle Bells' together, and then convene for a hot cuppa (or something stronger) and hear about that year's chosen cause. It's also a time for meeting up with people you might not have seen since the previous year's splashing about, a time for sharing stories and silly moments—an hour or so of pure smile-inducing loveliness.

Each year, the countdown before it is the exact opposite of the one I'm part of twelve hours earlier. Typically, somewhere around 11.55 someone will shout that there's five minutes before the swimmers should be in the water. At this point, surrounded by familiar faces and funny costumes (there are prizes awarded for the best) and my big bro, this is where my internal countdown of regret begins, stretching all the way back to that night in 2006.

Ten seconds of wondering why I agreed to this. Twenty seconds of cursing my (cold) outfit of a Batman T-shirt, a pair of shorts, and a black-and-white Santa-style hat that says 'Bah humbug'. Thirty seconds of trying to figure out the quickest route in (and out!). Around then, someone shouts that there's less than a minute … and most typically, just before the actual count begins, I realise that I can no longer feel my feet or my fingers and that this might make the whole swimming element a little tricky.

The actual ten-second countdown is the most Irish of things; there could be up to 60 people getting ready to go in the water, and with a lack of amplification, save for the loud voice of Terry Hayes, the count mumbles its way across the crowd. So while those closest to Terry are in time, those farthest away are shouting 'TEN … NINE …' while he's at 'FIVE …'.

Then there's a loud cheer and the masses start to move; if the tide is out, this means a walk across the stones whilst hoping that those in the front keep going far enough for you to get to the water.

In the meantime, the crowd onshore are cheering, but this doesn't drown out the shrieks and yells and occasional swear words of those ahead of me hitting the water. Then somehow the water is splashing around my feet, knees and waist, and breathing becomes trickier as I try to persuade myself to keep moving forward and that—despite the fact that I'm already numb below the waist—I am having fun. Inside my brain, my internal clock is counting down. I know I'll be in the water for five minutes max., and I know that the trick is get my head underwater as quickly as possible; so, time to take a deep breath and dive down under the waves.

Once this is achieved, the mental block and internal monologue of 'Oh dear God, what am I doing?!' disappears. Usually around this point, too, the splashing has started, so as I come up for air I'm met with skites of water from all sides. Somehow an unofficial linked circle begins and I find myself arm-in-arm jumping up and down, with a stranger on one side of me and my big bro on the other, and we all sing a chorus of 'Jingle Bells' before another spate of splashing begins.

Christmas swim, Sligo 2016.

This is typically when my big brother and I go 'feet up'. He's an excellent sea swimmer and I can paddle a bit, so we swim a few metres away from everyone else, lie back in the Atlantic and put our feet up to watch the shenanigans. One year, a seal did likewise about twenty feet away. Other years there have been rainbows across the mountains, and one year there was snow and frost on the sands.

'Feet up', despite being the coldest time, is my favourite time. The shrieks and cheers and silliness just a few metres away, combined with the Atlantic air and Knocknarea, and Benbulben wrapped around our wee stretch of water like a hug, brings a warmth to my soul that is indescribable. The stress of the countdown from the previous night washes away, and the joy and hilarity of the most recent countdown fills me with Christmas spirit. It's a strange place to find contentment, but it is one of the few places where I can instantly just let go and let God, and appreciate all that I have—nature, laughter, life and love. This is Christmas.

CHRISTMAS AND THE IRISH JEWS

Natalie Wynn

Christmas may seem an unlikely theme for an essay about Jews—after all, on the face of it, what could be less Jewish? As these reflections will show, however, it is a surprisingly effective prism for highlighting some of the more subtle issues relating to day-to-day Jewish life in the diaspora (i.e. outside of the state of Israel) that can be less obvious within more abstract and academic discussions about acculturation, integration and representation.

Robert Popper's comedy *Friday Night Dinner*, which aired on Channel Four between 2011 and 2020, encapsulates many of the realities of life for secular Jews living in non-Jewish countries as seen through the eyes of the Goodman family, characters that Popper claims to have modelled on his own immediate family. The Goodmans' weird neighbour Jim illustrates very effectively the prurient curiosity that is displayed by some non-Jewish people, underpinned by an assumption that Jews are radically different, or other, to themselves, a phenomenon sometimes described as allosemitism (derived from the Greek word for 'other' [*allos*] and coined by the Polish writer and academic Artur Sandauer). For example, when Jim is nosing around the back of the Goodmans' house and comes across Jackie and Martin (played by Tamsin Greig and Paul Ritter) trying out their new hot tub, he immediately assumes that Jews have different bathing habits to non-Jews (series 5, episode 1). Sometimes

Jim's curiosity is deflected back onto him with hilarious results, as in the case of the fictional Jewish birthday tradition of the 'shmoigel' (season 1, episode 5) or 'Jewish' rice pudding (season 6, episode 5).

One of the episodes of *Friday Night Dinner* that, to me, best encapsulates the contradictions of contemporary diaspora Jewishness is 'Christmas' (season 2, episode 7), where the Goodmans are gathering for Christmas lunch with all the trimmings, complete with gifts and Christmas decorations. Nevertheless, Jackie is disgusted when the gloriously eccentric Martin arrives home with the biggest Christmas tree he could find, as, for Jackie, the tree represents an invisible demarcation line with respect to her sense of Jewishness. Many Jewish families in Ireland and elsewhere acknowledge Christmas in some form by gathering together, with or without gifts, to share a roast dinner, minus the ham for those who avoid it, like the Goodmans. In my family, trees and decorations might, likewise, be a step too far, but the festive season nevertheless offers us an opportunity to rest and enjoy seasonal fare, festive television and, most importantly, time together as a family. I have always exchanged gifts and cards with non-Jewish friends, relatives and my non-Jewish husband. Our daughter even receives two sets of presents, for Chanukah from her Jewish family and for Christmas from non-Jewish relatives and friends. Some Jewish people I know see no conflict between the two festivals and celebrate Christmas with all the trimmings. Some love the music and have no problem singing carols with the choirs in which they participate, on the grounds that these have no particular religious significance for them.

Most readers will probably have heard of the Jewish festival of lights, Chanukah ('dedication'), an eight-day celebration that can fall anytime between late November and early January depending on the vagaries of the Hebrew calendar. Chanukah commemorates the reconsecration of the temple in Jerusalem in 164 BCE following the Maccabean revolt against the Hellenistic Seleucid regime. The length of the festival is popularly associated with a miracle whereby a small container of consecrated oil for the temple's menorah was supposed to have lasted for eight days, the time required to prepare a new batch. It is more likely, however, to reflect the timing of the rededication of the temple during the eight-day harvest festival of Sukkot (meaning 'booths' or 'tabernacles'). Chanukah mostly falls during the month of December, which means that it often intersects with Christmas. A few years ago, when the two coincided, I made potato *latkes* to accompany our meal instead of roast potatoes. In 2022, when we were invited for Christmas lunch by my Church of Ireland cousins, they very thoughtfully adapted their menorah for Chanukah (see photo) to allow us to mark both sets of festivals together as a family.

Just as Jewish behaviour at Christmas has been influenced by the majority culture, the celebration of Chanukah in the diaspora has also been influenced. Nowadays, it is probably more common to give gifts than the traditional *gelt* (money), something that my daughter's Israeli schoolfriend, when they were both around six years old, could barely comprehend. In America, Chanukah jumpers, decorations, cards and 'Chanukah bushes' (decorated trees) are becoming increasingly common.

However, while this crossover is a sure indication of gradual Jewish acculturation to non-Jewish society, it can also be a source of significant confusion and even some subtle othering. In countries with small Jewish communities, such as Ireland, where there is less general familiarity with Jewish culture, the timing of Chanukah fosters the impression that it is a form of Jewish equivalent to Christmas, even though the origins, traditions and significance of the two festivals could not be more different. This can be particularly uncomfortable in work situations, where it is hard, without embarking on too much fuss or explanation, to convey why seemingly innocuous things such as Christmas jumpers, trees or decorations might be a cause of discomfort in certain contexts, in an age where the religious significance of Christmas has become largely irrelevant for many people. This highlights the inadequacy of fashionable principles of 'tolerance', 'inclusion' and 'multiculturalism', with their implicit expectation that minorities should conform to majority culture, which falls far short of genuine acceptance, pluralism and sensitivity towards and respect for difference.

These are issues that are reflected in *Friday Night Dinner*, which, for all its brilliance and understated accuracy in portraying aspects of Jewish identity and Jewish/non-Jewish relations, raises some serious questions regarding the representation of minorities in popular culture. The American Jewish comedian, actor and writer Sarah Silverman has coined the term 'Jewface', referencing the racist tradition of 'blackface', to describe the preference for casting non-Jews to play characters with strong Jewish identities, over and above equally talented Jewish actors. One recent example is the choice of Helen Mirren for the lead role in a biopic about the Israeli politician Golda Meir, due for release in August 2023. As Silverman explained to David Baddiel in his documentary *Jews Don't Count*, broadcast on Channel 4 in November 2022, Jewish actors tend to be relegated to peripheral, often typecast roles, such as the mouthy and somewhat annoying best friend, literary agent or such-like. While the casting of Zoe Saldana to play Nina Simone attracted significant and entirely justified criticism owing to Saldana's need for 'blackface' make-up and prosthetics, the issue of 'Jewface' remains off the public political correctness radar. Despite the intrinsic Jewishness of *Friday Night Dinner*, none of the main actors were Jewish while some of the supporting actors were, most notably Tracy-Ann Oberman, who repeatedly appeared as Jackie's neurotic and slightly annoying best friend 'Auntie' Val.

Each year I relish the opportunity that Christmas offers to pause, rest, meet with friends and spend time with my family, yet it is also a regular reminder of the personal boundaries that are inherent in identity and are different for each of us. Each person's experience of acculturation is individual and unique, and the acculturation of Jews and their integration into non-Jewish society, whether in Ireland or elsewhere, is an ongoing, as-yet-incomplete process. This is reflected in contemporary debates on the meaning and significance of Jewish identity, religion and culture, and the multiplicity of ways in which 'Jewishness' can be defined today,

Menorah. Image © Karin Morrow.

whether as religion, ethnicity, culture or civilisation, or something else entirely.

Contemporary Jewish practices surrounding Christmas and Chanukah reflect the fact that exchange has been a reality of diaspora life since Antiquity, and that many of the things that Jews now consider typically Jewish were influenced by external beliefs and practices. The food that is central to the celebration of Jewish festivals is an excellent example of how Jews have adapted to non-Jewish society and absorbed certain of its elements over two millennia of dispersion. There is no better case in point than that quintessential traditional Chanukah dish, the *latke*, which is also found in the non-Jewish cuisine of central and eastern Europe. According to the musical storyteller Daniel Cainer, the positive and negative aspects of Jewish experience are encapsulated in another iconic Jewish food, the bagel, whose roundness represents continuity but whose 'hole' represents the mark that centuries of transience, otherness, misrepresentation and conditional acceptance have left at the 'centre' of the Jewish soul.

SOURCES AND FURTHER READING

All series of *Friday Night Dinner*, its anniversary special, 'Ten Years and a Lovely Bit of Squirrel', and David Baddiel's *Jews Don't Count* can be viewed on All4 (https://www.channel4.com/).

For more information on Daniel Cainer and examples of his work, see www.danielcainer.com.

For an overview of the meaning and celebration of Chanukah, see 'Hanukkah 101', *My Jewish Learning* (https://www.myjewishlearning.com/article/hanukkah-101/; accessed 25 January 2023).

Jordan Hoffman, 'Nina review: problems more than skin-deep in cliche-ridden Nina Simone biopic', *The Guardian*, 20 April 2016 (https://www.theguardian.com/film/2016/apr/20/nina-simone-biopic-review-zoe-saldana).

THE ORGANIST'S
CHRISTMAS CAROLS

Ida Milne

My sister, the doyenne of our mother's social calendar, phoned:
'Ma would like to go to a carol service; would you like to
bring her'?

Our mother is 91. For more than 50 years she played the quirky organ
in St Edan's, the cathedral in the Church of Ireland diocese of Ferns. She
has sat stoically—and, yes, even regally—on the organ seat high in the
gallery, her back to the rest of the church, but watching for signals from
the dean in her organ mirror or checking up on the rest of the congregation below. Who might prefer what melody for the hymns? Whom
could she count on to add to the voices of the small choir, her loyal
assistants? When we were younger, she would monitor what we were up
to in the family pew, technically under the care of Da, but he often had a
snooze during the sermon, off duty from farm work. Were we behaving
like dutiful attentive little Christians or up to mischief? Had we snuck
in an Enid Blyton to read and were fishing it furtively out of our little
handbags, only to be rumbled by that mirror? She has played through
funerals and weddings, baptisms and her real favourite, the dour Holy
Week services. But the annual carol service was her *pièce de resistance*,
the day she was in charge; all the current dean had to do was to keep
announcing the readings and the hymns and carols that she had chosen,
to the 'airs' she liked. For me, it was what kept me from abandoning

religion. It was hard not to believe in the Christmas air of St Edan's. Even the silence had a noise of presence.

More than 50 years, until Covid stopped her. So this would be her first appearance at a carol service since 2019, when she was boss at the organ. That day, as she played the last notes of 'Hark the Herald Angels', the congregation chattered their way out down the aisle below. Snapping the organ lid shut and collecting her hymn-books, a time-honoured end-of-service ritual, she laughed and said, 'I've gotten cocky, I don't even practise anymore'. No one would have noticed. We never suspected that it would be her last carol service as organist, but Covid had other ideas. By some instinct, I stole a video of that final joyous voluntary on my phone.

And here I was bringing her back to church after the pandemic absence, loosening the strings protecting her from infection. Of course we were late—we could hear the dean calling the first hymn as we fumbled, Ma now on her stick, through the tall doorway. I thought that she'd head for the nave, with the main congregation—the easy option. But no, she dived at something of a gallop for the stairs, excited to be back. Towards the top she faltered, caught her breath and continued. She had not climbed stairs in two years, but she was climbing these ones, determined. We opened the door, the noise as ever seeming deliberately louder to embarrass late entrants, and shuffled to the cramped gallery seats to the right of the silent organ. Music sprang from the church compact disc player beside it, and familiar faces operating it smiled welcomes at her. 'It cannot replace you', they whispered affectionately. The hymn-books were swiftly passed back, rustling to find the page. Fully alert, Ma, who had barely left the house during the pandemic, stretched to look over the gallery railing to see who was where below, sorting families through generations. Eyes and ears rapt on the proceedings, even though in the rush to leave the house we had forgotten her hearing aids.

The service in December 2022 was seven carols and readings, a cutback from the days when there were twelve, the twelve days of Christmas marathon. As we moved from reading to hymn, Ma sang clearly in her soprano voice, word and note perfect: female or no, I am more of a tenor. I could hear my brother at the other side of the gallery singing out too. Lord knows what exalted choir we were drowning out on the compact disc. The Lord also knows how often we had complained at having to do this. Now we are full of emotion, regretting the past reluctance.

As we passed through it, my mind drifted back to earlier carol services, sitting in the same spot, often glancing over to check whether Ma needed help at her perch: there would be urgent but controlled signals, if someone had put up the wrong carol number on the plaque or removed a vital music book. We would resolve the issue. The performance should appear seamless.

Watchful of her present, my memories of services past reeled by in my mind's eye. The wonder of a more crowded church as a small child, nervous and excited to bring the toys that we were donating to the Sunshine homes up to lay under the Christmas tree which held centre stage between the pulpit—not used on that day—and the oak eagle lectern, hiding the altar. Da would push his shy brood out into the aisle below the gallery, clutching our gifts—wrapped, like all our presents, in well-used Christmas paper—and joining the other children. Then we would turn to the audience and timidly sing 'Away in a-a manger', overawed at the privilege. We waited nervously for the assessment of the organist. As the last organ notes died away, she would swivel around, giving a quick approval before preparing for the next hymn. We relaxed, glad not to have disgraced her.

At nine, I was promoted to read a lesson. I loved reading, but public speaking terrified me. 'Just do it, you will be fine.' I was anything but fine but obeyed. As we reached our teens, those of the five of us who could sing were promoted to the gallery for the carol service, assisting Ma's regular choir. We perhaps had more volume than music in our voices, but she was indifferent to our protests. 'It all helps.' She instructed us in which lines of the carols needed to be sung staccato: 'all:seat:ted:on:the:ground'. In our twenties, sometimes the hangovers were a challenge for a morning carol service. We all preferred it held in the evening, mother included, although she did not join us in Dunbar's for a libation to loosen the vocal cords. Most of the carols are truly more appropriate for evening. Shepherds weren't visited by angels during the day, and the Magi could only see the guiding star in the night sky. And 'In the Bleak Midwinter' was more of a night-time carol. Christina Rosetti, sister of Dante Gabriel and author of 'Bleak Midwinter', always outshines her more famous brother's legacy at Christmas. Hers are Ma's favourites, and mine too. Rosetti's poem 'Love came down at Christmas', to the Irish traditional air 'Garton', is lilting perfection, demanding presentism, whomsoever sings it. 'Stars and angels gave the sign.'

In my thirties, our infant daughters joined me on this gallery for the carols. They too got the magic. That life decade also marked the last carol services with our maternal grandmother, herself an organist into her nineties in Rossdroit. Her blue eyes would purse and twinkle, charmed by the atmosphere and the music; I recall her bemused glance as my deep voice hit the lower notes. But now it was the turn of the younger generation to sing. When our eldest, Constance, was ten, she and her father Eoghan gave a particularly rousing opening to the service with 'Once in Royal David's City', as Ma pulled out all the stops on the organ to give it full throttle. Síofra (daughter number two) and I beamed with pride. Later they both sang in the King's Hospital choir, but there Jedward got the honour of kickstarting the carol service with the same hymn. In my fifties, family circumstances changed. My marriage failed; the carol service was one of the rocks of security and joy for me, and for my daughters.

Through all those decades Ma, while wife, mother and grandmother, had filled her other role on that organ seat, persuading the ancient bellows to pump the pipes into action. Until now. In December 2022, at 62 years of age, I finally got to sit beside my mammy at the carol service, enjoying her joy at the proceedings. The organ chair was empty, heavy with history, but somehow still carried her authority. The air was still thick with Christmas magic. The sky had not fallen.

She looked longingly at her former constant companion as the dean bid the farewell blessing. I whispered: 'Would you like to have a little play?' She thought for a second and responded: 'There are too many people still here, but maybe next year. I will practise.'

NOTES ON CONTRIBUTORS

Keith Adams is Penal Policy Advocate at the Jesuit Centre for Faith and Justice, Dublin (Ireland), and a doctoral candidate in the Leuven Institute of Criminology.

Linda-May Ballard is a writer and folklorist based in Bangor, Northern Ireland.

Siobhán Barrett is the post-doctoral researcher on the LEIGHEAS Project in the Department of Early Irish at Maynooth University.

Catherine Barry is a Ph.D candidate in the Department of Philosophy in Maynooth University, working on religious toleration in eighteenth-century Ireland. She also blogs on Irish philosophy at IrishPhilosophy.com.

Sparky Booker is a historian of law, culture and society in late medieval Ireland. She is an assistant professor in History at the School of History and Geography, Dublin City University.

Béibhinn Breathnach holds an MPhil. in Public History and Cultural Heritage from Trinity College Dublin. She currently works in RTÉ.

Conor Brockbank is a recent MA Modern History graduate from Aberystwyth University, UK, whose research focuses on the Irish in Wales, specifically the activities of the Irish Province of the Calced Carmelite Order in Britain, Ireland and Zimbabwe.

Mary M. Burke is a professor of English at the University of Connecticut.

Bairbre Cahill is a writer and facilitator with a particular interest in the spirituality of everyday life.

Ita Callagy has been working across all elements of video and audio production for longer than she cares to remember and still finds it all far too enjoyable.

Denis Casey is a collaborator with the Bulevafuentes research group at the Universidad de Burgos, Spain.

Caitriona Clear is an independent scholar.

Patrick Comerford is an Anglican priest now living in retirement in Stony Stratford, near Milton Keynes, Buckinghamshire. He is a former adjunct assistant professor at Trinity College Dublin.

Ian d'Alton is a visiting research fellow at the Centre for Contemporary Irish History, Trinity College Dublin.

Seamus Dooley, from Ferbane, Co. Offaly, is assistant general secretary of the National Union of Journalists (UK and Ireland) and is a former reporter and regional newspaper editor.

Helen Doyle is a PhD student at the Department of History, Maynooth University. She is from Bagenalstown, Co. Carlow.

Michelle Dunne was awarded a Ph.D in Modern Irish (Folklore) by Dublin City University in March 2023. Her thesis focused on the role and representation of women in Seán Mac Mathúna's folklore collection.

Nicole Gallagher is the Church of Ireland general synod officer. She graduated with a Ph.D from Technological University Dublin in 2022.

Seán William Gannon is a historian of twentieth-century Ireland, the British Empire and their intersections.

Norrie Gibney (1936–2009) spent her life in Dublin, where she raised four children and helped to found the adult education group KLEAR (Kilbarrack Local Education for Adult Renewal).

Crawford Gribben teaches History at Queen's University Belfast.

Brian Griffin is an adjunct associate professor in the Department of History, Maynooth University.

James Hendicott is a freelance writer from England, but long based in Dublin. He met his Irish wife while living and working in the Seoul English teaching community.

Mary Hilary is a freelance writer and musician, with a background in Irish radio and television performances.

Fiona Hurley is Norrie Gibney's niece. She lives in Galway, where she works as a technical writer.

Francis Kelly is an author and historian. He was awarded his Ph.D from University College Cork and is a native of Manorhamilton, Co. Leitrim.

Laurence Kirkpatrick is retired professor of Church History in the Institute of Theology, Queen's University Belfast.

Felix M. Larkin is a historian and retired public servant.

Patricia Lysaght is professor emerita of European Ethnology and Folklore, University College Dublin.

Ciarán McCabe lectures in Modern Irish History at Queen's University Belfast.

Mícheál Mac Craith is a Franciscan priest and professor emeritus of Modern Irish, University of Galway.

Max McCoubrey is a writer and songwriter who uses her experience in show business and the media as a source for her writing.

Nell McDonagh holds a Master's degree from Dublin City University and has an interest in Traveller community and cultural issues and Traveller history.

Conor McDonough OP is a Dominican friar of the Irish Province, assigned to St Saviour's Priory, Dublin.

Yvonne McDermott lectures on the History and Geography programme in ATU Mayo.

Ultan McGoohan is a priest of the diocese of Kilmore based in Bailieborough, Co. Cavan.

Ciarán Mac Murchaidh is professor at Fiontar & Scoil na Gaeilge, Dublin City University.

Ida Milne is a social historian, History lecturer at Carlow College, and a visiting research fellow at the School of Histories and Humanities, Trinity College Dublin.

Miriam Moffitt has taught Church history across a number of third-level institutions for many years.

Pauline Murphy is a freelance writer from Cork.

Ríona Ní Churtáin is a lecturer in Modern Irish at University College Cork.

Adrian Ó Ceallaigh is a graduate of Maynooth University. Recently he received an award from Foras na Gaeilge for writers in the Irish language.

Tadhg Ó Dúshláine is a poet and an academic writer, and formerly senior lecturer in Modern Irish at Maynooth University.

Pádraig Ó Héalaí is a retired senior lecturer at the School of Irish, University of Galway.

Thomas O'Loughlin is professor emeritus of Historical Theology at the University of Nottingham.

Pádraig Ó Macháin is professor of Modern Irish at University College Cork.

Denise O'Meara lives in Tramore, Co. Waterford, and teaches Biology at the local university.

Victoria Anne Pearson is a Ph.D candidate in the School of Arts and Humanities, Ulster University. Her thesis focuses on the life and work of Dr Francis Moylan (1735–1815), bishop of Kerry and later of Cork.

E. Moore Quinn is a professor of Anthropology at the College of Charleston, South Carolina.

Padraic Rooney is a 68-year-old retired man from Sligo town. He has always liked stories. This is his first to be published.

JP Ryan is an Irish educator and artist living in the Czech Republic.

Salvador Ryan is professor of Ecclesiastical History at St Patrick's Pontifical University, Maynooth.

Brendan Scott is manager of the Irish Family History Foundation.

Diarmuid Scully is a lecturer at the School of History, University College Cork.

Yvonne Seale is associate professor of Medieval History at SUNY Geneseo.

Regina Sexton is a food and culinary historian, food writer, broadcaster and cook. She lectures at University College Cork, where she is the Programme Manager of the MA in Food Studies and Irish Foodways.

John-Paul Sheridan is director of education programmes, St Patrick's Pontifical University, Maynooth.

Tara Shields is a DfE-funded Ph.D candidate at Queen's University Belfast.

Damian Shiels is a historian and archaeologist and is currently a Research Fellow in History at the Department of Humanities, Northumbria University.

David Stifter is professor of Old and Middle Irish at Maynooth University.

Clodagh Tait is a lecturer in the Department of History, Mary Immaculate College, University of Limerick.

Sonja Tiernan is a fellow of the Royal Historical Society and was the Eamon Cleary Professor of Irish Studies and co-director of the Centre for Irish and Scottish Studies, University of Otago, New Zealand, until 2023.

Marie Whelton is a lecturer in Irish Language and Literature at the Marino Institute of Education, Dublin.

Kevin Williams is senior research fellow at the Centre for Evaluation, Quality and Inspection, School of Policy and Practice, Institute of Education, Dublin City University.

Patrick A. Williams is a doctor in the University Hospital, Waterford. His main interests are in brain-imaging and interpretive judgement.

Penelope Woods was formerly in charge of early printed books and manuscripts at the Russell Library, Maynooth. She writes on book history.

Niamh Wycherley is a medieval historian in the Department of Early Irish, Maynooth University.

Natalie Wynn is a research associate of the Herzog Centre for Jewish and Near Eastern Religions and Culture, Trinity College Dublin, specialising in Irish Jewish history, identity and experience from the late nineteenth century to the present day.